ME and MR JONES

ME
and
MR JONES

MY LIFE WITH DAVID BOWIE AND THE SPIDERS FROM MARS

SUZI RONSON

PEGASUS BOOKS

NEW YORK LONDON

ME AND MR. JONES

Pegasus Books, Ltd.
148 West 37th Street, 13th Floor
New York, NY 10018

First Pegasus Books cloth edition April 2024

ISBN: 978-1-63936-656-9

10 9 8 7 6 5 4 3 2 1

Printed in the United States of America
Distributed by Simon & Schuster
www.pegasusbooks.com

Dedicated to my daughter, Lisa Ronson,
so she knows how life was.

And to my darling husband, Mick Ronson,
who is missed every day.

contents

PLATES

PREFACE

25 April 1963

I scream and scream and scream and for the first time in my life make as much noise as I want without anyone telling me to be quiet. I'm fourteen years old at a Beatles concert in Croydon and, along with every other fan in the hall, I am mad with excitement.

I get my ticket through sheer luck. My schoolfriend Marlene's older brother is going to Fairfield Halls to buy tickets and she asks me if I want one. Yes, I do – I have a Saturday job and I can pay the 6/6* tomorrow. Dying with excitement, I rush home to tell my mum. I'm worried she'll say no, but instead she says, 'Can I come?'

'I've only got one ticket.' I can feel my face going red.

She turns her back to me.

'Well, you're a bit young to go to Croydon on your own.'

'I'm meeting Marlene and her brother there, I'll be fine.'

Who wants to see The Beatles with their mum?

I search for something cool to wear and as I look at my reflection in the full-length mirror on the wardrobe door, I fantasise about Paul McCartney: he catches my eye in the crowd and sends someone to look for me; his new girlfriend, the glamorous Jane Asher, is

---

* The metric equivalent of 6/6 is 32.5p, and the equivalent today is approximately £9.

XI

forgotten as we fall madly in love. Staring at my reflection, I can't help but wish I looked like Jean Shrimpton. I'm well rounded, with thick, frizzy hair; she's skinny and beautiful, with straight flat hair. I'd die to look like her. I finally decide on a purple corduroy mini skirt that hangs on my hips with a decorative black belt, along with a ribbed top and long black boots.

On the day of the concert, I leave school after religious education, bike home and rush to get ready. I wind my frizzy hair into large rollers, hoping to calm it down, sellotape my fringe and kiss curls to my forehead and cheeks, and spray everything with Mum's lacquer. My hair is a bleached-blonde mess – Mum combed in some Sun In, hoping for blonde highlights, but it went a bit yellow instead. After I get into my skirt and boots and hide some make-up in my handbag, I take out the rollers and peel off the tape. I'm going for the Brigitte Bardot look and pray it doesn't rain.

I'm ready, and as I'm calling goodbye from the front door, Mum offers to drive me to the bus stop at Bromley South station. There's no saying no and she complains bitterly about her life all the way there.

'It's all right for you, going out. I never go out. You'd think your father would take me somewhere, but he never gets out of that bloody chair.' This isn't anything I haven't heard before. My parents don't get along and my mum complains about it all the time. As she drops me off at the bus stop, she squeezes my hand and says, 'I hope you have a lovely time,' and I can tell she means it.

When the bus comes, I push my way upstairs along with the other kids that get on. There's a ton of people around my age on the top deck; we're all going to see The Beatles, and everyone is buzzing with anticipation. Some of the boys comb their hair forward like The Beatles, but the back is short, and the front – cut for a much more conventional side parting – slopes diagonally across their foreheads.

Fairfield Halls is quite a large venue, and tonight it's packed with kids. Our seats are right behind the drums, and I can see presents for Ringo on the drum kit: socks, and some aftershave. I feel guilty that I haven't brought anything.

The lights go down and as The Beatles walk onstage, we scream. Ringo smiles as he slips behind the drums – he's so close I can almost touch him – and we scream some more. We scream for the entire forty-five-minute set; there are moments when I hear snippets of songs over the noise, 'Please Please Me' or 'She Loves You'. They shake their heads as they sing 'ooh' and it sends us mad. John tries to get us to be quiet but hearing his voice, his Liverpudlian accent, makes us scream even louder.

At the end of the show everyone rushes round to the stage door, hoping for an autograph or even just a glimpse of the boys. They come out and we scream; they wave to us, we scream louder, and when they get into the car and pull out of the gates, we're on it like dogs. I'm on the bonnet, others are on the roof. I can see them in the car – they look scared. It takes the police to get us off. The moment leaves me in tears, and I don't know why. It could be teenage angst, or hormones, or maybe just adrenaline, but in my heart I feel a freedom I've never felt before. It's at that moment I *know*: I don't want a normal life. I don't know how to change it, but I don't want to live the life of my parents.

The night comes back to me vividly some years later. It's 1972 and I'm getting into a limo with David Bowie and the Spiders from Mars. We've just finished a show in Scotland, and the car is waiting in the narrow alley behind the theatre. The band leave the dressing room and come straight to the car followed by Stuey, David's bodyguard. David and lead guitarist Mick Ronson are in the car, and I'm about to get in with Woody Woodmansey and Trevor Bolder – the drummer and bass player – right behind me. I hear a roar and glimpse a crowd of fans, who barrel round the corner and bear down on us at lightning speed.

'Fur fuck's sake!' shouts Stuey, pushing me, Woody and Trevor into the car before crashing in on top of us. He manages to close the door in their faces, and as he does a howl of despair rises up from the crowd; they'd been so close. They try the door handles. I hold down a lock on one side of the car, my finger white with the pressure. Everything goes dark as fans pound on the doors and windows, unleashing their frustration on the car. Screaming, squashed faces press up against the windows inches from my face. The car shudders with the weight of people jumping on top of it, bodies on top of bodies. It begins to rock and I'm sure it's about to go over.

'Drive! Drive!' David yells to the chauffeur, but he can't drive, he's hiding in the front well of the car in fear of his life. It takes forever for the police to get them off. As we get away, there's quiet in the car, until Mick Ronson says, 'I guess they liked us then.'

We explode into laughter. He's right, they did like us, it was another fantastic show. This band is on fire. The night I jumped on The Beatles' car, their faces looked as scared as ours must have been.

1
EARLY LIFE

I'm not good at school. I don't like it, and I leave for good at fifteen. My headmistress thinks it's for the best and my mum's okay with it on one condition: I must learn a trade. I can either go to secretarial school at Pitman College in Bromley or train to become a hairdresser. Hairdressing wins.

School breaks up in late July and I walk out of Marian Vian Secondary Modern school for the last time. There are no tearful goodbyes, no sorrowful exchanges of phone numbers with other girls. I'm happy not to be coming back and feel as if I've finally grown up. Mum finds me a course at Evelyn Paget College of Hair and Beauty in Bromley; she and Dad are willing to pay one hundred pounds for the six-month course that will allow me to skip the three years of drudgery that come with starting as a junior. I'll start proper hairdressing faster and make better money than the poor juniors who have to work earning a pittance for all that time.

Evelyn Paget College sits two floors above Bromley High Street. You enter through a narrow stairway leading up to the reception; it's lined with photos of the hairstyles of the day in gold frames. The top floor of the college is for beginners and paid students. I've been moved to the main floor, which is for more experienced hairdressers. Everything here is cut price: perms, cuts, tints, and shampoo and sets. The place is always crowded.

Most of us are girls, but there are a couple of men training as well. Colin, who's a mod, wears a pink paisley shirt and a parka jacket – he rides a scooter with a furry tail on the aerial, it's so cool. The other bloke is Peter, tall with a square jaw and large hands, who rides a BSA motorbike. He's a rocker. Mods and rockers have a dreadful name in the papers. They're sworn enemies and fight in gangs on the beach in seaside towns like Brighton and Margate, but Colin and Peter aren't too serious about it. Everyone loves Peter, he's funny and charming. We go out for a while, and I lose my virginity to him on the floor of my attic.

I'm popular with clients and quickly rack it up with both wages and tips. I put money on the table at the end of the week for Mum, and the rest is mine. Bromley is an ordinary London suburb with a market square that Medhursts department store sits on; Woolworths and the usual assortment of shops make up a typical high street, along with a couple of cinemas. I'm happy at work, I like the girls and enjoy doing hair. I feel confident in my choice.

Home is a different story. I have one brother and though we don't have much in common, the one thing we do talk about is Mum's moods. 'Is Mum all right?' is a mantra around the house. Mum and Dad live together but apart. They have separate bedrooms in our suburban semi-detached house. While they do normal things – go to work, eat meals, watch TV – to say they're happy is a stretch.

My parents married straight after the war. Everyone did – the churches had never been busier. The government encouraged families and provided free milk and cheap lunches for children at school. Dad came back from France grateful to be alive and in one piece. He'd followed the front through France in a tank with his crew, repairing tanks, guns and whatever else was broken or left behind. One moonless night, they got lost and became separated from their battalion. Dad, in charge, decided to drive his tank across an empty field and into some woods. He carefully manoeuvred his way through the woods and on the other side lay a small village. They rolled with trepidation into the village and were surprised and delighted at the effusive welcome they received. Dad and his men were drunk for three days before they were found and rejoined the battalion.

When Dad was asked for a report, the senior officer couldn't believe his story. The field he crossed was full of mines, the woods he crept through full of German soldiers. How did he do it and survive? He didn't like to tell them what he told us: that spirits guided him. He was a spiritualist, a believer (his mother was a medium). To his officers, a hero. I've got his medals to prove it, and a certificate of bravery signed by Lord Montgomery.

Mum was a driver at Biggin Hill Airport during the war. Her job was to ferry silent pilots to their planes. As the sun went down, she would watch them take off for France, never knowing if they would come back. The waiting was endless, the thrill of their return monumental. She watched the Battle of Britain out on the street with her sisters and neighbours, dogfights in the sky. When the war ended, she missed the drama and excitement of her life at Biggin Hill. There wasn't much of that at her mother's house in Orpington. She met Dad in a local dance hall – they both loved to dance and flew around the floor in each other's arms under the mirror ball, and before too long they walked down the aisle and tied the knot at a local church in Bromley.

They moved into 96 Cumberland Road and rented out the first floor to a family with children and the attic to one of Dad's friends. I became best friends with their daughter Linda. When we were very little, Dad drove a huge, refrigerated truck all over England, delivering meat. He was away for days at a time, while Mum was at home with us. Eventually, he changed his job and became a chauffeur to Mr Robertson of the Hawker Siddeley Group, a company that primarily built planes; the Hawker Hurricane had great success in the Second World War.

There are still many late nights, but at least Dad sleeps at home now. At the weekends, he takes my brother out on his boat, his one great passion, while I'm left with my mum to sympathise about her thoughtless husband. The two of them come home late, smelling of salt – I want to go with them but it's not on the cards.

One bit of light relief is the pirate radio stations. Radio Caroline and Radio London are a breath of fresh air in England. We all listen to them, Mum singing along to Ketty Lester or Ray Charles while doing the ironing. I pass my driving test when I'm seventeen and Dad helps me get my first car, an Austin A40. I love music, and with a car there's live music everywhere. Linda – the girl who used to live upstairs – and I go to the Tiger's Head or the Savoy in Catford. The floors are soft and sticky, the bars crowded and full of howling semi-drunk boys. My mum would call them 'common' or 'oiks' and would not like me to bring one home.

Linda and I try the Bromel Club in the Bromley Court Hotel. So many great bands play here: Pink Floyd, who drip oil on a revolving wheel that sends psychedelic shapes to a white sheet onstage, are like nothing else I've seen; I love Georgie Fame and The Blue Flames and the synchronised dancing of Geno Washington and The Ram Jam Band. The night Jimi Hendrix is scheduled to play, Linda has an earache and her mum won't let her go. To my disappointment, we miss seeing what became, according to Bill Wyman at least, a truly historic performance.

◆

When I finish training at Evelyn Paget, I'm sent to their Beckenham branch. Beckenham is a small town south-east of London, with St George's Church at one end and the Regal Cinema at the other. It's dotted with pubs and is full of young mums with prams and older people with shopping baskets. It's a safe, prosperous suburb, posher than Bromley. Mum encourages me to say that we live in Beckenham or Park Langley, but Park Langley's only claim to fame is the Chinese Garage, built like a pagoda in 1928. Beckenham hangs on to its middle-class status with no Wimpy Bar and only one or two 1960s-type coffee shops that serve foamy coffee, cheese and tomato sandwiches or beans on toast.

The road to London goes through Beckenham, past the Regal, and over Clock House Bridge. My mum thinks the world ends at Clock House Bridge and warns me about the perils of Penge on the other side. She says Penge is 'common' too, but she has no words for Brixton or Herne Hill and hopes I never break down there.

Traffic is moving at a crawl. I know I'll be late, so I quickly apply mascara at the traffic lights before I park by St George's Church. It is a quarter past nine when I walk through the salon door, and Doris, our elderly receptionist, glares at me. My first client is at the basin.

'Good morning, Mrs Taylor.'

Mrs Taylor responds with an exasperated sigh. I give the nod to Heather, our junior, and walk into the staff room. Heather's only been here a week and I should be watching her, but I need time to get into my dark-blue nylon uniform. I adjust my hair in the mirror and quickly apply some pale-pink lipstick before going out to check my trolley for rollers and pins.

Mrs Taylor comes up red and watery from the shampoo and says, 'My neck's wet and I wouldn't be surprised if it's not all down my back.' She's right, but I quickly put a dry towel around her neck and walk her to the chair.

'It looks all right to me,' I lie, flashing a murderous look at Heather. 'Are you having a trim, Mrs Taylor, or just a shampoo and set today?'

'Just a shampoo and set today, thank you, I haven't got time for a trim,' she says, pointedly looking at her watch. Mrs Taylor is a little older but likes a smart set; no waves and curls for her, she prefers a little height and some wings at the side to lift her face. I roll her up and lead her to the dryer.

Bob the towel man walks in, smelling of laundry. He sits down and carefully rolls a cigarette with tobacco-stained fingers, then lights up and takes a long drag. He clamps the cigarette between his lips as he piles the clean towels on to the bench and takes down the sacks of dirty ones. I go out to the front desk and look at the book with Doris to see my appointments for the day. Today should be a good day. Most of my clients are young mothers, who make for more interesting work than the pensioners that come in on Mondays and Tuesdays – we give them a great deal, and the blue brigade arrive in full force. They all want a similar look. Waves and curls and 'something that will last until the weekend'. They chat about their families, their health and what's in the news.

I want to try new things. The girls and I want to keep up with the times; it's the end of the 1960s and styles are changing so quickly. I've been cutting boys' hair on the side for quite a while and men seem to prefer my haircuts to a barber's. I bring it up at the salon and we're all on board. We talk to our boss, Mrs Fine, and decide on a 'Man's Night' on a Tuesday from 6 to 8 p.m. Doris isn't happy – she doesn't want to stay late, and we don't make her. We dim the salon lights and light some candles, buy some wine. All of us touch up our make-up and wear regular clothes instead of uniforms. Evelyn Paget put a notice in the front reception and a small ad in the local paper.

The first night is a slow trickle, maybe eight men in all. We all laugh, it's so silly, but as we discuss it the next day, we agree: times have changed; barbers cut hair differently to us, they use clippers, which none of us use – scissors work better on longer styles. After a few weeks, the novelty of working these nights soon wears off. We haven't been offered any more money to do it and decide it's not worth giving up an evening, so we shut it down after a couple of months. I manage to get a few more private clients out of it before it's over.

It's just another day when I get asked to help out with a later client, Mrs Jones. She arrives just before a quarter to five. She's a woman of about my mum's age, wearing a tweed skirt with sensible shoes and the ever-present English cardigan. Her hair is thick and I'm sure it will take forever to dry. Like most other customers, she starts talking about her family the moment I get started.

'My David is such an artistic boy,' she says. 'He's always been that way, plays guitar and piano. He doesn't have a lot of time to see me but I'm so proud of him.' She rattles on and on as I'm rolling her up, and I smile and nod. I put on the hairnet and motion to Heather to put her under the dryer. Mrs Jones opens a *Woman's Own* and settles in comfortably.

'Put it on hot,' I whisper to Heather, 'we don't want to be here all night!' Half an hour later, when she's dry and I'm combing her out, she's back to her son.

'He was in the top ten, you know,' she tells me.

'Really?' I ask, listening properly now. 'What was the song?'

'"Space Oddity",' she says with a smile.

'Really?' I ask again, and she nods. I meet her eyes in the mirror. 'Are we talking about David Bowie?'

'Yes,' she says. 'I'm his mum!'

I've heard of David Bowie from kids in the pub. He's a musician who plays at The Three Tuns, a local pub on Beckenham High Street. David has an arty thing going on and it seems a bit niche to me. I haven't been myself.

I know 'Space Oddity' was a hit – in the top ten, as his mum says – but that was over a year ago now. A one-hit wonder, maybe? I don't say this to his mum, of course; I give her the reaction she wants, surprise and delight. After a final spray of lacquer, I show her the back of her head with a flash of a hand mirror, pull the gown off and give her the bill.

'I love it,' she says, as she pats her head. 'I'll come to you next week.'

2
A CHANCE ENCOUNTER

1971

It's Saturday, always a busy day at the salon, and just as I'm sitting down with a cup of tea, I hear Doris say from the front, 'Well I never did!' I watch Heather's face register shock and disbelief.

'Come and have a look,' she says, laughing, beckoning me over. A man and woman are walking down Beckenham High Street, the man pushing a pram – not that unusual. I can't see what the fuss is about, but then I realise he's wearing a dress. It's a dull gold midi, which flows as he walks. The top is covered by a jacket, and with it he wears knee-length boots and a floppy hat with long blond hair falling out of it. He's with a skinny girl with short blonde hair, wearing black jeans and a bronze, waist-length furry jacket. Shopkeepers, staff and customers alike turn to have a look.

'It's David Bowie,' I hear someone whisper behind me. Builders across the street can't resist calling out 'Hello darling' and whistling at him.

'Look at that, whatever's next?!' Doris huffs.

We can't get over it at the salon, and every client who walks through the door hears the same story about the man in a dress and what nerve he has. I don't say anything out loud, but inside I think they look amazing.

The following week, Mrs Jones comes in for her set with the same girl that was with David in the High Street.

'I'd like to introduce you to my daughter-in-law,' she says gingerly. 'This is Angie.'

She waves her forward. I can't tell if she's proud or embarrassed. Angie's tall and thin, as thin as I'd like to be. I love her narrow blue eyes and generous smile. Her skin is whiter than white, almost translucent, and you can see blue veins running under it. She's wearing the same black jeans and furry jacket she had on the other day. I wonder where she shops – you don't see clothes like that in Beckenham. Angie doesn't have classic good looks, but to me she's stunning. When she speaks it's with a weird accent, kind of American with a touch of cockney on the side. She's cool and confident. I've never met anyone like her.

Angie sits at my mirror. I'm a little nervous as I ask her what she'd like me to do with her hair. I feel sure it won't be what my regulars are after.

'Something outrageous,' she says with a sweet smile. 'How about some colour?'

You don't have to ask me twice! I love playing with colour and rarely get the chance to be inventive; Angie is the perfect person to try out ideas on. A lot of my older clients have grey hair, and I use a water rinse on them to brighten it up. I also have clients whose hair is a little brassy from bleach, and they need a rinse to dampen down the gold. Undiluted, the colours are fierce, and when I spill a drop on a white towel it's a brilliant jewel colour.

I start by bleaching out white stripes on the side of Angie's head. I ask about her life, as I do with all my customers, only this time I'm truly interested. Angie is eager to talk. She tells me about David and his band. Angie helps them dress for their shows, and if there are lights or a follow spot at the venue, she's not above using them, convincing the promoter she has experience with stage lights. I imagine Angie never letting an opportunity pass her by and whether she has or hasn't used a follow spot before, I'm sure she did a good job.

After a show, she and David run around London all night, hanging out in the cool clubs and coming home at all hours with whoever they've met in tow. She's outrageously loud and funny, and David's biggest fan. Her life sounds unbelievably exciting.

After the bleach has taken, I use the watercolours neat and create short stripes of bright pink, soft blue and frosty silver. It comes out great. Angie loves it. She gives me a big tip and says she'll be back next week.

◆

It's a couple of months before Angie comes back to the salon; it's Christmas week. I hear her out front and look over the swing doors as she talks to Doris. Her hair has grown, but a bit of the pink stripe is still visible. She wears silvery-blue trousers with short boots and has her fur jacket pulled around her face. 'Nothing before Christmas, I'm afraid,' I hear Doris say. Angie sees me and waves.

'I want a perm,' she tells me, 'before Christmas, but it seems you are all booked up.' I look at the book and Doris is right: we're jammed. I follow her out of the salon.

'Hey Angie,' I call softly. 'I can come to your house tonight if you like, and give you a perm?' Her eyes light up. 'I'll come after work, about seven – okay?' Angie shoots a look at the salon as she tells me her address before leaving. I return to Doris's curious gaze. 'Just told her to call again tomorrow and see if we have any cancellations.'

Nicking clients is strictly forbidden; I have private clients, I always have, but I don't take them from the salon. Angie is different, she'll find somewhere else to go if I don't fit her in. I don't want to lose her. During the afternoon I sneak some perm curlers, papers and perm solution into a bag, and as soon as my last client is out the door I leave and drive to Haddon Hall.

Haddon Hall is one of those huge mansions that families used to live in during the olden days. David and Angie live on the ground floor. I knock at the oak front door and Angie answers. She doesn't seem to recognise me. I'm not sure what to say but as I turn to leave, she smiles and invites me in for tea.

I follow her into a massive entrance hall and look up at the tall stained-glass windows that provide a backdrop for a sweeping, Hollywood-style staircase leading from the ground floor to the minstrels' gallery. I feel as if I'm in a church. We go from the hall into the living room. The sheer size of it is intimidating, but it's more the way it's decorated that impresses me. The carpet is midnight blue, the walls the same colour; they rise up to an ornate silver ceiling. I can smell fragrant candles. There's a long couch with gold-trimmed blue velvet cushions, and on the wall behind corresponding cushions hang from hooks. A pink chaise longue sits on the opposite side of the room. In front of the couch is a low chest that serves as a coffee table, covered with magazines, cups and glasses. More cushions are scattered on the floor, along with colourful album covers.

David sits in the bay window, flicking through a magazine. His guitar rests on a stand close by and there is some sound equipment and a cassette tape recorder on the floor. He's wearing a soft velvet shirt with rolled-up sleeves and fitted trousers. His skin is as white as Angie's, his face finely boned. Long blond hair spills over his shoulders, casting shadows over his face and eyes. He greets me, and without further ado he nods to Angie and they both leave the room. They don't return for what feels like an eternity, but it's very possibly only twenty minutes or so; I find out later that this is something they do quite regularly to their guests, to see who will stay and who will go. I flip through the magazines on the floor; they are from Europe, foreign words on their covers. The clothes in them are rich, exquisite – even I can tell that this is high fashion. I look at the models and realise that they aren't classic beauties, and it makes them all the more interesting. David and Angie finally return with a tray of tea and act as if nothing unusual has taken place. I play along.

Angie begins by apologising and saying she's changed her mind about the perm. I'm relieved; I'm not sure a perm would look so great on her anyway. We chat about style, fashion and music – well, they do, while I listen and agree with everything they say. The truth is that I'm in the dark. I haven't heard of anyone David is talking about, Lou Reed and The Velvet Underground, Iggy Pop. I'm trying to think of something interesting to say, so when he mentions Marc Bolan, I'm delighted – I've heard of Marc Bolan – and I jump right in.

'Oh yes, I saw him on *Top of the Pops*,' I start happily. 'I love the way he looks.'

It was true. On *Top of the Pops*, Marc wore a top hat, satin trousers and a feather boa around his neck, with glitter on his cheeks; he smiled and flirted with the camera and the audience. No one looks, acts or sounds like Marc Bolan. When I finish my fan-like accolade, though, David doesn't respond. The atmosphere shifts and he

13

changes the subject. I thought I was on common ground here and I'm not sure what's gone wrong. I didn't know then that Marc and David went to each other's gigs, to the same clubs. Although they seemed friendly, they were also fierce competitors. David is quiet as he sits and flips through the magazines on the floor.

Angie is taken with the idea of how wonderful he would look with short hair. She says it again and when she gets no reaction from him, she throws it over to me.

'What do you think, Suzi?'

'Well, no one has short hair.' I think of Donovan, The Rolling Stones, The Who: they all have long, flowing locks. The Beatles might have started long hair for men, but the hippies took it to a whole different level. David would be the first to break that trend.

'It would look really different,' I go on. 'It might look really good.' It would certainly be new. David gets up slowly and comes over to show me a photograph in a magazine of a model with a red spiky hairdo.

'Can you do that?' he asks.

I look more closely at the photo. The girl looks incredible; her style is credited to someone called Kansai Yamamoto, a designer from Japan. It's a woman's hairstyle! I say yes instantly and try to keep the surprise from my face. As crazy as it is, I think David's the perfect person to pull this off. He's tall and rock-star thin, with high cheekbones and translucent white skin, his neck long and slim, his body almost feminine. We start immediately, clearing a space and laying down newspaper. It takes me about half an hour to chop off his long blond hair, and as it falls round my feet I am cautiously optimistic. The feeling's short-lived though, as when I finish, his hair won't stand up – it just flops to one side.

I'm panicking and David doesn't look too bright, so I say with a confidence I don't feel, 'Don't worry, Dave, as soon as we tint it, the texture will change, and it will stand up.'

I'm praying I'm right.

The next day, I experiment with colour at the salon. I snip a bit of Heather's hair – it's the same mousy shade as David's – and find the right colour almost immediately. It's from the Fantasy range by Schwarzkopf: Red Hot Red. I try it with both 20- and 30-volume peroxide and, as I thought, the 30 volume lifts the colour up and makes it very bright. Now all I have to worry about is how to make it stand up. There are soft setting lotions at the salon, but they won't do. I need something stronger. I remember using a product called GARD before, an anti-dandruff treatment from Germany. It doesn't just cure dandruff – it sets hair like stone.

Angie calls me at the salon a few days later and says in a bright but slightly strained voice that David isn't happy; she asks when I'll be back.

'Tonight,' I say, and with hair dye and confidence I go back to Haddon Hall.

David greets me in silence. His hair looks like a schoolboy's haircut. I timidly hold out the swatches of bright-red hair that I did the experiment on: 'Look, David, it's just like the photo.' He looks marginally more interested but is still quiet. I put on the cape and apply the colour, and David still doesn't say a word as we wait for it to take. Lucky for me Angie is here, chatting away as usual, though I'm not really listening – I'm too nervous to listen. When it's time, I wash it off and the tint runs like blood down the sink. I do a little dance inside: it's a brilliant red. If the GARD works like I remember, I'll be home and dry.

I pour a liberal amount into my hands and spread it into his hair. I start to dry it and as I do, I pull it up and away from his head. To my delight and relief, I feel the texture change in my hands. Any doubts David might have had disappear the second he looks in the mirror at his short spiky red hair. He looks amazing. It's standing up like a brush on his head. I start to smile as Angie screams and David dances round the room, posing, shaking his head, loving it. Angie says 'numma numma' and purrs into his ear, then laughs up at him.

'You look amazing, and . . . taller,' she says in that funny voice of hers. The style does add a couple of inches to his head. He looks at himself in the mirror again and again, running his fingers through his hair, and then, with a final laugh, he walks out the door, calling over his shoulder to Angie:

'Let's go up to the Sombrero.'

3
BOYS WILL BE BOYS

Angie calls to invite me back to Haddon Hall.

'We're having friends over on Friday,' she says, 'and there's some-one I want you to meet.' She doesn't give me any more information, but I don't care, I'm just thrilled to be invited.

I arrive and see a gorgeous man twirling Angie in the entrance hall, both of them laughing away. He's tall and slim with ash-blond hair and a beautiful smile. Angie calls him Rudolph Valentino. Rudolph's real name is Freddie Burretti. We walk together to the bedroom, and I watch her sort through fabric on the rumpled bed as she keeps talk-ing. The bedroom is a mirror image of the living room, except for the colour. It's painted in a soft rosy pink and has a dark raspberry carpet that glows from subtle lamps. A gold ceiling reflects the light and makes it feel like Aladdin's cave. There's a bay window behind the bed, full of net and taffeta, and by the far wall there's a rail full of shiny costumes. A dress hangs in front of a mirrored wardrobe – it's unbelievably beautiful, so much so that I'm scared to touch it, but when I do the soft fabric slips through my fingers like water. The pale-blue motif is of a different texture to the heavy beige satin and the gold frog fastenings. The way it's cut makes it almost alive on the hanger. Angie turns to look at me and asks me if I like it.

'It's beautiful.'

'It's David's,' she laughs. 'Mr Fish from London.' She picks up an album from the side of the bed, *The Man Who Sold the World*. The cover has David lounging on a couch in the very dress I'm looking at. I don't say anything, but wish I knew who Mr Fish was.

Angie is telling Freddie and me about Trident Studios in London and how amazing the songs are sounding. I'm in awe of her and her attitude: she says what she wants, whenever she wants, without a care in the world. I think we're about the same age but she's way more sophisticated and worldly than I am. I'm fascinated by the way she carries herself.

'Freddie's a clothing designer and helped design all of these,' she says, making a grand gesture towards the rail.

I'm impressed, and as the three of us go into the living room to join the others, I wonder whether Freddie works for them all the time. There are eight or nine people in the living room, and David nods and smiles at me as I enter. I'm introduced to Freddie's girlfriend, Daniella, a West Indian girl, small and slim with short hair the colour of an egg yolk. I'm surprised when she speaks – she sounds as if she's from the East End, and the accent doesn't seem to go with her almond-shaped, liquid brown eyes, or her exotic appearance. Her friend Maxine says hello, and we sit together and talk about the house, about David and Angie. Maxine tells me they all met at the club David mentioned, the Sombrero, and I instantly decide that this is the club to go to – forget the Speakeasy, where my friends and I usually end up.

David and Angie's friends look so effortlessly stylish and I long to look as if I belong with this crowd. The room is coloured with soft lights and perfumed candles, and people are drinking and smoking. On the coffee table there's a couple of bottles of wine with glasses, and all the fabulous magazines I'd seen before. Freddie and David sit close together on the couch, and while I stand and chat to Daniella I'm confused and more than a bit shocked when David leans over and kisses Freddie full on the mouth, a proper kiss! I know Daniella sees this but she says nothing and just smiles at me as I glance towards Angie, who laughs as she says:

'Boys will be boys!'

It's at this moment it's apparent: I'm not like these people at all. I'm completely out of my depth. I'm only three miles from home but I might as well be in a foreign land. It's pitiful.

Angie smiles and walks me over to a group of boys who are lingering to one side of the room. She introduces me to 'the boys who play with David' as 'the girl who cut David's hair'.

''ello,' they say in unison. They're in regular T-shirts and jeans and don't look like David or his glamorous friends in the slightest.

'When are you going to cum cut my 'air then?' one of them asks, laughing. Woody, Mick and Trevor introduce themselves in their northern accents and explain that they're from ''ull', which requires translating into Hull. Mick is gorgeous, with long blond hair and smooth muscular arms. They tell me they lived in Haddon Hall with the Bowies before they got their own flat at the other end of Beckenham.

I ask them if they like David's hair. The silence that follows is short, and Mick says, 'It's not for everyone.' They all laugh. They're nice and polite, and they seem more like me than the other people here. I begin to breathe easier. A glass of wine appears for me and we continue chatting away. Woody chuckles as he tells me about what it was like when they lived here.

'It were busy,' he laughs. 'People cummin' and goin' at all hours.' He pauses, looking at Trev.

'Yeah,' Trev agrees, 'all sorts going on.'

'Where did you sleep?' I ask, knowing there aren't any other bedrooms.

'You know where you cum in,' starts Woody, 'that big staircase?' I nod. 'There's a balcony up there, and Angie give us curtains and mattresses.'

'You mean the minstrels' gallery,' chimes in Trevor with a smile.

'We got a great view,' says Woody slyly. That sends them all into fits of laughter.

Angie overhears him and says, 'You should have come down and joined us.'

They go quiet until she passes, then Woody whispers, 'No fuckin' way.' That draws a smile from both Trevor and Mick. I don't ask questions but the innuendo in the air is obvious. Woody and Mick laugh a lot and smoke roll-ups from an Old Holborn tin; their fingers are brown from the tobacco. I talk to Woody about Hull and how it's different from Beckenham. 'Better fish and chips in 'ull,' he says.

'And not so bloody expensive,' adds Trevor.

'No, I like it down 'ere,' Woody goes on, 'there's more t' do.' They're not like the local boys in Beckenham either, now that I think about it. They seem sharp in a way, on guard and focused.

There's more loud laughter from the other side of the room. A young boy, Billy, is trading insults with Freddie and another man I don't know. It's all light-hearted enough but the banter is very sexual in nature. David still has his arm draped around Freddie's shoulders.

A short while after this, the band look ready to leave; and as things seem to be getting more boisterous on the couch, I decide to go as well. I ask them if they want a ride home. Mick and Trev squeeze in the back, Woody comes in the front. They direct me to go past the Regal and round the roundabout, and point out a driveway just beyond. I pull on to the gravel and they all get out.

'Night!' they call as they go up steps into the house. I drive home, hoping I was cool enough with David and Freddie. Before I left, Angie took me to one side and asked if I wanted to work with them. I said yes, but I'm not sure if she's serious. To be fair, I'm still a bit shocked at the kiss, but the rest of it was okay and I'm hoping to get invited again. The next day, as I'm driving to work, I decide I'm going to ignore the kiss and pretend it didn't happen. It's a blast hanging out with them at Haddon Hall. Mick is gorgeous, true, but I'm not even looking at him like that, I'm there for something else entirely. I pull into the car park. It's Saturday, and I bet everyone else is asleep. I yawn and make my way to Evelyn Paget.

4
COMING OUT

January 1972

Mum comes home with the *Melody Maker*. It's the January issue and David's on the front cover, looking wonderful – with my haircut! I almost can't believe it. This is my first brush with fame, the first time I've known someone who's not only in the paper but on the front page. I want to dive in and read the article, but I have to face Mum first.

'Is this who your friends are?' she asks, hands on hips, lips trembling. I can see that she's almost in tears. I've been dreading this moment. I know my mum; she's going to take a dim view of me being involved with what she calls a 'poof'.

'Yes,' I say, and I hope she leaves it at that, though it's unlikely.

'I'm the laughing stock of the shop! Mr Jutton' – Mum's elderly boss – 'is hardly speaking to me, and neither is his daughter!' His daughter is the other part-timer. 'Goodness knows what poor Mrs Jones is going through.' There's a pregnant pause. 'What do you think, Ken?' She shoots a look at my dad, and he looks down at the front cover.

'Is he a poof then?' He's got a face on that looks as if he's smelled something bad. My brother laughs, until I glare at him.

'No, Dad, he's married with a child, he can't be.'

I look at the front cover and yes, there it is, on the front page of the *Melody Maker*, and inside, by another photo with the caption

'Oh You Pretty Things', he says: 'I'm gay and I always have been, even when I was David Jones.' I jump in with both feet.

'Mum, you've met Angie.' I know she has, Angie shops at Juttons. 'You said you liked her.' I'm desperate. Mum has a lot of influence over me – I live at home, and she can make my life a misery. 'He's married, they have a son. It's just for show, for the papers.'

I hadn't told her about the kiss I'd seen at Haddon Hall between Freddie and David, nor about the mixed crowd that hangs out there. I don't tell her much at all, and that seems to upset her more than anything. I know she's curious, but I also know that she won't understand. I don't see any point in telling her what's really going on. I keep quiet.

She turns her back to me and starts peeling potatoes for dinner. There'll be more to come, she's just recharging. My brother, Mick, minces out the door, his eyes rolling back in his head. He leaves the kitchen with a laugh as I turn away.

'Well, at least we know he won't be after you then, Suzi,' Mum says, her hands busy in the sink. I don't say anything – it's better she doesn't know that David's after everything!

5

CHICKEN SHACK

The Golden Arrow is up the road from where I work. It's a new pub, large, comfortable and modern.

It's Friday night and I meet Judy and Wendy at the pub, but it's quiet and none of our friends are here so we go across the road to the Mistrale Club. The Mistrale Club is close to the station and has a couple of bars and a live-music stage. Whoever's playing tonight isn't pulling a crowd.

'It's dead in here, let's go up the Speak,' Wendy says. She's right, it's totally dead, and to top it off, Kim, the boy I have a crush on, walks in with another girl. I'm devastated. He was a bit of a muso and had lovely eyes and blondish curly hair. We'd looked at each other over our drink glasses in the pub and spoken a couple of times. I'd even offered to cut his hair. He took me up on it and I went to his house, cut his hair and fooled around with him in his bedroom a bit, but when I left, he didn't ask to see me again – he never called, and since then I hadn't seen him at the pub. I cut my eyes at him as I leave.

Wendy leads the way out. She works at a dress shop and wears black Goth clothes, stacked high heels, tons of eye make-up and dark-red lips. Tonight, as she walks out of the club, she looks like a pirate ship in full sail. Her long hair falls around her moonlike face like a curtain. She has a habit of twisting her hair in her fingers, silver rings flashing as she slides them through it. Judy and I are both wearing black flares; her heels are higher than mine, but I'm taller. She's all in black, but I break it up with a turquoise T-shirt under my jacket. My hair is still long, still blonde, and backcombed madly at the crown.

'Come on, Suzi, we won't be late. We'll have a great time.' It's about 10 p.m.; the pub will be kicking out soon and really I should go home. Kim's still on my mind: what did I do wrong?

'I've got a joint for the car,' adds Judy, trying to entice me.

'I've got to work tomorrow,' I groan.

'Come on, Suzi,' begs Wendy, and before I know it we're piling into my old Austin A40 and driving up to town. I've known these girls for a while now and they're a lot more fun than the old crowd I used to hang out with. I know the car has a lot to do with the relationship – I have one and they don't – but most of the time I don't care. Going out with them is more exciting than anything I've done before. I'd never go up to London at night if it wasn't for them.

Judy's a blast. Before I met her, she was a young tennis star at Beckenham Tennis Club. There was talk of Wimbledon, but that's all it amounted to: talk. Now she works in an office and gets the weekends off. Her hair is short and shaggy, her shoulders are large, and she has a slim, tight body and taut legs. She's 'a bit of a goer', according to my brother. I don't care what she does, I'm going along for the ride, and she's certainly broadened my experience as to what 'going out' is all about. We puff the joint on the way up to town and finally get to the Speakeasy. The Speakeasy is on Margaret Street in central London; it's a hip club full of musicians. Judy smiles at the doorman as we squeeze into the Friday night crowd.

'Who's that?' I ask Wendy as Judy runs over to say hello to someone who looks like a walking skeleton. His jacket hangs off his shoulders as if they're a clothes hanger and his drainpipe trousers look like they've been painted on, ending with black winkle-picker shoes. He's older than us, smokes incessantly and seems nervous, his eyes darting about the club. I look at his hair – I always look at hair – and it seems his is thinning. He wears it in frizzy curls, pulled forward to hide the receding hairline.

'Oh, it's Stan the Man from Chicken Shack,' Wendy says, 'and he's with the divine drummer, Paul.' She widens her eyes suggestively. 'Judy and I have been to a couple of their gigs. We told you about them, Suzi!'

I remember Judy saying something about a band that they had seen, and how she likes the lead singer. Judy likes a lot of boys, so I hadn't paid much attention. I look over and see Paul at the bar. He's quite handsome, about my height, with long curly hair, wearing tight blue jeans with a denim jacket. As he walks from the bar, he holds my eyes with his.

'Hi,' he says, looking me up and down.

'Hello yourself,' I quip back.

Wendy joins Judy, who by now has a drink and is laughing loudly as she looks up into Stan's face, his arm around her shoulders. As they get lost in the crowd, Paul offers me a drink. This means a lot, given that drinks cost a fortune in here. We stand and talk about his band, Chicken Shack. He tells me that 'Shack' has a long history – the only original member is Stan Webb, nodding in his direction.

'I've only been with them a few months,' Paul says, 'but I love it and think we have a chance. Christine Perfect used to play with Stan and she's amazing.'

He pauses as we move to a less crowded area. I'm silent. I'd like to say I know who Christine Perfect is, but I don't, though I love hearing about touring, about how good they're getting now that they're playing every night. I'm impressed with anything that isn't a normal life, and I'm impressed with Paul.

'Let's get out of here,' he says, taking my hand.

Stan, Judy and Wendy follow us out the door, and we walk to their flat, which is right off the King's Road. It's a small place on the third floor with a couple of bedrooms and a tiny living room. It's a mess: clothes all over the floor and full of empty beer bottles and fags. Nothing smells good. It's 1 a.m. Judy goes off to Stan's room, Wendy dozes on the couch and Paul continues to tell me about life on the road.

'Yeah, well, we just got back from Germany, you know. We're really big out there. You'd never believe all the women – they're wild for us.' He's smiling as he gets closer. 'I much prefer English girls though.' I want to believe him. He starts to kiss and touch me. He's so handsome, he gives me the shivers. 'Come into the bedroom,' he whispers.

I follow him into his room and we start to fool around on the bed. You know that feeling when you really want to but wonder: is this a good idea? Although he's sexy and says things I want to hear, I'd like to know more about him than him just being hot in Germany. It only feels right for a minute, and then it feels all wrong. All of a sudden, I want to be at home in my own bed with my dog, Ringo, cuddled up beside me.

'What's wrong?' he asks when I refuse to take off my knickers.

'Got to go,' I mumble, 'got to go to work in the morning.' He asks me if I can't take the day off and I say I can't possibly. I'm going home. I go out to the living room and wake Wendy up, and call out to Judy, 'I'm leaving.'

27

I hear Stan tell her that she can't stay. 'Me wife's coming in tomorrow. I'll call you next week.'

The girls both go to sleep as soon as they are in the car – typical – and as I race home down the South Circular, I wonder if Paul will call me again. I wonder if he likes me. I haven't been with that many boys. Mum warns me of the dangers of being too easy and I half believe her. I long to go out with someone exciting, someone who calls when they say they will. I want to be sure they're really interested before I go all the way with them.

I wait in the next night and he doesn't call. I tell myself to give him a chance and go to the Golden Arrow to meet the girls again. Mum tells me Paul called while I was out and that he'll call back, and when he does – the next evening – I try hard to be cool but I'm so happy that I'm sure he can hear it in my voice. When he asks me out to the pictures to see the new James Bond, *Diamonds Are Forever*, I'm over the moon.

He wants to take me out, not just 'bring a bottle of wine to mine'!

At the flat, I get a frosty reception from a blonde girl I haven't met before. It's not until I'm upstairs and see Stan standing in the hallway that I twig it's his wife. Stan looks at me imploringly, though there's no need. I'm not here to make trouble. Judy will be upset but she already knows he's married. I'm introduced as Paul's girlfriend, which is a thrill. We go to the pictures, me stepping into my new role, and I love the film: Sean Connery is suave and sexy; Shirley Bassey – who my dad loves – sings the theme song. Best of all, Paul is actually acting like a boyfriend, like someone who likes me. He persuades me to stay the night and take off work the next day; I call in at 9 a.m. and with a pathetic voice tell Doris I'm ill and can't make it in. After sleeping most of the day, we go down King's

Road with Stan and his wife. God only knows what I'm going to tell Judy.

The World's End is one of the trendy pubs on King's Road. As we're eating American hamburgers and drinking beer, I look at Paul and Stan in a new light. They travel all over Europe, live in a great flat in London – how do they do it? I have no idea, but it looks good to me. Before I go home, I buy their record *Imagination Lady*. Paul wants to see me again tomorrow, but my happiness is short-lived as he doesn't call. I waste the night looking at the phone.

I don't hear from him all week, and when Judy tells me the Shack are playing a gig on Friday I'm undecided about going, but she's keen to see Stan again and uses all her powers of persuasion. It's a small, crowded gig, lots of people are drunk and Shack don't come on until after midnight. Paul seems surprised to see me, but in a good way. After they come off, we leave and he walks towards my car. I tell him I have work in the morning again.

'Come on, Suzi,' says Judy, her eyes begging me to stay. 'You can stay, they won't mind.'

'I took off last Saturday, I can't do it again.'

Paul doesn't seem to care that much and walks towards a minicab office in the high street. At 2.30 a.m. I'm sick of saying I'm sorry and leave them to wait. I drive down the South Circular exhausted with everything.

Paul calls a couple of days later and he seems okay. He tells me there's another gig coming up. I start to see him here and there and I'm around the flat enough to feel comfortable talking to Maggi, their roadie. It's crowded in the small flat with the three of them there, and all they talk about is making it. Their record is in the charts in Germany, and they want to tour again. I sit and listen to their hopes and dreams.

Paul and I are hot and heavy on and off for a few weeks. Then he stops calling. I try to call him but there's no answer, and it's another few days before I hear from him. He invites me to the flat. I feel a bit nervous, uncertain as to why, but by the tone of his voice I feel like something's up. I arrive and Maggi lets me in to an almost empty flat.

'What happened?'

'They've got a tour, in Germany. I ain't been asked,' he says sadly. 'Tol' me the flat's over at the weekend and I have to leave.'

I don't know what to say. As I wait for Paul, Maggi tells me it's been a shock to them all, getting the tour and having to leave here. Paul and Stan come back from the pub and they're both a bit slaughtered. Stan staggers into his room while Paul, after seeing my face, gives me a hug and reassures me that he'll be back in London soon.

'This all happened so fast!' he says, pulling me into his room, bare except for the bed. All the colourful posters are gone, and his clothes are already packed. Afterwards, as I'm lying close to him, he tells me more. A promoter who had a spot to fill asked them to tour Europe with other British bands. He's so excited, and I can't blame him. He lives for this. 'No point in keeping this place, it's too expensive. I'm taking me stuff up to Birmingham and staying at me mate's house until we leave.'

There's no thought of me; not for a second are my feelings considered. We've been together only a few weeks, I know, but we'd had some fun, and now it's over. It's not a choice, it's a given. There's nothing I can say. This is his dream and, funnily enough, I understand. There's such joy in his face. Who wouldn't choose touring

Germany over – what? Without his band, what will he do here? And then, with piercing clarity, I see the life of a musician's girlfriend or wife laid out in front of me, and I know that's not where I want to be.

In the years to come I see this scenario played out repeatedly, and it happens to me too.

6
STARMAN

I start advertising on noticeboards for private clients. I like the extra cash and it's easy. Angie calls when David needs a touch-up or a trim; I'm always free for them. As I'm doing his hair or waiting for the tint to take, I listen to them planning their future. It's mostly about shows, or how David should look, what he should wear, who's going to come to the shows. What about press? Tony Defries's name comes up often. He's David's manager and full of ideas. Everybody seems sure David will make it.

One night, as Angie opens the door for me, I hear music coming from the living room. Freddie and Daniella are at the foot of the stairs with Maxine, and we walk in together. Mick Ronson is sat by David, both of them smoking cigarettes, a song floating out of the small cassette player on the floor between them; our conversation slows to a silence. David's voice is ethereal, and as he sings the chorus of 'Starman' I notice how different the music sounds from most of his other songs. I think it sounds extraordinary.

When the song ends, Angie screams and we break into applause. David and Mick sit in silence, smiling at each other. Angie is sure it'll be a big hit when it's released.

David is full of nervous energy, alternately pacing the room or sitting down smoking. It's rare to see him so animated; he usually sits on the floor, quiet and reflective. I hear my name mentioned from the other side of the room; it's Angie, talking to Freddie Burretti.

'Suzi, can you help with that?'

'Help with what?' I ask.

'The costumes and shows. We need someone to take care of the boys.'

My heart leaps: 'I'd love to do that.' I'm not sure if David is listening but I don't care – at least Angie knows how I feel. David suddenly says that he wants a full-length mirror in his dressing room and that he needs privacy.

'I can't see myself in a small mirror,' he complains. Mick nods in agreement and Angie is right there with them. I blurt out an idea that pops into my head about how they can get full-length mirrors cheap from Marley Tile, a hardware shop in Bromley, and bring them to the gigs. There's silence from the boys, but Angie says it's a great thought. Emboldened, I continue:

'I think they're about twelve and six each.'

'Let's get two,' instructs David. 'When we come off, I want a place to change. I don't want fans to see me with make-up running down my face.'

'There's so much to do,' says Angie, looking at Ronno (as Mick is often called). 'We have to transform these boys.' She walks over and strokes his hair. He pulls away, laughs, and looks at me. I think: yeah, I wouldn't mind transforming him!

'Let's get the band's hair done and see what we can do with make-up,' says Angie. 'When can you do their hair?'

'I can come Wednesday, or any evening,' I stammer.

'Why not tomorrow?'

'I've got a job,' I remind her, 'at the hairdresser's.'

'Oh, you have to stop working for them and come and work for us.'

I look at David and he flashes me a grin. Mick winks and I'm ecstatic. I go home with my heart racing, dreaming about touring, about America. Maybe I'll be part of all that, maybe I'll get the job and go on the road with them. I can hardly sleep.

In the cold light of day, though, I decide not to give in my notice. Angie hadn't even mentioned wages; no details had been discussed. I live in a world where if you want a job or someone wants to hire you, you interview, discuss the hours and wages, and then take the job or not. It was so airy-fairy with this lot. I want the job if there's one to be had, but that's the question: is there even one to be had? Part of me thinks this dream of going on the road with them is within reach, but I'm hesitant; days pass before I pluck up enough courage to call Haddon Hall. A stranger answers the phone and says that Angie has gone to Cyprus, and David's recording in London.

I trudge to work the next day deflated, frustrated by the whole situation. My ship seems to have sailed and I'm not on it. Mrs Jones comes in for her appointment, but she isn't telling me anything. When I mention Angie, she purses her lips in disapproval. Even a mention of David isn't getting the usual smile, so I roll her hair up in silence and put her under the dryer.

Christmas comes and goes with no word from them. I start to stalk Haddon Hall. I drive by before work, after work, before the pub, after the pub. I can't see the house from the road as the drive-way curves, trees and overgrown bushes hiding the windows and front door. After a few days, though, I'm confident, pulling into the driveway as if I live there. I get out and have a look around. No one's home; there's no sign of life. I cruise past the band's flat too

– there are lights on, but I don't have a reason to drop by. I haunt the local pubs hoping to bump into one of them, with no luck.

This goes on for about a week, until one night the lights at Haddon Hall are back on. I brake in the shadow of the trees and very slowly reverse out of the driveway. I don't want to look desperate; I'm praying they haven't heard my car. The next day, Angie calls me at the salon and asks me to come and give David a touch-up and trim, and it's as if we talked yesterday. They're back.

When I walk in that evening, there are suitcases in the hall and the smell of cooking in the air. Angie is free with her 'darling's and 'how lovely to see you's . . . and it is lovely to see the both of them, it really is, Angie with her confidence and style and David just being David. I touch up his roots and listen to some music he plays on a cassette.

'We're playing in London next week,' David says. 'Why don't you come?'

'Bring some friends,' Angie says.

I can't imagine what kind of a show they'll be putting on. I call Judy, who I've been neglecting.

'David Bowie's playing a gig in London, and I've been invited. Do you and Wendy feel like coming?'

'Are they any good?' asks Judy.

'Don't know. I've done his hair and heard some of the music – it sounds great, but I haven't seen them play.'

'Oh well,' says Judy, 'if they're no good, we can go on to the Speak.'

We drive up to town in my car, and my God, it's a mob, really full. Chicken Shack gigs are never full. Angie has left me tickets at the door so we park the car and go straight in. A screech to my right and here's Angie bouncing through the crowd. I catch a glimpse of Wendy's amazed face as Angie pulls all of us to where she's sitting on the floor. She's wearing pink jeans and a feather top, and everybody seems to know her. I try to play it cool. Angie isn't cool; she's just loud and crazy.

The lights go down, some classical music comes on and the band walks on to the stage in the dark. Angie screams and jumps to her feet; I follow, along with the rest of the audience.

I can see David as he waits in the wings while the band slide on their guitars and Woody settles behind his kit. The classical music fades out, the stage lights come on and they start and settle into a strong, loud beat with a wailing guitar. David walks to the centre mic and as the spotlight hits him, the audience collectively gasp.

His hair glows fire-engine red and sticks straight up like bright feathers, his white face in full make-up giving him the appearance of being from another planet. He's wearing a tight red two-piece suit made from quilted nursery fabric, strewn with yellow, blue and green ABCs. His feet are laced up in red plastic boots. It's a real eye-opener for me, seeing him in place onstage; he looks like an exotic bird. He stands stock still at first, letting us all have a good look, and then he launches into the first song.

David and the Spiders are electrifying, and the tension builds in the crowd. Onstage, Mick's even more gorgeous, spinning and twisting as his muscled arms rip the hell out of his Les Paul. The band wear velvet suits a bit like David's but each a different colour – curtain material from Liberty's, I find out later. As they play, the whole place rocks. This isn't folk music: it's unbelievably loud, exhilarating. I didn't know what to expect but it isn't this. I look at Wendy and see it in her face too.

'Why didn't you tell us?!' screams Judy, clapping and jumping up and down with Wendy.

'I didn't know!' I yell back, clapping and dancing along with them. The audience are of the same opinion, the place in an uproar.

At the end of the show, Angie takes me to meet David's manager, Tony Defries. He's tall and slightly stooped, with a huge afro and a large cigar hanging between the fingers of his right hand.

'This is Suzi Fussey, she cut David's hair.'

'Did you enjoy the show?' he asks softly.

'Oh yes I did,' I start to enthuse, but he walks away, leaving me talking to myself. As we're about to leave, Angie turns to me.

'Well, that's all settled. Come and work for us full time after we get back from Cyprus.'

And with that she's gone, leaving Wendy, Judy and me standing among the beer bottles and fag ends.

'Angie just offered me a job.'

'Are you going to take it?' asks Judy. 'What kind of a job?'

'I'm not sure, but I think it's to do with hair and costumes.'

'On the road?' cries Wendy.

'I think so, but I don't know. We didn't talk about wages or anything.'

We go out to the car and as we get in, Wendy asks if I want some money for petrol. This is a first, and I realise to my great delight that I have gone up in their estimation, something more than 'the girl with the car'. Wendy and Judy can't stop talking about Angie and David on the way home.

◆

A week later and the reviews in *New Musical Express* and *Melody Maker* are raving about the gig. I can't wait to hear from Angie again, if only to find out more about the job offer and terms of employment, but when she calls she doesn't mention it and invites me to another gig instead. I'm hooked and go with them to every gig I can. Judy and Wendy are almost forgotten, as is Paul. He doesn't think too much of Bowie and his band and he kind of reminds me of my mum with his attitude, but I don't care. He didn't think twice about dumping me to go on tour. Maybe he's sorry he left me; he certainly calls more now that I'm never home.

Mum and Dad ask me where I'm going; sometimes I tell them, but sometimes I lie and tell them I'm going to Judy's, or out with the girls for the night. I can only go to the gigs if they're not too far away, given that I'm still working at the salon every day.

Angie calls again. 'Can you come tonight?' she asks eagerly. 'To do David's hair?'

I dress as cool as I can and go over with all my hairdressing stuff. David and Angie are sitting on the floor of the living room, baby Zowie crawling around on the carpet and hanging on to the coffee table. No one's paying him much attention, though, and soon Sue Frost – who lives downstairs and helps with sewing the costumes – picks him up, tucks him under her arm and off they go.

Angie makes tea as I slap tint on the roots of David's hair. I'm eager to let him know how great I think the shows are.

'I love the costumes, especially the boots,' I say, while trimming his hair, 'but the way the band looks, they need to have more of a look.' He's quiet. 'They need help with their hair.' I have his attention now. 'Mick looks okay, his hair has a little style, but the other two!' I roll my eyes, and David's laughing in agreement.

It's true: the long straight hippie look that Trevor has does not go with the smart costume he wears, and the same is true of Woody, his hair a mess of dry, sticking-out frizz.

'Go do their hair,' says David, laughter in his eyes. 'Let's see what you can come up with.'

It's what I was hoping he would say. It's an opportunity to impress him. I feel butterflies; I might talk a good one, but I'm nervous. I have to come up with the goods. Mick has a certain style, but I wonder how daring the rest of the band will be. Angie calls and tells me I'm booked with the band for next Saturday night.

◆

My heart's in my mouth as I drive to the band's flat near the Regal. Trev comes down to let me in and I walk up the stairs into the living room. I immediately smell pot, and smile. I'm introduced to Stuey, who's smoking the most enormous joint I've ever seen. A bouncer from Hull, he joined David after they were overwhelmed by an unfriendly audience in a working men's pub; their look didn't go down too well, and they were chased offstage. Mick suggested Stuey come to London to look after them.

The living room is crowded with people, and I can't help but wonder how everyone fits in this small flat. Apart from Woody and Trev, there are two girls. The one sitting with Woody is introduced to me as June, and when she says 'hello' she sounds the same as the boys; it's an accent that predominates in the room. The other girl is Trev's wife, Anne, pretty and shy with long blonde hair. Someone else is sitting on the couch, a tall and skinny man, his hair long and greasy, and he's introduced as Pete Hunsley, their roadie.

Stuey laughs as he looks at me, and says, ''ow's it goin'?'

He's about my height, very powerful-looking in his arms and shoulders, thick in the legs. I've never met a black person before, let alone one with a Yorkshire accent – can you imagine? Stuey makes me smile right away: 'When you're dun wi' 'em, I'd like summat stylish meself.'

He bends forward and laughs at my reaction. I'm lost: not only have I never met a black person before, I've got no idea about his hair, but I play along.

'Sure,' I say blithely, as if this is the kind of thing I do all the time. 'I'll give it a go,' and with that he smiles and hands me the joint.

I look around the living room. There's no sign of Mick, and I can't help but be a little disappointed. My God, he looks amazing onstage, and somehow he's just as good in person. I find myself wondering if he has a girlfriend, before chiding myself. I can't even entertain the thought. I want a job with them, and fancying Mick Ronson won't help. Thankfully, he makes it easy for me: he doesn't give me any encouragement whatsoever.

Everyone seems curious as to what I might do to their hair. They're not the only ones!

Woody is first up. He's whippet-thin, with a James Caan-type body and wonderfully shaped shoulders (probably a result of constant drumming). His hair isn't easy though. I cut it close to his head, a bit like David's style, but it's coarse and dry and little curls keep springing up around his ears and neck. After shaping it I use some GARD lotion, hoping to knock the curl out of it, and it stands up.

He walks to the mirror, followed by June. They both seem happy with the result.

Now for Trevor. His shiny brown hair is parted in the middle, hanging down well past his shoulders.

'I don't want me 'air short,' he says, and I can understand why. I have a brainwave.

'Let's just cut the top off and spike it up. We can blend the top into the rest with long layers.'

'Eh?'

'It'll look great. And then we can dye it black.' There's a pause.

'Blue-black?' he asks.

'Yes, blue-black.' I'm surprised; he's obviously given this some thought. It's a fantastic haircut. Trevor loves it and wears it with panache.

Mick, who materialises while I'm styling Trevor's hair, won't let me touch his hair.

'You're all right,' he says.

'Who does your hair then?'

'I do it meself,' he flashes back, with a steely look that invites no questions.

'If you ever want help with the colour . . . ?'

He doesn't say more, so I leave it. I have a feeling he doesn't want to look like David, but I find him more handsome than David anyway. He has fine features with large grey-green eyes, an aquiline nose, high cheekbones and fine, fair skin. While the details are delicate, the end result is very masculine. The powerful performance I saw is completely at odds with the man standing in front of me now. Onstage he's passionate and confident, but here he seems almost shy. We're both in the kitchen; I'm putting my stuff away and he's making tea for everyone. I'm hoping to win him round, so he'll let me cut his hair and impress David in the process, but he's fast with the tea and out the door with his mug as soon as he can go.

I leave, saying to Trev, 'I'll be in touch about the colour. See you soon!'

Stuey calls out, 'Guess you'll do my 'air next time?'

Gales of laughter follow me downstairs.

7

DAVID AND ANGIE

Late May / Early June 1972

I've heard 'Changes' on the radio at home – it's Tony Blackburn's record of the week – and I'm elated as I rush out to get a *Hunky Dory* cassette. 'Changes' and 'Life on Mars' are the standouts, and I listen to the album over and over again.

I find myself navigating two lives, one that's normal and frankly a little boring, the other full of possibility. I still see my friends at the pub but will drop everything to go to Haddon Hall; hanging out with David and Angie is just intoxicating. David's rarely home these days, and when he is he's often shut up in the back room, loosely called 'the studio'. Tonight, though, he's here. I can feel it as I walk in: there's an electricity in the air, Angie's bubbly, and I can hear music. The house feels alive, guitars and laughter filtering out from the studio. Angie beckons me into the kitchen and we make tea and take it in to them. Mick's sitting at the piano, David on a stool holding an acoustic guitar. Mick looks so smart, in an open-collar white shirt and Stirling Cooper black jeans. David, on the other hand, looks tired and has a hat on to cover his greasy hair. He's wearing floppy trousers and a ratty T-shirt. They don't say anything to me besides thanking me for the tea, and that's only from Mick. Angie and I leave the rehearsal room and go into the living room.

'"Starman" is doing great,' she squeaks. 'It's only going up from here.'

I feel as if I should know about this, how the song's doing, but I don't. I act excited, and I am excited, but I wish I knew more about charts and what's coming up. I resolve to learn. As if she read my mind, Angie shows me the cover of the next album: *The Rise and Fall of Ziggy Stardust and the Spiders from Mars*. I gasp. My haircut is on the album cover! I can't help but wonder when this photo was taken – it's identical to the style I copied from the Kansai photo. The colour isn't quite right, and it's not really standing up, but it still looks great; David looks out of this world. I'm knocked out my haircut is on the front and the back of the album cover.

I suddenly feel so grateful to Angie. Without her I wouldn't be here, would never have done David's hair. Her suggestions, her ideas and endless energy give this adventure wings. She tells me they all love David's hair, his manager, Tony, included.

'I never cut Mick's hair,' I admit, suddenly embarrassed.

'Oh, I know, it's okay. He'll get there, and in the meantime, he still looks fabulous, doesn't he?' I have to agree with that. 'David and I love the boys' hair too!'

'I'm so glad, I think they came out really well.' I'm dying to ask about the job, but I don't want to be pushy and I don't want to be a nuisance. What if they've changed their minds? In a way, I'd rather not know – I'm here now and I'm happy with that.

◆

A string of dates is coming up, but most of them are miles away. While they're away on tour I don't go to Haddon Hall much, so I'm pleasantly surprised when Angie calls and asks me to come over and do her hair. She has a special date and says she must look great.

It's Wednesday – my day off – so I go over late morning armed to the teeth with hair dye, razors and scissors, all wrapped in my cape. She greets me in her dressing gown and nods me into the kitchen. As we sip our tea, she leans in and confides in me.

'I saw Mickey Finn last night,' she giggles. My face registers surprise and incredulity: I've heard of Mickey Finn, seen him on the telly, he plays percussion for T. Rex. 'I didn't get home until 6 a.m.!'

She laughs, crossing to the bathroom directly opposite the kitchen. There's a steaming bath waiting; the room smells of lilacs and there's candles burning. In my mind I compare my bathroom to hers, and mine comes up wanting. She slips off her robe, gets into the bath and continues.

'Oh, it's okay, David knows all about Mickey. He encourages me! We have an open marriage; we both have fun. Darling . . . life is too boring to be with just one person.' She tosses her head back and slides under the water. It feels a bit unfair – it's as if she's sleeping with the enemy.

'It's no secret,' she says, coming up drenched with suds, 'it's just the way we are. We're both liberated, both happy and free to do whatever we like.' One of her long legs stretches over the lip of the bath, toes dripping water on the floor. 'It's better than lies and deceit, don't you think?'

I'm at a loss as to what to say, so I don't say anything. 'My first great love was a girlfriend from my school in Connecticut,' she sighs, giving me a wicked grin. 'We were caught together in bed and I was expelled from school!' I'm not sure what reaction she's looking for, but if it's shock, she's succeeding – and it must be written all over my face, judging by the way she keeps laughing.

She gets out of the bath, dries off and slides back into her dressing gown. As she sits in front of the mirror, I get out my scissors and slim down the sides of her hair close to her head. I watch her dress. I'm not attracted to Angie – I'm not attracted to girls – but I love the way she looks; everything about her is just effortlessly stunning.

The subject's dropped, and we go on to more important things. How are the shows going? When can we go and see them? Does Sue have enough fabric? When's Freddie coming? . . . When am I getting a job? It's on the tip of my tongue but I don't ask.

It's not long afterwards, maybe a few days, when David calls and asks if I can come over and do his hair. I wash my hair and wear the nicest things I have: a long cotton skirt that wraps tight around my hips and flares out to the floor and a pale green crossover ballet top with long sleeves. When I get to Haddon Hall, David opens the front door to greet me with a big grin, holding my shoulders as he kisses me on both cheeks.

'You look nice,' he says.

Alarm bells go off: David never does this, never opens the door, never kisses me. I look around for Angie and ask where she is. 'Oh, she's off being her usual fabulous self,' he laughs. 'I don't know where she is half the time.'

I think of Mickey Finn as he gently takes my hand and walks me to the living room. I sit on the couch, he on the floor. 'I don't really want my hair cut. I wanted to see you.' He smiles sheepishly as he looks up at me.

'Oh,' I say, and then stop . . . I've no clue what else to say.

'Let's go up to town and have dinner. I know this great place Tony takes me to, Mimo's, you'll love it.' He looks so earnest. I can't help but smile and I'm flattered he wants to spend time with me, but I sense there's more to this than meets the eye.

I'm nervous about being alone with him – what will we talk about? Usually when I'm with David and Angie it's them carrying the conversation, talking about Andy Warhol, or William Burroughs and his book *The Naked Lunch*, or clubs and events in London that are coming up (which I might have heard of but haven't seen for myself). I'm a bit in awe of these conversations. I want to contribute, I try and make a comment here and there and I laugh when I think they're funny; but my opinion is rarely sought, and only in the realm of fashion and hair or a perceived slight about David in the papers. I'm panicking. What will I say if David talks about Rimbaud, or Nietzsche?

I need not worry, though, as tonight I meet a different David, charming and sweet, and before I know it his arm is around my waist and we're out the door, in his car and on our way to London. It's easier going than I think; David seems interested in what I have to say and he puts me at ease. When we arrive at the restaurant, I can tell he's a regular by the way they greet him:

'Good evening, David, right this way, David, your table is waiting.'

He laughs as he takes my hand and walks in with me. Everyone stares, his hair and clothes bright against the white linens and fine china. The way David dresses is unusual, to say the least, and tonight he's wearing his jeans tucked into boots; his shirt is loose and patterned and covered by a purple jacket that's made of velvet. The restaurant itself is small but bustling with waiters and diners, and there's fresh flowers in the middle of the room that spill out alongside bottles of wine and a great basket of fruit.

We sit at a corner table. David orders wine, and we get menus. He leans over and whispers in my ear, 'Everything tastes good. I hope you like it here.'

I'm basking in the attention from him. David is as charming as ever but when I mention the band he changes the subject, and it feels as if he doesn't want to discuss music with me. I'm dying to know how the tour is going, what's coming up next, but he doesn't want to talk about that either. Instead, I remark on how good his hair looks and he just laughs, and in a way he almost seems shy, but I can still sense the confidence that makes him who he is. We do talk about his manager, and David's almost reverent about the way Defries makes things happen, about the way he creates opportunities. Finally, though, we talk about Angie.

'I don't know what I'd do without her, she's so outrageous and brave,' he laughs, running his hand through his hair. He looks so young at that moment, almost vulnerable. 'Not a jealous bone in her body,' he adds, giving my knee a squeeze under the table.

On the way back to Beckenham, I think about what's coming up. I want a job with him far more than a night in bed, but leaving gracefully feels complicated. We get to Haddon Hall, back to where my car is, and pull into the driveway. He turns to me as the engine goes silent, and we sit in the dark until he says:

'Well, Suzi, are you coming in?'

I know, I could get in my car and go home, but part of me is curious. I'm not that attracted to him, but as he holds my eyes the distance between us closes and suddenly he's kissing me. It's a rush, the passion rises, and before I know what I'm doing I'm in the house and in his bedroom. The soft lighting is romantic and I let my inhibitions go as he undresses me; I bask in the golden pink glow that is their bedroom. He's a tender, romantic lover who tells me my body is Rubenesque, that I'm beautiful. I feel as if I've crossed a line I didn't mean to cross, and when it's over and the room comes back into focus he says that he loves being with me, that he'll have fun telling Angie all about it the next morning. I freeze.

'You're going to tell her?'

'Of course,' he answers, 'I tell her everything and she me, we have no secrets.' Shame washes over me. How can I face Angie? 'She'll understand,' he says, seeing my reaction. 'She expects it – we have an understanding, it'd be worse if I didn't tell her.' He seems a little impatient with me now, and a bit amused. 'Don't be silly. I thought you understood.' I dress to leave. He doesn't get up to see me to the door, he doesn't say anything else except goodnight as he turns over to go to sleep.

Have I blown it? Will Angie feel betrayed? What was I thinking? I replay the evening in my head as I cuddle up in bed with Ringo. I remember what Angie said:

'Isn't it better than lies and deceit?'

She's right, she told David about Mickey and now David will tell her about me. I suddenly hope I get a good report. If I'm going to take part in this new world with new permissive trends, I must squash my grey suburban ideas and embrace it. Fidelity is not expected, nor wanted. Can I be happy with this? The idea of a man I love wanting to sleep with whomever – and expecting me to do the same – feels foreign to me. All I can do is wait for the fallout.

A couple of suspenseful days go by before Angie calls to talk about the next gig, as if nothing happened. She doesn't say a word about my night with David, and as far as I know never says a word to anyone else. I'm grateful; I don't want to come on like a groupie, I want a job with them. David – apart from a soft smile and a kiss on the cheek – behaves as he always does, concerned about tuning his guitar and the show.

The whole thing leaves me with questions: does everyone sleep with everyone together or do they seek privacy? Is everyone promiscuous? What I hear and what I see are two different things. I once felt a silent invitation from Daniella, Freddie's girl, a seductive look I chose to ignore. Freddie witnessed the brief interaction, he laughed, and the moment passed . . .

When the band lived at Haddon Hall, they saw half-naked girls walking around downstairs, part of an all-night party. They were invited to join in, but didn't go, preferring to watch from the gallery. I wonder why they didn't go: are they shy? The gay element might have put them off, or maybe they prefer their sex in private, I don't know.

I know David and Angie both like to mark their territory, but whether it's for show or it's really the way they feel is a mystery to me.

8
EARLY GIGS

Back at work, I catch Doris looking at me under her heavily pen-cilled eyebrows. She doesn't say a word, but I can tell they're all agog, bursting with curiosity. I don't tell them I slept with David, obviously. I just talk about the music and how much I love it there, how exciting it is to be in their company. Inevitably, they ask about the gay thing, and I shrug it off just like I did with my mum and dad:

'He has a wife and a child – how can it be true?'

They don't have an answer to that, and it's dropped. David is tongue in cheek about the whole thing anyway. He doesn't act like a gay man in the same way that Freddie and other boys do. He teases with his gay friends, and they might horse around a bit at home, but there's little action, just a lot of innuendo. I guess he is, as he says, bisexual. And besides, the primary focus with them is the music, and David's career.

Living together without being married used to be frowned upon, but it seems tame in comparison to whatever David is ushering in.

◆

The mirrors from Marley Tile travel with me in my new car, a black Triumph Herald. When I'm at a show, I set up the mirrors, take out my hairdryer and get drinks from the bar – anything the band or David want, I'll do it or get it. The gigs are small, the dressing rooms grungy, one or two rooms at best with a grotty bathroom in between. They're thick with smoke and Elnett hair lacquer.

As the band get ready, the audience's cheers can be plainly heard, adding a dose of adrenaline to the mix. I spray Trevor's sidies silver while Mick tunes up in the corner. He gives his guitar to Pete, the roadie, to put onstage and sprays his hair one more time; it's a golden helmet by now. Then he stands with David and the others at the side of the stage. I watch them furiously puff their final cigarettes and can see the sparks fly as they stub them out.

They go on to a roar, and I slip into the crowd as they rip into the first number, 'Hang On to Yourself'. This isn't a bunch of blokes getting up from the bar to play a gig – this is a proper show. David is ethereal, his make-up full and perfect, his hair like a traffic light. Mick – a god on guitar, with his shirt open to the waist – is posing and strutting. No one moves onstage like they do. The interaction between the two of them is electrifying, so rare and sexy.

At one of these gigs, I meet a photographer. He's tall and skinny with dark-brown curly hair. I'm told it's Mick Rock. Cameras hang around his neck and a huge black bag slips off his shoulder. As Angie and I scream in the audience, I watch him jump all over the place, snapping away. He's on the stage one minute, in the audience the next, and right down the front when he can get there. After the show we talk for a while, and he eventually asks me for a lift home. I agree – he lives miles from me, but I don't care. I ask him how I can get a proper job with David, but he doesn't know and we're too stoned to care. I drop him off and it's 4 a.m. as I drive down Cumberland Road. Foxes run in the early-morning light, it's nearly dawn, and I have to be up in a few hours to go to Evelyn Paget and roll up some old girl's hair . . . it's killing me.

Girlfriends and wives come to some gigs; groupies are always around, variations of the same girl, but they're not touring with the band or working at shows. Mum doesn't understand and worries that I'm out too much, not getting enough sleep. She's right, of course, but I'm waiting.

9

CRASH AND BURN

Paul calls after ages and invites me to a Chicken Shack gig. I'm curious to see him again. Wendy and Judy are desperate to come, though they haven't been asked themselves – Stan seems to have cooled towards Judy.

Paul greets me with a smile and a kiss on the cheek and seems to have forgotten how casually he dumped me. I'm pleasantly surprised that I don't find him that attractive any more. They get up and play, Stan takes a beer onstage, they chat to each other between songs, no one knows what's coming next. They all laugh when the bass player starts a song in the wrong key: it's so unprofessional, and boring to boot. The audience chat over the band and only stop when the music's too loud to talk over. Judy and Wendy sing along and dance at the bar.

After the set, Paul is attentive; he buys me a drink, tells me he missed me, that he's glad I came. I flutter my eyelashes and flirt with him – what's the harm? They get up and do another set, and when they've finished we wait for them to pack up what little gear they have and go to the Speak for a drink. Paul asks me about David – Judy told him I'd cut his hair – and I tell him that I love the music and try to describe a gig, but it falls on deaf ears.

'Is he queer then . . . ?' he asks. This again.

'He's bisexual,' I say, but he persists.

'Does he go with men?' He looks at Stan, and they both wait for me to answer.

I toss my eyes impatiently. Judy tries to help but they don't take any notice of her. I laugh inside. It's so obvious they haven't seen David and the Spiders in action. If they had, they might not be so fixated on the gay thing. I think they could learn a lot from David. The detail that goes into every performance makes the show what it is. You add adrenaline to all that hard work and you get a seamless show, a show that has the audience on their feet. Everything is carefully planned; nothing is left to chance. It sets him apart from everyone.

I tell Paul I'm going to get a job with them and he says, 'Come on, Suzi, what would you even do?' I say I've been asked to take care of hair and costumes, but he thinks I'm talking rubbish and changes the subject back to their tour in Germany.

I tune him out. I couldn't care less. His attitude towards David reminds me of my mum. It makes me all the more determined to get this bloody job. Paul invites me to stay the night and I make a weak excuse about work; this time he knows what I mean without me having to tell him. Stan doesn't ask Judy to stay, and by 2 a.m. I'm ready to leave.

We say our farewells, and I swear Judy's crying as she follows Wendy into the back of the car. Before long, they're both asleep – some things never change. I speed down the South Circular, zip through the tollgate by Dulwich College and continue up to Crystal Palace. At the top of the hill, I make a left towards Penge. I'm only a few miles from home when it happens. My eyes close, I don't feel anything. There's the crunch of metal on metal.

'What the fuck?!' yells Judy.

'What's happening?' cries Wendy from the back. I don't know and I don't stop.

'I think I hit something,' I mumble, 'maybe a parked car?' It's the only answer.

The car feels fine. I reassure myself that it can't be that bad. When I get to Judy's house, I get out and take a look and . . . oh God, it's much worse than I expected. The side of the car looks like a tin can with the top peeled back.

'Shit . . . what am I going to tell my mum?'

A chill settles over me as I drive home, more awake now than I've been all night. I creep into the house; Ringo greets me with a small woof. I quiet him and crawl upstairs to bed.

When I wake up in the morning, I look at the time and swear under my breath: I'm late. My friends might not have to work on Saturdays, but I do. I struggle into my clothes and, with my head pounding, go downstairs. The milkman's at the door to collect the weekly bill. He asks what happened to the car.

'What car?' my mother asks, looking out the door.

'Suzi's, I think.'

'Is there something wrong with your car?' she asks. I look blankly at her as I try to think of something to say.

'Someone hit me in the car park.'

She goes out to have a look. I follow, and yes, it is quite a mess. I hear her gasp, then with her lips pressed together she says, 'I don't know what your father's going to say.' It's an empty threat and she knows it. 'In a car park, are you sure?' She studies me closely.

'Yes . . . No note or anything. It was parked by the Golden Arrow.'

Mum isn't convinced, but what can she say? I gulp down some tea, and as it starts to rain I get into the damaged car and drive off. I regret staying out so late. I regret wrecking my car. Wendy and Judy are probably still sleeping. I can't keep doing this.

◆

Even when I'm not with David or the band I'm out all the time, looking for something to do. I date furiously and my latest boy-friend is the manager of a club: deep-sea diver John. He's handsome, and after some years working on an oil rig he's now the manager of the Mistrale Club. Linda, who also likes the Mistrale, is keen on Phil, John's friend, who works there too. We get free entry into the club and free drinks. It's local and I'm glad of it; David and the band are local, and I want to be close in case they call. I'm privy to the management of the venue: I see who's playing, meet the band and, in general, feel pretty important.

All the boys who work at the Mistrale have hot cars: Mike Loveday – the owner, an ex-racing car driver – has a Rolls-Royce, Phil's got a black Austin Healey, and John has a white E-Type Jag. I like John, but really it's his car I'm in love with.

When the Mistrale closes, we head to Mike's private club and watch belly dancers while drinking vodka-oranges and eating moussaka. There are problems on the horizon though: Mike uses the till as his personal piggy bank. John takes issue with this and, after a huge row, leaves. He takes me down to Broadstairs to visit his parents, and I'm terrified he might propose. It's quiet and still, and apart from the sea I'm not feeling it. I can't wait to leave. Now more than ever, I know I'm not ready to settle down.

A week or so later, I talk John into coming to see David play at The Greyhound in Croydon. It's sold out, kids clambering at the door. My name's on the list at the back, but it's just one name and it's mine. I try to call to Stuey but he's not listening. Angie's nowhere to be seen, and when I look at John, I feel disappointed. I can't leave him outside, so we go to the pub, have a few drinks and I miss the gig. He tries to make light of it but I'm despondent and act like a child. It's the kiss of death. I know where I want to be and it's not with John. Soon after that, we break up. I look forward to the calls from Haddon Hall more and more.

◆

I haven't heard from Wendy and Judy for a while but one Friday I meet Judy at the Golden Arrow. The pub's busy and over in the corner I see a crowd of people, and in the middle of them a blond head: Mick Ronson. He's with Woody and Stuey, and they're pleased to see me. To my surprise, Mick offers me a drink. Judy comes over to say hello and bats her eyelashes at them. It's annoying, but only to be expected. It's not long before other girls gravitate towards us. I know most of them by sight, and tonight they all seem to know me.

'You didn't tell us you had such nice friends,' Woody says, laughing as he eyes up the talent around him. I want to tell him that I didn't know I had so many friends either, but instead I tell him that this is my local. Some of the blokes in the pub are checking out what's going on in the lounge. I hear my brother laughing at the bar, oblivious to it all.

A girl I know by sight called Pat sidles up behind me and greets me as if we are old friends. She's tall and model-thin, with long straight blonde hair. She knows she looks good, and all the boys – including my brother – want her. I look at her in amazement. She never usually speaks to me, preferring to hang with Beckenham's more wealthy set, the girls with nicer clothes, better cars and posh accents. They all stick together; their parents hang out at the Beckenham Place Park golf club, or the tennis club on Foxgrove Road. I see Pat look at Mick, who holds her gaze. When he motions for her to come and sit on a stool beside him, something inside me snaps and suddenly I feel furious.

She smiles at me as she takes a seat, and as I smile back I turn to Judy. Within the space of a minute she's laughing away with Woody, flirting with both him and Mick. How could she? Now I'm really upset – she's coming on like a groupie! I have to remind myself quickly that this is not what I want; I want to work with them as part of their crew, not sleep with them and be forgotten. Yet if that's what I want, then why am I cross? The pub closes and Woody invites all of us back to their flat, and as soon as we get there he immediately disappears into his room with Judy. Mick and Pat get cosy on the couch. Stuey's nowhere to be seen. I know I'm jealous.

'I'm going.'

'Oh, okay then, if you must,' says Mick as he stands up with a smile. He gives me a peck on the cheek goodbye and as I turn to leave, I ask Pat if she wants a ride.

'No, I'm fine. I'll get a minicab.'

'I'll get you a cab,' Mick says to her, sitting down. 'See you soon, Suzi.' There's nothing else to say so I leave. I curse in the car.

Judy and I have a row the next day. She says I should relax and have a good time.

'You're never getting a job with them, you're dreaming.'

I'm starting to wonder if she's right. I spitefully tell her that Woody has a girlfriend in Hull, but she doesn't care, she's more concerned about the local competition than anyone in Hull. There's another girl who's in the mix now as well, Sharon. She adores Mick and I know he's seen her more than once.

A few days later, Mick calls to ask for help with his hair. It's the first time he's asked me and I silently cheer. When I get to the flat, he isn't there, but surprise, surprise, his girlfriend is down from Hull – and she has a baby with her! I had no idea – and my first wicked thought is that I bet Pat doesn't know about this. I'm relieved for some reason. I dye Trevor's roots, Woody thinks about a blonder look, and by the time I'm finished with them, Mick is home. He doesn't look himself; I can tell he's had a few drinks.

''ello,' he says to me slowly, smiling and leaning against the back of the couch.

He sits down heavily on a chair and stretches out his legs. Denise, his girlfriend, asks him if he's eaten. 'I've 'ad me tea,' he answers, smiling again at me. ''ave you cum to do me 'air?' He gets up slowly and weaves into the kitchen, where he sits on a chair. 'Do whatever you want.'

Here's my chance to do something different, something to impress. The old girls' water rinse worked so well on Angie, and I want to try it again. I carefully dye his hair with multicoloured streaks. It takes a while, and as I'm finishing he's almost asleep. The next day, he calls me at the salon in a panic.

'Can you cum and take this oout?' he asks in a desperate whisper.

'Of course I can,' I say, feeling hurt. 'I'll be down right after work.'

When I get to the flat, Mick's pacing, his hair shining with bright feathers of blue, purple and pink colour. He's nervous, and

I understand – it's too much, even I can see that. I feel terrible and quickly mix up a 30-volume hydrogen peroxide shampoo. It does the trick, and when only a vestige of colour is left, he's happy and grateful.

Woody's in the corner, chuckling: ''e nearly 'ad a fucking 'eart attack when 'e woke up!'

10

SHOCK AND AWE

9–10 June 1972

Angie calls in a high state of excitement: they're going to see Elvis at Madison Square Garden in New York City. 'Come over, David must look wonderful!' I want to go with them . . . there's no chance of that happening, but still, a girl can dream. As I drive to Haddon Hall, I can't help but think over and over . . . they're going to see ELVIS!

When I get there, David is full of nervous energy, pacing up and down, smoking one cigarette after another. All he talks about is meeting Elvis – how it will be, what he should say, what he should wear and, above all else, how can he look really young? He wants to be seen as the heir apparent; he's planning a photo of him and Elvis where he'll be looking up at the older man.

'I'd sell my soul to be famous.' It just comes out.

Angie and I look at each other in silence. I feel as if I'm in a melodramatic black-and-white 1940s movie. It doesn't feel quite serious, like he's trying out saying it. Elvis has been a huge star my whole life. Even before The Beatles there was Elvis, so it's a surprise to me that David compares himself to Elvis and I marvel at his confidence. I mean, David's good, he's really good – but Elvis?!

It's a fast trip, there and back, just to see Elvis. They're flying – something David said he'd never do again, citing Buddy Holly and Ritchie Valens's deaths, each of them just as their star is rising. They pack; Angie must look good too, she's got a part to play, and Mick and Tony are going as well. I make sure there's enough GARD and hair spray and off they go.

''e's unbelievable,' Mick says when they get back. 'The women are mad for 'im, they throw their knickers at 'im an' Elvis mops 'is brow wi' 'em!' He can't stop laughing. 'When he cums on for t'encore, there's such a kerfuffle down front, security blokes tryin' to keep the gurls from jumpin' up on t'stage, Elvis leanin' down to 'em, encouragin' 'em. They go mad! Those security blokes 'ave a really tough job.' He shakes his head at the memory of it. 'I were nervous. I thought we'd be crushed, there's 42,000 people in Madison Square Garden, and when everybody stood up and pushed forward, we couldn't move.' It's obvious he's completely in awe of Elvis's charisma. 'After t'last number he runs off t'stage, gurls are screamin' and cryin', and then, over the loudspeakers, an announcement: "Elvis has left the building!"' He waves his hands as if holding back traffic. 'And just like that, 'e's gone, the audience are goin' crazy, sum gurls are faintin'.' He can't get over it.

It's affected them all, and none more so than David's manager, Tony Defries.

◆

Even though I haven't got a proper job with David yet, I'm loving my life, I love it all. It feels like I've arrived, bearing witness to the get-in and set-up at each venue I manage to go to. The sound check, the slow build to the show. The band just get better and better, their sound more powerful than ever. Tickets sell, people are talking – there's never been a band like this, so glamorous, so controversial.

They shock people, they get more and more attention. And then later that month comes Oxford.

The show kicks off at the Town Hall, students crowding the front and pressing against the stage. It's going to be a good show; they're all good shows. I'm at the side of the stage having a great time, and as I watch the band I'm dancing, inside and out. The photographer Mick Rock's here too, snapping away.

The last song of the set is 'Suffragette City', and as Mick goes into his solo David walks over to him and bends his face down towards the guitar strings. My jaw drops – what is he doing? Mick shuts his eyes as David uses his teeth on the strings, his hands reaching around and grabbing Mick's arse . . . OH MY GOD! My first thought is for Mick: he's been called gay a few times and hates it. Did he know David was going to do this? Whatever he's thinking, he plays with his eyes closed.

Stuey, who's crouched down behind a monitor, glances at me and we both have one of those 'what in the world' laughs in surprise. The crowd is silent . . . before bursting into a roar and going wild! Stuey has his job cut out for him protecting David and the band from their fans. Mick Rock is still snapping away behind me; I can see flashes over my shoulder. The look between Woody and Trevor is priceless. Mick's face is unfathomable, his eyes still closed.

David releases him and with a 'wham bam thank you ma'am' comes off, grabbing the cigarette from me and shouting to Mick Rock: 'Did you get it? Did you get it?'

Mick follows us back to the dressing room, saying in his slow way, 'What were that about, David?' He looks perplexed.

'Did you get it?' David repeats.

'Well, I'll know tomorrow,' Mick Rock says. 'I certainly got something.'

The band is unusually quiet when I go to their room. Mick puffs on a cigarette and looks white under his make-up. I ask him if he's okay.

'I suppose.' Then with a sigh, 'But me parents . . .'

He doesn't need to say more. I'm also thinking about my parents, and I'm just the hairdresser.

Within the week, the photo is plastered as a full-page ad in *Melody Maker*. It's from David, thanking the fans and crew, and it's an amazing photo – solid shock and awe, just what David needs. But Mick is upset, he threatens to quit; he's threatened before, over costumes and such, but this time it feels more serious.

I wonder if David's worried about losing Mick. He was a folk singer before Mick came along; Mick transformed him both onstage and in the studio. Onstage, Mick's masculine sex appeal plays off against David's femininity. It's thrilling, irreverent, and oh-so appealing. Somehow, they talk it out, and whatever David says seems to work. The move ends up being a part of every show.

I think David would be lost without him.

11
LOU AND IGGY

8 July 1972

I walk in from work and dinner's cooking: sausage and chips. Dad's
having a whisky and I can hear my brother upstairs. It's Thursday,
and Dad heads into the living room with his dinner and sinks into
his chair. My brother comes down and I can hear the TV on. It's
Top of the Pops . . . wait, what am I hearing? I run in and, yes,
David's on *Top of the Pops* singing 'Starman'! David's on *Top . . .
of . . . the . . . Pops* – I can't believe it!

'Is that . . . ?' my mother starts from behind me.

'Yes, yes! That's him, that's David Bowie!'

I'm so proud. Everyone takes notice. David casually drapes his
arm around Mick's shoulder during the song, and I give my dad a
sideways look but he doesn't say anything. If they only knew what
went on at the shows. Mum says she likes the song. David's seductive
stare as he points his finger into the camera mesmerises millions. He's
a calculated performer, and if you didn't know who David Bowie
was before the show, you certainly do after. The band looks so cool
in their costumes, David and Mick so handsome. The other bands
all look boring and safe in their denim, with long hair and no style.

The appearance catapults 'Starman' into the charts, and the Ziggy
album along with it. It changes everything. We're hastily invited to
perform at a charity event called Save the Whale organised by the

environmental group Friends of the Earth. Tony Defries tells me that a good charity gig is always worth doing.

The concert takes place at the Royal Festival Hall, a very classy venue, and it sells out within hours. We run on the best fuel: adrenaline. Kenny Everett, a huge fan of David's, is the host, and there are some back-up bands, Marmalade being one of them, but we don't mix with them; I don't know why, but we don't. Lou Reed is here and is planning to join David and the Spiders onstage. Lou is talked about almost religiously by David and Angie, and I hear a little about Nico too, a reclusive singer who made music with Lou in New York.

I picture Lou being a huge star in the States, but when I meet him he doesn't seem like that. He's pale and sweaty, walking around backstage with a couple of people he brought with him. He still looks great though. Angie chooses a black velvet Spanish suit complete with a bolero jacket for him to wear. There are a handful of diamantes on the front lapels and sleeves. I'm eyeing up his hair, thinking about what I can say to break the ice.

'Do you want me to help you with your make-up?'

I don't have much experience, but I've helped the band here and there and watched make-up artists work with David. How hard can it be? His hair is easy, short, soft, dark and curly. I think of it as a halo, then go to work on the make-up.

I ask him if he's nervous and get no response. I've about given up when after a while he says, 'How many people out there?'

'It's sold out, about three thousand, I think.'

He's silent. I don't know what else to say. I thought he'd be thrilled. David and the boys are always knocked out when I tell them a show's sold out. I ask him if he likes his hair and offer him a trim. He doesn't say anything, but his friend Eddie nods and says, 'Yeah, come over to our place.' I take his number.

When it's time for Lou to go on, I walk him to the side of the stage in the dark, torch in hand. The band is roaring, the audience up and dancing, and that buzz gets me every time. The lights go down and Mick starts playing the throbbing riff . . . 'I'm Waiting for the Man'. Lou steps on the stage, the lights go up and the crowd kicks it up another notch.

It's an incredible gig. They play so fiercely, so gorgeously, the band all sparkle and Lou all rock-and-roll darkness. It's one of the best nights yet and lots of press are in attendance; everyone's charged up. Tony mentions a party later that week to discuss plans to meet the American press. How fast we all run towards the future.

◆

All I want to do is impress David and Angie, so going round to Lou's is a plus in my book. Lou's staying in Wimbledon, home of tennis champions, pristine hedges and well-manicured lawns. I can't help but wonder why he's living here. He's doing a couple of shows while he's over – a month or so from now he'll play Friars in Aylesbury; David's immensely popular there. The house is typically suburban: two floors, quite a large kitchen, a back garden. The kitchen sink is full of dishes and there's open food containers on the side.

A tiny, beautiful girl, no taller than a child, comes into the kitchen wearing a dressing gown that's far too big for her; it drags on the floor as she walks. Her soft, curly, ash-blonde hair frames a perfect face with a small nose, huge blue eyes and porcelain skin. She's a mini sex bomb; completely stunning.

The band struggle up and one by one I do their hair in the kitchen. Nothing too crazy, they're not David and the Spiders, but everyone's happy. I don't see anything out of the ordinary. I've heard rumours about Lou and drugs and the like. I like a bit of a puff with the roadies but have no experience with anything harder.

We hang out for the rest of the afternoon. Eddie plays music, dark and loud. They tell me they're going to a restaurant and then a club, and ask if I want to come along. We get into the car; Lou doesn't say much on the drive, so I listen to stories about America from Eddie. Iggy Pop's name comes up – he's also playing in London. I've heard a lot about Iggy from David and Angie and want to see if he lives up to the hype.

Lou's due to play a show at King's Cross the following Saturday and it's agreed that I'll come over to help him with hair and make-up before going there together. I drive to Wimbledon in my car that now has a lavender wing, thanks to Dad. It looks scruffy, and even more so when I see a white Rolls-Royce in front of their house. Eddie's as surprised as I am. Tony Defries is pulling out all the stops for Lou's gig. My dad drives cars like this for a living; he won't believe I'm going to ride in a Rolls. Lou wears the suit Angie bought for the Save the Whale concert and he looks great. His hair and make-up go smoothly, his hair a soft black cloud around a pale face with dark, almost panda-like eyes. We pile in and sit in silence on our way to London. Eddie cracks gum that sounds like pistol shots.

I look out of the window and see a girl with her boyfriend at a bus stop. She's laughing up at him as he's saying something to her and holds her close. Suddenly, a wave of nostalgia washes over me as I think about John and my friends at the Mistrale Club; I think about my dog, about home, and I feel sad. I think this is the life I want but frankly I'm exhausted, constantly trying to be someone I'm not and seeing things I maybe shouldn't be seeing. My mood does lighten as we get into the city, though, and my memories of John disappear as quickly as they came to mind.

Lou isn't as nervous as he was last time, but then this isn't the Royal Festival Hall. It's a crazy little gig by the railway station and I can hear the trains rattling from the back of the venue. Inside, it's dark and cold and feels a bit damp, and all I can smell are the toilets and stale beer. I walk across the sticky black floor towards the dressing room and say hi to a few Bowie fans. Backstage smells worse than the main room, so after a minute or two I go out front to see if anyone I know has arrived. I figure a lot of Bowie people will be here, and maybe some journalists. Mick Rock's at the side of the stage. I go and say hello, and though he's nice enough he's busy with his cameras, so I walk to the back and wait around. The audience are a darker version of glam. It's mostly boys or young men wearing black leather. They look a little out of it, but I don't know if it's real or for effect. There are a few girls here too, also wearing black, with a lot of dark eye make-up.

The time has come: Lou steps on to the stage and picks up his guitar. The band join him, and they start with 'White Light/White Heat'. The audience pick up and move towards the stage; 'I'm Waiting for the Man' comes soon after and gets a lot of applause. I like both these songs; they sound different without Mick Ronson's playing, but it's still good. I begin to understand what the fuss is about. Lou is magnetic, he pours over the mic as he sings, and his band is solid. The audience are loving it, dancing a bit to the fast ones and silent for the rest. 'Sweet Jane' starts, and I feel myself drawn in.

At some point, David and Mick sneak in – they're with a few people, maybe the promised press. I see them at the end of the gig and watch while they say hello to Lou and the band. Mick spots me and says hi – he looks surprised that I'm here – but as soon as people start to point at them, they both disappear, along with Stuey. After an encore, I head back to Wimbledon with Lou, Eddie, the band and the mini-Marilyn. I'm running on empty.

We're in Aylesbury the following night; I've heard a lot about David and Aylesbury and I can't wait to see it for myself. Mum's a bit worried and asks me if I'll spend a night in at some point – what was I doing, out all night every night? Angie tells me David's planning to work on a more ambitious show in London, and I'm beyond happy since it means they'll be closer to home – plus I'll have a chance to be involved in whatever they're doing. I try to explain this to Mum and she tries to understand, but it's all a bit of a lost cause. To her credit, though, she never tries to stop me, and for that I'm eternally grateful.

When I get to Friars it's bedlam, and after I've made sure everyone has everything they need backstage, I run out front to find a good spot by the sound booth. The club is packed to the gills with overexcited, expectant kids, and tons of fans have waited for hours to get in. It's a total crush inside and out.

The press from America *is* here, staying together and looking around. They stick out like a sore thumb and seem a bit bewildered, as if they didn't expect a gig like this. Maybe it's the size of the club, or the fact there's no seats, only the floor to sit on; maybe the raucous fans aren't what they expect. They're standing together, making faces at the warm beer.

'Ode to Joy', the Beethoven piece that David nicked from the movie *Clockwork Orange*, starts up – he uses it to open every show. As it plays, some of the fans beat and stamp their feet in time to the music. David and the band take their places in the dark, and as it finishes David steps forward to the mic and says:

'I'm David Bowie, and this is some of our rock.'

They launch into 'Hang On to Yourself', the guitar blistering hot, David sounding great, Mick amazing, and the bass and drums lock it all in place. It's fast and furious and the fans love it. The place is rocking and as I steal a look at the journalists, I can see they love it as well. By the end of the show, the Americans seem to be just as in love with David and the Spiders as everyone else.

Iggy Pop is playing at King's Cross later that night. David and Angie leave in a car after the gig – I don't know where they're going, maybe to see him perform. A bus for the journalists pulls up and they get on it and leave. King's Cross is a long way away from Aylesbury and I'll have to drive back to Bromley after. I'm exhausted, so I decide to give the gig a miss and go home.

Angie tells me Iggy Pop is like no other live entertainer she's ever seen, and according to the music press from that night she isn't wrong. In the photos he's snarling, wearing silver leather trousers that hang low on his snake-like hips, his chest bare; and apparently he threw himself into the crowd at one point, landing on them and then the hard cement floor. When he got back to the stage, he leered at the audience upside down while doing a back bend. He was threatening, insulting, and he encouraged the audience to be the same. When an amp broke down in the middle of his set, Iggy changed his tune and stood alone and sang 'The Shadow of Your Smile' a cappella in the centre of the stage.

. . . I wish I'd gone.

12

DORCHESTER HOTEL

16 July 1972

Everything's been carefully planned by Tony Defries. He tells me RCA, Elvis's label, have signed up David and there's going to be a press party at the Dorchester Hotel, to which I'm invited.

The Dorchester is elegant and exclusive, and as I approach on foot from Marble Arch I've got butterflies in my stomach. I should have taken a taxi, I think to myself; no one *walks* into the Dorchester. My mother and I used to pass it on our way to the West End and she speaks about it in awe.

'Most expensive hotel in the world,' she nods at me as we pass. I believe her – why wouldn't I?

As I get closer, I see one gleaming car after another pull into the entrance, where the doormen welcome the hotel guests and collect their luggage. I can't wait to tell my dad – his job has him sitting outside hotels like this, waiting for his boss, and now I'm here as a guest.

We drink tea, eat small things from big plates and congratulate everyone on the success of the previous week. David, Lou and Iggy are in fine form. David's dressed to impress with a tight-fitting purple velvet jacket, zipped at the front and paired with flowing, patterned satin trousers and his red boots. This outfit is one of three he'll wear during the afternoon. Lou wears a laced-up shirt with pink trousers, and Iggy has on jeans with a Marc Bolan T-shirt.

David is animated, Lou sulky, and Iggy – arriving late – tells people he wants to fly out the hotel window. David holds court sitting next to Lou, telling the reporters that they're both heralding in a new era. The press eats it up. They pose for photos and I see Mick Rock again, his camera flashing as he takes photo after photo. After a while I take a walk outside and join Tony Defries, who's puffing on an enormous cigar. It's a surprisingly warm evening and there's other people lingering too, escaping the hotel heat. Hyde Park stretches out across the street and the lights of the hotel spill out behind us. Tony starts to talk to me about money: who has it and who doesn't, what it can do, how to get it, how to spend it. We talk about my parents, about Bromley.

'Look at all these residences,' he says, gesturing with his cigar. 'Do you know how much it is to own or rent one of these flats?'

He tells me the values and I gape. I look around at the blocks and blocks of flats near to the hotel and overlooking the park.

'How can people afford it?'

'They have the means.' He smiles. 'And guess what, Suzi, they're all full.'

He nods as he puffs on his cigar. I walk back with him into the hotel. It's something I never forget.

◆

The class system in England is secure and comfortable – if you're in the right part of it. The middle class think they are sandwiched evenly between lower class and upper class. Most people, and I include myself here, think wealth is more evenly distributed than it is.

My parents have a normal life. They think they're well off – and to some they are – but they, like so many other people, have no idea what real money is. I don't either, but I'm learning. The only way my family is getting any money is to win it. Dad plays 'Spot the Ball' in the *News of the World* on Sundays and tries his luck on the football pools; Mum's happy as long as she thinks she is better off than her sister. She runs our house on a tight budget, and every penny counts. You can't use the telephone without her breathing down your neck, one eye on you, the other on the clock. She buys a freezer and fills it with what she grows in the back garden; beans and berries, after being carefully prepared, make their way into the freezer, and apples and plums from our fruit trees do the same, or sit in glass jars in the pantry. Meat, bought in bulk, is trimmed and frozen too, and the same goes for bread. Our freezer groans with the weight of so much food.

My parents wouldn't understand David and Angie, the way they spend. It's hard to explain their complete disregard for money; they would despair at the waste. Mum doesn't waste a thing. Whatever's left on the table makes its way to Ringo's bowl and then to the foxes at the top of the garden or the compost heap. I admire her now, but back then it was a pain in the arse.

I feel as if I'm seeing life at its most raw and most celebrated. From King's Cross Underground station to the Dorchester Hotel in Mayfair, I'm navigating my future. My head spins as I try to understand how to straddle my values with what's around me. I instinctively know I must maintain my reputation, not be seen as someone who might be disruptive within this small, intimate circle of people. I see it first-hand, how girls are treated. They're left behind; they're here to have fun with but they don't get to tour and they're not a part of what's really going on. I try to explain to my parents about the way other people live, but it falls on deaf ears.

Mums says: 'You think you're better than us.'

I'm not better, but I am different.

My dad, as a chauffeur, sees the other side of life more clearly. He drives to Sir Thomas Sopwith's estate in Scotland for a week-long fishing trip every spring; Dad gaffs the salmon out of the river for his boss, Mr Robertson. Later in the year they go shooting on Mountbatten's estate in the country; Mr Robertson shoots, Dad holds the pheasants. He sends a large salmon home from Scotland and a brace of pheasant from the country. We eat these so many ways that we get sick of it.

'It's a pound a pound,' Mum will say when my brother and I make a face at fishcakes again. Fishcakes are usually the last of it, and Ringo sits patiently under the kitchen table waiting for them. The pheasants hang in the garage, dripping blood from their beaks, until they're ripe, after which they get taken to the local butcher to be dressed. My grandmother knows how to cook them and she teaches Mum.

Dad lives on overtime and has such patience, but he has no expectations of rising up the ranks. In his book, he's already made it: he's survived the war and he owns his house. He has a wife, two children and a boat – he's happy enough. Wealth is a club that is closed to people like Dad. It isn't like that for me. It isn't all about the money; it's about expressing oneself in an artistic way. Art is the great leveller.

13
THE JOB

Defries, 26 July 1972

I get an unexpected call from Angie one night shortly after the Dorchester party.

'Suzi: David and I have been talking and we need you to come and work with us all the time. We have a lot of shows coming up, there's tons to do . . .' She stops. 'Suzi?'

'Yes?' I say quietly. Is this really it? My breath catches in my throat as she goes on.

'Tony's the one to talk to about wages and everything, so go and see him, okay? You can even do his hair!'

She laughs her laugh, and as I laugh along with her I wonder what on earth I'm going to do with that enormous afro.

The next day, I drive to London, rehearsing what to say in the car. After I park, I knock on the door of Gunter Hall, my heart racing. Tony answers wearing a dressing gown; it's the middle of the afternoon. He smiles like a crocodile as he asks me in. I want the job, but I don't want to sleep with the manager to get it. As I press past him, he doesn't move an inch.

Tony waves me into the living room and asks if I want tea. I decide to take no notice of his dressing gown and with a 'yes, please' to tea, I walk into a large room with double-height ceilings and a staircase that leads to a space overlooking the main room.

A small, slim girl bounces downstairs and jumps on the cushions;

she's in her pyjamas too and I immediately feel better for it. Tony brings in a tray of tea and biscuits and introduces Melanie as his girlfriend. Tony doesn't seem to be in any rush to get his hair cut and sits back, expansive in his bathrobe. He's not a classically handsome man but intelligence radiates from him, and his eyes, like steel-grey marbles, weigh me up.

'I'm going to make David Bowie a huge star.' He talks about David and Angie as if they are naughty children. 'When I found those two, they had nowhere to live, an ineffectual manager and no idea how to go forward. I felt sorry for them. They came here and David was huddled in the corner' – he points to where Melanie is sitting – 'they were lost. I'm looking after them now, and if I'm not wrong, by this time next year they'll be banging down the doors to get him to America. You saw the gig at Aylesbury.'

Tony says he has complete control; his plan is to make David unreachable, mysterious, otherworldly. 'Nothing is done unless it comes from here,' he says. 'All interview requests must be directed here. No photos are permitted when they interview, and none must be taken at the gigs. We will provide a suitable photo if needed.'

This demand and expectation of total control is part of the reason he hires people with little to no experience. He prefers people who work with him not to have any preconceived ideas; everything must be done his way. His ideas on management and touring are groundbreaking, and no one questions him. Everything he asks for seems normal. The rider he lays down for a gig is long and specific: if the piano is not in tune or the right size or an inferior brand, we can cancel the gig; if the dressing rooms are not equipped properly, or the access to and from the stage is not viable, we can cancel the gig; if the stage is too high or too low, the lights or sound inferior, we can cancel the gig. Of course, we never do cancel, but it scares the pants off people at the venue. Despite the fact most venues think we're nuts, they usually scramble to rectify any problems; after the show, they look at us in a different light. The attention to detail makes for a professional, exciting performance without any fuck-ups.

I remember what David said about Tony the night I had dinner with him: Tony's confidence and the way he says things makes me believe him. After a while, he asks me to cut his hair and stands up to clear a space. He keeps going as I trim his giant curls.

'All David should be doing is creating. That's what he is good at. We need a team of people that believe in what we are trying to do and who will give it their all.' We talk about David's haircut; he says he's impressed with the fact I didn't leave my job at Angie's beckoning but chose to see the offer first. I didn't say it was because I was scared of my mum, and that having money on the table at the end of the week was too important to give up for my family.

'I can't give up my job unless I get paid.'

He looks surprised. 'How much do you make now?'

'About eleven pounds a week, plus tips.' There's a silence, and I'm about to say that I'd take less when he says:

'We'll give you twenty pounds a week, plus per diems when you are away.'

I don't know what per diems are, but I don't care either. This is a huge raise for me and Mum will be pleased with the extra cash.

It's hard to believe I'm finally here, that it's all coming together. On the drive back home, it starts to sink in. Life is about to change. I'm going on the road with a rock 'n' roll band. I can scarcely believe it. Mum tries to be excited for me, but I can tell she isn't that keen.

'I suppose we'll never see you now,' she says with a sigh. 'Well, please be careful, Suzi.'

I hear a catch in her voice as I go out the door, but I don't care. I give in my notice at the salon the next morning. My boss, Mrs Fine, looks disapproving.

'You should think twice before giving up a secure well-paying job,' she tells me.

'I have,' I say softly, and after I work out my week's notice under the incredulous eyes of Doris and the staff, I walk out of Evelyn Paget for good.

◆

Monday morning, the first day of my new job, and I'm in the kitchen with Mum, talking over a cup of tea.

'What time are you going to work then?'

'I don't know, they're going to call me,' I answer, hoping they will.

She leaves for work and says over her shoulder, 'At least do the washing-up or something.'

I can't go to Haddon Hall yet, it's way too early. I think about David and Angie, the way they look. My wardrobe is limited to jeans, T-shirts and a skirt or two. I need to look more stylish. I'm determined to go up to the West End to get some cool clothes, to Miss Selfridge, or maybe Biba in Kensington.

When Angie calls, I drive to Haddon Hall, and she answers the door in her dressing gown. We go into the living room; it's dark in here and smells of stale smoke. I pull back the curtains as she half-heartedly starts to pick up the litter that's strewn across the floor. God knows what went on here last night. The place is a wreck – empty bottles, full ashtrays, glasses on every surface. Angie cackles as she picks up some satin knickers, nodding her head as I tell her about my visit with Tony. She isn't surprised when I tell her he answered the door in his dressing gown and laughs when I tell her about his haircut. David calls for tea and I follow Angie to the kitchen.

We carry tea and toast into the pink bedroom. David's awake but still in bed; he doesn't say much, just smokes and seems exhausted, his hair a giant baby quiff in the middle of his head. He abruptly gets up from the bed and, naked, balancing a teacup in his hand, leaves the room. I hear water running. Angie follows him and asks what he wants to wear, offering suggestions. There's a knock at the door and it's our local minicab company, Clockhouse Cars. David's going to rehearse at the Rainbow Theatre in Finsbury Park, the venue for the huge show he's planning. He leaves in tight jeans, a cool jacket and a butcher-boy hat.

After he's gone, Angie and I go back to the bedroom. She throws costumes and fabric on to the bed, talking the entire time.

'Freddie and I love Liberty's, it's our favourite place to shop.'

I wish I knew London the way she did. Mum and I take one route to London: we park at the same garage close to Marble Arch and walk down Oxford Street looking in all the shops, Selfridges being the favourite. I'm ready to see other parts of London, Chelsea, King's Road – and Liberty's!

As if by magic, Tony calls the day after with a strange request.

'Can you take Angie shopping? David needs some space to concentrate on this show, she's driving him mad!'

I'm surprised he puts it like that, but I'm only too pleased to go shopping with Angie. When I arrive at Haddon Hall, David's just getting up and there's a limo burbling in the driveway. Tony's final words ring in my ears: 'Don't come home until the car is full!'

What a wonderful job, I think to myself as we swish past the Golden Arrow and Evelyn Paget on our way to London. We drop David at the Rainbow Theatre then drive to the West End. Angie explains to me that our shopping trip is primarily for unusual items for the show. The limo takes us first to Oxford Street, where we buy shoes for the band at Russell & Bromley – black patent leather with a heel – before going on to Selfridges.

When we get to Selfridges, it's as if royalty has arrived: it's partly because of the limo outside, but it's also the way Angie looks and acts. Her short blonde hair and big fluffy coat are an attention grabber and soon we have the undivided attention of all the assistants in the underwear department, as well as curiosity from other customers. I'm not quite sure what underwear is needed for the show, but I watch as bras with matching knickers, suspender belts and stockings are taken to the till. Angie laughs at my expression. They pack them up and we move on to the make-up department.

I love the make-up department and watch as she plays with the pots and powders on display. She dips a brush into dark-blue eyeshadow, and as she applies it she talks non-stop about the Rainbow, about David and the wonderful show he's producing. She invites all the salesgirls to come, along with any customers that are within earshot.

'It'll be something you'll never forget,' she promises. 'What do you think, Suzi?'

She gazes at me through smoky eyes. I think she looks wonderful. I start looking for make-up that might work for David and the boys; I get mascara for Mick and some gold and silver eyeshadow for the others. We both look for as much glitter as we can find.

We break for afternoon tea before going on to Regent Street and the elegant Liberty's of London. As we walk into the store, Angie gives a contented sigh, and a feeling of peace comes over me too. There's an overwhelming sense of old England within these walls; wooden beams and decorated panels stretch and spiral up to windows at the top, where light floods in. Each floor has the promise of amazing things to look at and buy. I can smell jasmine soap and scented candles on this floor, and I see scarves being shown to a customer, the colours like jewels on the counter. Angie walks towards the staircase, me following close behind. On the third floor we step into a room full of shelves packed with bolt after bolt of colourful fabric.

A man hastens over to greet Angie as a long-lost friend.

'I'm so pleased to see you again,' he says, and then, looking at me: 'Where's Freddie?'

Angie smiles as she introduces me, tells him about Freddie, and with lots of 'darling's and kisses in the air, we walk towards a counter.

'I *have* to show you this fabric,' he says as he pulls out a beautiful metallic cloth. We both 'ooh' and 'aah' as Angie examines it; her eyes narrow as she makes her selection. Soon enough, packets are being wrapped and boxes are being filled, with more and more material being shown. We buy and buy and then it's off to the haberdashery department to pick up buttons and fastenings, zips and ribbons.

After Liberty's, we continue on to Mayfair, to Mr Fish's shop. It's small, with a round wooden sign outside, and inside it's just like any other shop – except for the clothes. I glance along the rails loaded with beautiful items before spotting the eye-watering prices.

I watch Angie as she talks to the assistant and tells him about David wearing one of the dresses on the cover of *Hunky Dory.*

And so it goes on, shop after shop. I trail Angie with boxes and bags, and as we finally start for home, the phrase 'Shop 'til you drop' certainly comes into my mind. Last stop, Penge, to buy cat litter for the cat downstairs and milk for the house. Mission accomplished: the car is full.

14

THE RAINBOW

19/20 August 1972

I walk through the stage door of the Rainbow Theatre the next morning feeling triumphant. I'm now a full-time employee of Tony's company, MainMan, and, as a result, of David Bowie. I go up some steps and out on to the brightly lit stage. The theatre smells of smoke, beer, and humanity. It's at least as big as the Royal Festival Hall and from where I stand I can see row after row of red velvet seats. They seem to go on forever before fading into darkness at the back of the theatre. I glance up at the wide, empty balcony, imagining it full of kids.

I go and check out the dressing rooms, which look plenty big enough for David and the band. A truck carrying scaffolding arrives and it's brought to the stage by sweaty men to be installed. The sounds of power tools start up and hammers ring out over the theatre. Slowly, the structure rises: steel towers, large screens with wooden walkways that lead from platform to platform, ladders that go up and down to the stage floor. The band's equipment comes next, pulled in by the roadies and set up onstage.

Lindsay Kemp's dancers have arrived in coats and scarves over their leotards. I'd heard about Lindsay from both David and Angie but hadn't met him in person yet. I know David studied mime with him and they worked with him on a production in the 1960s, and he's here now to help with this extravaganza. The dancers start to warm up on the side of the stage, and voices outside rise to a crescendo as car wheels spin on gravel: David, Angie and the band have arrived. There's a fuss and I hear loud voices throwing questions in the air, though no one answers them.

David smiles as he walks in next to Lindsay, cowering at the noise of the construction. They both laugh and David waves at the team to take a break. They walk around and under the installation, pointing and gesturing with their cigarettes. Lindsay's shortish, a little pudgy and a bit older than David. His cap covers what I suspect is a bald head. These two have been friends for years and were lovers when they first met, and now they'll be creating Ziggy's world onstage together.

The rehearsals are underway with both the band and the dancers. David and Lindsay suggest moves, change parts, and use flashes of energy to add something extra. Mick, who plays both guitar and piano in the show, has to work out how to get from one instrument to the other seamlessly.

David loves his little red suit from Kansai, but it's impossible to wear without the family jewels falling out. Angie has bought a jockstrap, but it's beige and shows, so I end up having to dye it brilliant red on the top of Mum's gas stove at home. The dancers take a break and float to the side of the stage, where they bend and stretch in the wings. Coloured lights wash over David and the band as they rehearse. I marvel at a follow spot that reduces to a pin prick and then extends back out, highlighting David's hands as he mimes.

Tony comes to the theatre in the afternoon. He walks around trying to gauge progress, puffing on his ever-present cigar. He calls the crew together by the sound booth.

'I don't want anyone talking to the press outside. What we're creating here is mystery and excitement, no one must give anything away.' We all look at each other as he goes on. 'None of you should take photos or record anything.' I look at my roadie friends: all of us are too busy to think about taking any photos or videos. 'There will be notices in the lobby forbidding cameras and recording equipment for the audience. If they do not obey, and we catch them, they will be ejected!' He seems delighted at the prospect. 'You're all doing a wonderful job helping David with this show.' His fur coat floats open as he walks off with a gait that's all his own.

We take over the Rainbow for three days before the actual performance. It's an unusual move but a necessary one given the show is so complicated. It's a circus outside, fans loitering near the stage door alongside the press. I walk past them, ignoring their questions and feeling oh-so important as they call out to me. I'm buzzing with anticipation. David is overjoyed, worried and just plain exhausted all at once. As I drive home, I've never felt more alive: no drinking, no pot, just pure adrenaline.

My job might have started as the hairdresser but now it's anything and everything. From hair and make-up to running errands. I take orders for lunch, grab coffee or tea, cigarettes, anything anyone wants. During rehearsals I watch David and the band play, the dancers moving fluidly, all in harmony with the song. It's coming together.

The morning of the show and I can hardly wait to get up there. I pack my make-up and slip into jeans and a Bowie shirt. I fluff my hair up, trying to embrace my curls, and arrive around the same time as the crew. We discuss the strong and weak points of the show over breakfast, the difficult ins and outs. Lindsay arrives and goes over the final moves with his dancers, followed shortly after by David and the band for a sound check. Roxy Music, our support band, have been hanging out all day and are politely asked to leave. They complain, and they have every right to. They're having a rough time: their sound check is non-existent, and they have to play in front of the curtain on a small strip of stage so as not to spoil the surprise of our set. They must be sick of us.

The house opens. Kids pour in down the aisles, some wearing make-up and sporting Ziggy haircuts. Roxy Music come on and are well received, but the greatest cheers are reserved for when they come off. There's a short break; our nerves are on fire. The audience start to call out and suddenly the moment is upon us. The lights go down and the audience's hum turns into a crescendo of sound as Beethoven's Ninth starts.

Lindsay and his troupe ripple to the side of the stage. The patter of feet, their ghostly figures and the smell of greasepaint pass by as they flitter to their places. We're all on our toes. David takes yet another cigarette and paces in a small circle. The tension on the side of the stage is so high, it almost has its own frequency. The band slip on next and pick up their instruments.

As the last few notes of the classical music echo away, the curtain parts and in a flash of light David strides on as Ziggy Stardust. He walks to the mic and begins the first song; Mick's piano plays in the background. One of the dancers, Annie, the only girl performing, bends and waves her body behind a screen as Lady Stardust, and it's as if she's doing moves from another planet.

David looks amazing – everyone does for that matter – and I'm transfixed as I watch the dancers spin and weave in the dry ice that billows off the stage. The shell-shocked audience spring to life as Mick slips on his guitar and rips into 'Hang On to Yourself'; the band play underneath the scaffold towers that David, Lindsay and the dancers are performing on. David sings songs about an alien who is lost in space, and he seems lost in himself at the same time. It's an extraordinary vision, David's imaginary world.

Lindsay as Starman looks like a fairy on acid – he has a clown face and huge black eyes, and he smiles at the audience as he puffs a massive joint. Jack Birkett, a blind – yes, blind – dancer, moves silently and without assistance up the scaffolding and out on to the set. I'm terrified he'll fall but Jack counts his steps. It's rock and roll theatre. Who knows if London is ready for it.

I feel as if I've held my breath for an hour before I slip into the audience to see the effect from the front. David delivers something so unusual, so unexpected, that it's hard to take it all in.

It's a long show and when it's done, after endless applause and demands for another encore, the crowd slowly filter out. Backstage is chaotic, everyone talking at once, Tony beaming, the band and crew delighted as they relive the show. Two more shows have been added for the next day, a matinee and evening performance, and both sell out instantly. I pick up the damp costumes and towels and straighten the dressing rooms ready for tomorrow. I'm exhausted and ecstatic, full of myself and the success of a show that I've been a part of. As I drive home, my mind goes over the whole awe-inspiring night. I sleep the sleep of the dead.

The next morning, I drive to Haddon Hall. Lindsay and David are in the living room and I can see the exhaustion and exultation on their faces as they sit together, smoking and talking quietly. The next two shows go just as well as if not better than the first one, and sure enough David wants to take it on the road.

The press reviews compare him to Judy Garland. 'A STAR IS BORN,' they rave, describing the shows as fantastical, theatrical and something altogether new.

David is the darling of London.

15
ALL THESE YOUNG FACES

At MainMan, I listen to Tony explain to David why Lindsay Kemp and his dancers, recently christened 'the Astronettes', will not be travelling with us any further: it'll be hard to find the right venues for the size of the set; it'll be difficult to set up and break down; and it'll be really expensive to travel with.

When I go back to the flat in Beckenham, it seems the band are relieved the show is being simplified. I ask where Mick is and Trevor tells me he's been in the toilet, writing, all morning. My curiosity gets the better of me – I have to see it for myself, so I knock on the toilet door. Mick answers in a cloud of smoke, headphones round his ears and a worried look on his face.

'I 'ave to finish this, Suzi, too noisy out there. We can cut me 'air later.'

And with that he closes the door. David and he, in the midst of all the Rainbow craziness, are producing Lou Reed at Trident Studios. Now, whenever I listen to *Transformer*, I think of that small toilet and Mick sitting on the loo, hunched over and writing music.

After a sellout show in Bristol the next day, we turn around and come back to the Rainbow. It's easy this time and goes down a storm; Bournemouth is our next stop, and from there, Doncaster. We'll be away for at least a week. As my suitcase goes underneath the bus, I clamber on and take a window seat. I look out as Woody and Trevor say fond farewells to June and Anne. Denise isn't with them, nor the baby, and I wonder about her and Mick's relationship. I feel a bit sorry for the girls being left behind, but I'd be lying if I said I wasn't glad that I was going with them.

I relish putting a Bowie photo pass around my neck the next morning. The crew and I settle into a rhythm, arriving early at each venue. As they load in, I take a look at the dressing rooms. Most of the time they're okay, but I want to make them extra special, so I polish the mirrors, clean the tops of the dressing tables and sweep the floor. The wardrobe trunks arrive, cold from the truck, and I open them up and pull out the costumes. The ironing board is set up and I watch steam rise as I press the wrinkles out of their outfits. Once pressed, I hang them up in each dressing room and put the shoes and accessories close by. Angie has given me some colourful throws to make the dressing rooms look more attractive; sometimes I use them on an ugly chair or to make a table look brighter. I plug in the hairdryer, lay out David's make-up and the trusty GARD. In the band's room, the silver spray waits for Trevor's whiskers alongside Elnett hair lacquer for Mick. When I've got everything set in the dressing rooms, I go to town for the finishing touches: wine and flowers. I love this part of my day; it's exciting looking around a new town, seeing different shops. It's not the generic high street of today, but something truer, more real, something that reflects the local community.

At every gig, fans start to gather at the stage door early in the afternoon. They'll wait for hours just to catch a glimpse of David or one of the band. Some have dyed their hair red, others blond, and they've all cut it short and tried to make it stand up. There's glitter on their cheeks and they wear anything that sparkles. Some do it better than others, but some go beyond the pale and look a bit bedraggled. They beg for an autograph, a signed photo if I can get one for them, or maybe a guitar pick from Mick. As I look at all these young faces covered in make-up and sparkles, I wonder what their parents think of all this, and I just hope they get home safely. Being outrageous and gay in London is one thing, but in the suburban towns of England it's a different story. We've all read about gay-bashing in the papers.

The band arrive in the late afternoon for a sound check before going out for dinner. Dinner's a daily ritual for David and the band and they eat together before every show. The serious business of getting ready starts as soon as they're back in the building. 'Doors open' comes crackling through the loudspeaker in the dressing room: it's thirty minutes until showtime. We hear the fans pour in, laughter and noise as they find their seats. 'Five minutes,' someone calls at the dressing-room door, the distant rumble of the audience erupting into a roar as 'Ode to Joy' starts. Every night the band is greeted by kids with wild expectations, and every night they deliver without fail. I watch the show from all over the venue, I love to buzz around the gig: I'm onstage one minute, off the next, out at the front by the sound booth or up on the balcony.

When it's time for a costume change, I'm on the side of the stage with a lit cigarette and a glass of wine for David. I light his way to the dressing room. The change is smooth, and as he smokes another cigarette, he asks me how the sound is and wants to know what the fans are saying. Sometimes he tells me which girl he fancies in the front row – after the show's over, I'll look out for her, and if she wants to come backstage to say hello I make sure she gets there.

If David has a complaint, it's usually about security and directed at Stuey. David likes his fans up and dancing so when he sees security stop them he gets upset, yelling at Stuey to tell the guards to back off. Stuey's job isn't easy. There's a fine line between fans who are dancing and a mob that might storm the stage. He also has to deal with the people who work at the venue. They have a certain way of doing things and don't want kids standing on the seats or running down the aisles willy-nilly. Fans can become obsessive, nice one minute and over the top the next. David's been caught before; he lost some hair and had a jacket torn apart. The band have nearly had their clothes ripped from their backs. Even with Stuey, the fans can get out of hand. I remember one gig where it takes not only him but the roadies and some venue security to get David and the boys into the car.

After that, a new strategy emerges: the Elvis Presley Exit. Defries has been dreaming about it since he saw Elvis at Madison Square Garden. The first night we try it, we succeed beyond all expectations. It goes like this: I wait at the side of the stage for the final notes of the encore to fade away, after which the band and David run off, Stuey alongside us. As we get whisked away, I hear the announcement echoing behind me: 'DAVID BOWIE HAS LEFT THE BUILDING.' With a loud bang of the stage door, we're out in the fresh air. It's so smooth, and the few fans that are out here barely react as we blow by them and jump into the car. We peel away and within fifteen minutes we're safely at the hotel. They walk in still wearing their costumes – that gets a few raised eyebrows – and go straight to their rooms. I follow them and the car waits as I collect everything to do with the show from each room: costumes, shoes, tights, bracelets, and even David's jockstrap.

When the crew and I get back after loading out, I see Mick and Woody alone at a table.

'We'd rather be mobbed,' Woody says to me. I laugh and can understand – they don't want to get ripped to pieces, but they do want to have fun.

Partway through the tour, a friend of the promoter comes to a show with an adorable-looking boy who can't take his eyes off David. He's slim, with an angelic face and long dark curly hair. David sees him too and casually asks me about him during a costume change.

'He's a huge fan,' I say, and am rewarded with a grin.

'I want to meet him after the show. Get him in the car for me, Suzi.'

'I think he's with someone.'

He gives me a sceptical look and tosses his eyes. 'Just tell him,' he says, with an impossible smirk.

We run back to the stage and when I tell the boy, as discreetly as possible, that David wants to meet him, he's so thrilled he can barely believe me.

'Meet me at the stage door when the encore starts.'

'How can I do that?' He gestures towards the man he came with.

'It's up to you,' I say. I feel sorry for him, he looks so torn.

As the encore begins, I see the boy sneaking his way back towards me and the stage door. I guess he's made up his mind. Mick, Woody and Trevor come flying out the stage door and jump in the front of the limo with the driver. I wonder why – there's just me and this scared-looking kid in the back. I'm about to say something when David comes rushing out of the door with Stuey close behind him. The boy beside me is shaking, I can feel it. David throws himself into the car and without a word launches himself at the boy. I can see David pushing his tongue down the boy's throat and his hand trying to open his trousers, all the while telling him what they'll be doing back at the hotel. I'm speechless; Stuey just sits and looks out of the window.

Mick asks me if I'm all right and extends his hand through the window to hold mine as David and the boy wrestle around with each other right next to me. Now I know why none of them sat at the back. I sit forward, trying not to look, but it's right in front of me. I hear a zip, see some skin, there's some moaning.

Fortunately, it's not a long drive to the hotel, and when we get there David tells me to bring the boy to his room. He straightens himself up and gets out with a laugh to greet some fans who are waiting. I feel violated, and I can't imagine what the boy's feeling as he sits next to me trying to regain his composure. As I walk with him to the hotel, I ask him if he's all right. He smiles and says he's okay, so I take him with me as I go to collect David's costumes. I knock gently on the door. David hands me his costume and with a long white arm pulls the boy into the room.

The next day on the bus David sits at the back, withdrawn, reflective and quiet. 'All the Young Dudes' comes on the radio; we listen and yell a bit as the DJ says it's on its way up the charts. I don't know Mott the Hoople, but David loves them, and they must be thrilled to hear their single on the radio.

When the tour is over, we return to Beckenham and the band start to rehearse for America. It's all anyone talks about, the American tour, and I'm dying to go. MainMan have the band's passports, they are there to get US visas, but they never asked for mine. I'm so depressed. Then, just when I've about given up, I get a call from Tony.

'We need your passport, Suzi, bring it up tomorrow.'
I nearly scream.

I'M GOING TO AMERICA WITH DAVID BOWIE AND THE
SPIDERS FROM MARS!

16

ACROSS THE POND

On 12 September 1972, with great waves of cheering from devoted fans at the dockside in Southampton, David and Angie leave for New York on the *Queen Elizabeth 2* with the artist George Underwood and his wife Birgit, with whom they're good friends.

I pick up my passport from the MainMan offices at Gunter Grove and almost sob looking at the precious visa stamped inside. There's little time for the costumes to be finished and packed along with everything else I'll need for the tour. I shop for glittery treasures, bracelets, earrings, frosty make-up and silver lurex tights; I get doubles of everything and more when I can. The American Tourister suitcases I used to haul the costumes around in are long gone, replaced by two wardrobe trunks in striped canvas and leather. They look as if they should be boarding the *Lusitania*, they're so smart and chic. It's a novelty to have drawers and hangers, and I carefully pack one for David and the other for the band. Each piece has a place, everything tightly arranged, and I chronicle it all with a handwritten inventory. A copy is in each trunk, and I have two with me. I lock the cases and slip brass keys on to a key ring and give a matching set to the driver. My steamer trunks leave without fanfare on the back of a lorry with all the other equipment.

I heave a sigh of relief after they've left and go to meet Judy and Wendy in the Golden Arrow. I park my car and see them through the window at the bar, and for a second I'm transported back to the many Friday nights that I've spent with them here.

Was it only a few months ago I met David and Angie? It doesn't seem possible. I've slipped into my new life as easily as I slip into my new clothes. I'm eternally grateful to David and Angie, who took a chance on me, but I fought to get here too and feel as if I deserve it. Now I'm living life, not sitting on the sidelines, and with that last thought I get out of the car and go into the bar.

We hug and squeak and make a big fuss; I haven't seen them in an age and we're eager to catch up on what's going on. We order a round of drinks at the bar and take them to a table. After the initial flood, we calm down and I take a look around at the pub.

Leaning against the bar is Kim. He catches my eye and raises a glass in a silent toast. I smile and nod. He's a one-night stand from long ago, and tonight he's here with Chris – tall, cool Chris. He follows Kim's gaze and looks over; Judy smiles and he gives her the 'do you want a drink?' motion with his hand. Judy nods at Wendy and me.

'Come on, Suzi, free drinks!'

We talk for a while, then as Chris starts to chat with Wendy and Judy, Kim looks directly at me and asks softly, 'Are you still with him then . . . David?'

He says it as if it's a secret. I look at him from under my eyelashes and nod.

'How is it?'

It's a long minute before I answer.

'It's amazing,' and then, with a grin, 'yeah, it's really good.'

We don't mention the past, but it hangs between us. It hurt at the time. I look at him and with another smile tell him that I'm leaving for New York tomorrow. It's a satisfying moment, and as I turn to talk to Wendy and Judy, I feel him slip behind me. He enters my line of sight for a second and, with a soft wave, says a silent goodbye.

The next day I fly with the crew into JFK and we're immediately whisked to rehearsals at an RCA studio in the middle of the city. It's here I meet a tall stranger who's talking to David and Mick; there's been talk of a piano player and I suppose this might be him. In the past, Mick has had to run from piano to guitar, filling in the parts; and though he plays piano well enough, as I listen to Mike Garson play through 'Changes', I'm transported. The song sounds more sophisticated, theatrical, even a bit jazzy. Mike adds another dimension to David's music; it occurs to me that he's a completely different kind of man from the rest of the band, not just musically but also in the way he looks. I'd never have put the two together.

I hear him say that he's a stranger to David's music, and I can't help but wonder where he came from. Later, I find out that Annette Peacock – a friend of David, Mick and Tony Defries – had suggested him. He seems friendly enough; a little uncomfortable around us, shy perhaps, but it all disappears when he sits down behind the piano. Whatever he plays is magic, it doesn't clash with the band, and the sound of them together is warm and full. Mick's smile is infectious as he listens to Mike play. I see them chatting easily between songs, and whatever Mick wants, Mike can do, with little effort and no mistakes. I'm thrilled for Mick; he seems to have met his musical match. I'm not trying to take anything away from Woody and Trevor, they're both fantastic players, but Mick, he's different.

'The call came out of the blue,' Mike admits. 'I was told I had to leave my house that instant, come to the RCA studios in New York to try out for the band.' He pauses, takes a breath, looking around as if he can hardly believe the course of events. 'I literally left a piano student holding my baby! I called my wife, who went right home. She doesn't know what to think, except maybe I've lost my mind, and now I'm here.' He looks around again, laughing to himself.

Mike asks me what he should wear and I'm at a bit of a loss. Tall and chubby, with grey curls, he doesn't look remotely like anyone else in the band. He seems older than us, but only by a few years. When I ask if he wants to get the grey out of his hair, he chuckles and tells me he went grey prematurely, and asks whether it really matters. I don't think so, but I do wish I could think how to style him. I draw a blank and suggest he wears black until something else is sorted out.

We leave New York and travel to Cleveland on a Greyhound bus for our first gig. We drive for hours and hours – we could have got to Scotland more quickly, and this is only a small part of the country! The scenery is bland: fields and fields, a patchwork quilt of farms and the endless highway. Being on tour is wonderful and being in America makes it all the more exciting. Mick is deep in conversation with Mike, David sits in the back with George and Birgit, and Angie takes on the role of tour mother. With much sashaying up and down the aisle, she checks on David before settling herself next to Anton.

Anton is a tall, handsome man with a huge afro and skin the colour of coffee and cream. They'd met him in Italy. He was their chef, and now he's David's bodyguard – who knows where life will take you? I'm sure Angie's told Anton, or he's seen for himself, the way they are with each other. They have separate bedrooms and she's as free to play as David is, so I'm not shocked when she slides into a seat next to Anton, though I am surprised to see them giggle and fool around under the blanket.

Later that night, at our hotel in Erie, they're found unashamedly cavorting in the pool. It's a shock to the staff of this small hotel and they demand they get out. There's talk of calling the police, but they call David instead. There's no real good reason – it's not that late, and they're not being *that* bad – but it's America in the early 1970s and interracial relationships aren't common . . . anywhere. David, no stranger to controversy, is calm and comes to the rescue of his wife and bodyguard.

The next day, we continue on towards Cleveland Music Hall. The hall looks massive from the outside and my heart races at the thought of it, but when we get inside I realise we're only playing a part of it. It's here I meet our incredible lighting crew. Bob See, the lighting designer, is a huge guy who handles his three-hundred-pound-plus bulky frame admirably. He has an all-American crew that travel separately from us. We all have a common goal: to make this an unmissable show. Will Cleveland be ready for Ziggy and the Spiders? I hope so.

When the lights go down, we're in the wings, still and silent. David shifts from foot to foot as the audience settle and start to whoop from behind the curtain. We all smoke and laugh nervously before the band slip onstage. Mick picks up his guitar in the dark and David looks at me and draws himself up to his full height. He takes a couple of deep breaths before handing me the stub of his cigarette and walking out. There's a huge roar, a follow spot picks him up and we're off to the races. I watch from the side for a while then go out to the sound desk, where it's all thumbs up. The sound has never been better, clearer, the vocals up front backed with the pounding bass and thundering drums. When Mick hits the solo run in 'Life on Mars', Robin Mayhew, the sound man, lifts him up and the sweet notes roll over the audience.

After the show, at the hotel, everyone is overjoyed; and although David might act cool, he seems relieved the first gig is over, as do the band. He soon disappears with a girl and no one else stays up late; we have an early start the next day, we're off to Elvis's home-town: Memphis. Memphis isn't really Bowie territory, and we hear from someone at the box office that the ticket sales are poor; but by the afternoon there's a queue snaking around the building, and come the evening we've sold out.

If Cleveland was good, tonight is even better, and it's on this high note that we go back to New York. When we get there, I peer out the bus windows to see the city that never sleeps. The bus pulls to a stop on Fifth Avenue opposite the Plaza Hotel and a blond man with long curly hair and baby-blue eyes is waiting to greet us. He gets on the bus and we all fall silent as he introduces himself in a sweet, soft, southern drawl.

'I'm Leee, please stay on the bus while I get your hotel keys.'

I look out of the window after him. While we wait, a shifty-looking woman with a cart walks by. She sits, then squats down by our front wheel. One of the crew leans out of the window and says in astonishment, 'She's taking a shit!'

It's hard to see through the dark bus windows, but it turns out he's right: she is pooping and scooping! She relieves then retrieves the item and places it tenderly on her cart. Willy and Pete get out and take a photo. For most of the crew, it's their first time in America; for all of us, it's the first time in New York, and it's a weird way to be introduced to it: a woman shitting on the street opposite one of the most famous hotels in the world.

We go from seeing this poor, lost soul to walking into the wildly beautiful, luxurious halls of the Plaza Hotel, up the wide red-carpeted stairs and in through the gold doors to the lobby. Staff and visitors stare alike as we stand with our luggage and hold our keys. The other guests seem older and more conservative, the men wearing suits and ties, the women classy dresses. Angie has her fur coat on with tight jeans and high heels, David is in velvet with satin trousers, and the band – with their unusual haircuts and rare clothes – are completely different to anyone else in sight. To say we look different is an understatement.

The Plaza Hotel is America's version of the Dorchester in London, sitting on the edge of Central Park and Fifth Avenue. The lobby is enormous, with high ceilings and huge chandeliers hanging low over lounge tables. I hear the tinkle of a piano over the soft hum of conversation. Porters load our luggage on to carts and invite us to follow them to the lift, where we meet smiling uniformed operators who take us up to our floor. David's suite and our rooms are together on the same floor; the band and the rest of the crew share with each other, two to a room, but as I'm the only girl I have a room to myself. The porter places my case on a luggage rack at the end of my bed and waits for a tip as I look around. The room is enormous, bigger than where we stayed last night and twice as grand as anything I've ever seen. Anton and Stuey take their posts, one by the lift and the other outside David's suite. I go down to David's rooms to see if he needs anything and it's here I meet Cyrinda Foxe.

Cyrinda is a sexy girl who wiggles up and down in a tight 1950s pencil skirt, tight sweater and high heels. Her hair is short and curls in platinum perfection, her white skin contrasting with her bright-red mouth. She looks like Marilyn Monroe and she's David's girl of the moment. I instantly want to look like her.

◆

New York is a revelation, the shops large and luxurious. I start at Bergdorf's then go to Bloomingdale's, and after that Angie takes me to Greenwich Village to the Pelican shoe shop. Angie picks up palm tree platform wedges for David and encourages me to try some shoes on. I slip on a pair and tower above everyone else, my legs looking endless. I can't decide between red glitter platforms with scarlet satin straps or black-and-white polka-dot platforms with white satin straps, so I get both in an uncharacteristic splurge. My mum would die at the price, but my mum isn't here, so I buy them with reckless abandon.

On the day of the show, Angie calls and tells me in a quiet voice that David isn't well, that he might have flu. I tell her I'll be there as soon as I've set up the dressing rooms. Carnegie Hall is a beautiful theatre with wonderful dressing rooms and doesn't need much from me. After lunch I go to David's suite, which is palatial and over-looks Central Park. Cyrinda is curled up in the corner on a chair, her feet tucked under her. She's silently flipping through a magazine and gives me a smile when she catches me looking at her. I still can't help but stare, she's so striking.

I hear voices that can only be David and Angie, one pleading and the other quiet. Trolleys of food and coffee are all over the main room, and as Angie comes out from the bedroom, she starts to move the trolleys to the door. As I get up to help her, I hear him say, 'I've got it covered, Angie, I really do. It's time for you to go do your own thing, baby.'

Angie doesn't say a word. I walk into the bathroom and find David sitting on a chair, looking at himself in the mirror. He's wearing a signature Plaza fluffy white bathrobe, which he shrugs off as I walk in. He's half naked in his underwear, as skinny and white as I've ever seen him. He feels hot under my hands, and as I throw a black cape over his shoulders I can see goosebumps forming. He continues talking to Angie.

'You know you have things to do, the film part you've been talking about. The papers are dying to have you for a photo session. You can help me so much more back in London, Angie, keeping people interested by being your fabulous self.'

Angie still doesn't answer.

I start to cut his hair, scissors slicing spikes in the top of his red head.

'Not too much,' warns David. I ignore him as I want his hair to really stand up tonight. 'Babe, think of all the fun you can have with Freddie and the girls.'

I think of all the fun she's going to miss. Angie's worked so hard, given so much energy, and has been completely involved with the creativity that has brought David here. Now, just when it's starting to get going, she's asked to leave. I wonder if her shenanigans with Anton in the pool in Cleveland helped or hurt her . . . I can't be sure. The noise of the hairdryer subdues the conversation, and when I finally finish his signature spiky red hairdo, Angie comes back to say joyfully how great he looks. She looks a bit pale, and I can see she's upset, but I ignore it. Angie doesn't want sympathy;

she wants to be wanted. David laughs at something Cyrinda says, and she laughs back at him with a tinkly little voice. I hate it for Angie.

I mix up some brilliant colours for her – I'm going to paint bright feathers in her hair tonight, a bit like I did for Mick.

'He's right,' she says quickly, looking at me in the mirror. 'This has been the plan all along. I have so much to do in London, I have to start my own career. I'm sure you'll look after David and the band. They'll miss me, but they'll all be okay.'

What worked well in Beckenham doesn't seem to be working quite so well for Angie now. She plays the game well, and if it hurts, she doesn't show it. Although I doubt she means what she says, I have to agree with her. I listen to her plans as I start working on her hair; she alternates between high and low, laughing hysterically at times and then catching herself and becoming as silent as the grave. It's hard to tell what she's really thinking.

I go to the lobby early and wait for David to come down. It's bound to be a spectacle, and there's press outside. The elevator doors open and David, with Angie on one arm and Cyrinda on the other, crosses the lobby, the other guests staring and parting like waves to let them through. I go ahead through the gold doors and turn as they pause on the steps of the Plaza. David, who's wearing a Freddie Burretti suit, looks affectionately at both of them. They all smile brilliantly as they pose for photos, and when they glide into a car I hail a waiting cab.

When I step out of the cab outside Carnegie Hall on 57th Street, a huge white spotlight washes over me. I feel as if I'm on the telly, and I watch as it makes lazy circles over the crowds of fans. I show my pass at the stage door and wait inside for David. The limo pulls up seconds later; David, with his head down, comes in flanked by Stuey, Angie and Cyrinda. He's quiet and withdrawn. Backstage, I make him lemon and honey tea that he drinks along with some red wine to give him a boost.

Tony Zanetta, our tour manager, rushes backstage into the dressing room, full of fiery excitement.

'Andy's here, David, Andy's here! He's so close to the front, you're bound to see him.'

He's talking about Andy Warhol, with whom he used to work. David looks as if he couldn't care less – he's a huge fan of Andy Warhol's so I figure it must be because he isn't feeling very well.

I met Tony – or Zee, for short – in London after he was flown in for the Rainbow show. Zee, Jamie Andrews, Leee Black Childers and Cherry Vanilla (aka Kathleen Dorritie) first met David and Angie while performing *Pork*, an Andy Warhol production, in London. They are all fabulous. Tony Ingrassia directed the show and Leee photographed the whole thing. Angie, David and Tony Defries loved their crazy energy and outrageous behaviour.

When *Pork* finished, they returned to New York and were persuaded to work for MainMan. Cherry and Zee, talented actors, became talented music businesspeople; Leee became a photographer and takes exclusive photos for MainMan; Zee, who had no idea of how to be a road manager, became ours.

Leee, Zee and Jamie are outrageous gay men with none of the subterfuge I've seen in London – these men are gay and proud of it. Cherry is a sex bomb with a pair of cherries tattooed on her breast, full of confidence, and has a raspy voice that I love. I have tons of fun with all of them.

◆

Anyway: back to New York and Carnegie Hall. After Zee rushes back out, David touches up his make-up as I dress him. I feel for him: here he is, about to play what might very well be the most important show of his life, and he's not feeling his best by any means of the word. Only a few people know David isn't well; he doesn't ask or get any sympathy, and there's no turning back.

It's showtime. The band follow the small pool of light from my torch to the side of the stage. As we stand behind the curtain, David starts to bounce on his toes, just as he always does. The band pass him in the dark, go on and pick up their guitars. Woody settles behind the drums. David walks on to Mick's blazing guitar; Mick turns on his heel as David approaches the centre mic, then twists away from the front row, all the time delivering strong, choppy chords. David starts to sing, and, with undeniably powerful support from the Spiders, goes right over the edge. Despite everything, he gives an extraordinary performance.

Then comes the first costume change. As he comes off, he's pale and shaking, dripping with sweat. He yells at Stuey about security; nothing new, we hear that all the time.

'I want them up and dancing, not sitting down!'

I'm not envious of Stuey's job tonight. This is Carnegie Hall: there are rules, and not even Bowie gets to do what he wants. He doesn't help by trying to whip the crowd into a frenzy, reaching out to them from the stage.

Cyrinda and Angie sit in the front row, screaming and dancing along with everyone else until they are pushed back into their seats. The New York audience are crazy for David. I've never seen so many people embrace the Ziggy look – it's a sea of glamorous, sparkly people. Many of them are dressed like David, some like Mick, and a lot of them – both boys and girls – are in full make-up. Others have gone the whole hog and cut, coloured and spiked their hair à la Ziggy. My haircut is everywhere! They give David the kind of adoration he's expecting, and it couldn't be at a better place. David, buoyed up with adrenaline, does an incredible show before collapsing in his dressing room.

Tonight, there's no need for a fast exit: the band change in the comfort of the Carnegie Hall dressing rooms and leave their sweaty costumes in a pile on the chair for me to collect. I go back and find David alone; I throw a dry towel round him as I find his clothes. Defries and Zee are in the dressing room first, followed by Angie and Cyrinda. There's loud congratulations and tons of praise for David, and as he sits and listens his pale face lights up. He dresses himself and, with both his wife and his girlfriend by his side, he walks to the stage door. I release them, along with Stuey and Anton, into a storm of fans. Cyrinda and Angie cling to him as they fight to get to the car. The band and Mike – who looks a little shell-shocked – are next, and after they've gone the crew and I finish the wine in the dressing room.

Back at the Plaza, Tony and the executives from RCA are over the moon. David holds court with the girls at a table while the crew and I join the band at the overflowing bar. It's a huge celebration, and as I look at David I think he must be made of steel. He and the band are extraordinary and richly deserve this adoration.

The next morning, it's bittersweet as I go to say goodbye to Angie. Angie had a lot to do with the rise of Ziggy. At Haddon Hall you couldn't tell who was more outrageous, her or him, and she always encouraged David to do things he was nervous about doing, whether it was cutting his hair or coming out as bisexual. It took a lot of courage for David to say he was bisexual back in the 1970s, and she was right behind him. I admire her tremendously and am surprised when Defries says aloud he finds Angie difficult. The whole thing seems a bit unfair, but who am I to comment? The roles she used to play have been taken over by professionals.

17

ON THE ROAD

We're all giddy with excitement and in high spirits on the bus as we leave New York City. Mike Garson gets to know everyone better, and we him. George and Birgit provide a welcome normalcy for David. David and George have been friends since school and chat away endlessly. Birgit, a Scandinavian beauty, is quiet, gazing out the window, her pale blonde hair a curtain around her face. Sometimes the guitars come out; it's often David and Mick, but sometimes George plays too.

Stuey, champion joint-roller, rolls joint after joint of tobacco with hash or grass. I have no idea where he gets it from, and no one else seems to care. He starts a challenge to see how big a joint he can master. Fifteen papers is the record. It looks like a torpedo, and he smokes it, for the most part, alone.

We're well appreciated in Boston, Chicago is fantastic, and as we roll into Detroit to play the Fisher Theatre, it all seems easy. For some reason, tonight the band decide to stay and wait for the show instead of going out for dinner; food is delivered to the hall. It's the beginning of October and it's been raining all day; the fans are getting drenched while queuing to get in. I'm in the band's dressing room when I hear the sound of breaking glass, and as I step into the hallway I feel Stuey and Anton rush past me towards David's room. There's a scuffle, and a low voice.

'Dave, it's me.'

Silence. I've known fans in England to get hysterical and stop at nothing to get close to David and the band, but the sheer determination of this man to get in is unusual. What an entrance: he comes in through the bloody window! It's over in a flash, and as he's being escorted out by Stuey and Anton, I hear him say again: 'Come on, David, you know me!'

Silence.

Later, Zee explains to me with a quizzical look that David did know the man. It was Calvin Lee, an influence from long ago who had been involved with both David and Angie. Zee said that Calvin claimed he had introduced the two of them to each other; but whatever the truth is, it's clear that he's a person David would rather forget. After he's gone and David is escorted away, I go into the dressing room to find fragments of glass all over the place. David looks a bit shaken up, but for some reason he has a smirk on his face.

After Detroit, we ditch the bus and fly across the dusty Midwest. As I look down from the plane, there's nothing but country and miles and miles of highway. Occasionally, a little village pops up, and once in a while a larger town, but for the most part it just looks empty.

David still isn't flying; he travels by car with his friends and Stuey. I like road trips as much as the next person, but with us flying and David driving we end up waiting for him, and without the daily gigs the electricity that propels us along starts to fade. By the time we get to St Louis and Kansas, we're brought to our knees. These are hard shows, the venues only half full; and despite David and the band giving it their all, they get no energy back from the audience. Days blend into each other, weekends are no different from a Monday or Tuesday.

In America, David's facing a different set of kids, a different set of values. A lot of them want to embrace his ideology but many people are fearful. America might be cool on the coasts, but the Bible Belt is conservative and dead set against anything that smacks of homosexuality.

◆

On a night off, David invites the band and me to a club somewhere outside of Chicago. Zee, Leee and Jamie join us, and along with Stuey and Anton we make quite a party. When we walk in, I hear great music, see men dancing with men. David and Anton immediately go to the dance floor. The waiters – who wear black hobnail boots, leather G-strings and some sort of harness – look a bit scary, but after a while I realise they're only waiters wearing a uniform. Jamie, Leee and Zee fit right in, but the band and I struggle. We sit together in uncomfortable silence; it's silly really, but that's how it is. Anton isn't gay but is happy to play the part while David checks out the action. Men come on to men much stronger than men come on to women, and here is no exception. If they know who David is, they don't acknowledge it, and I'm not sure whether David's pleased or upset that they don't make a fuss. Mick, Trev and Woody cling to my side.

18

LA LIFE

We fly into LA on 16 October and walk out into bright, warm sunshine. Limos are waiting courtesy of RCA, their uniformed drivers smiling as they take our luggage. I try to be cool, and no one says a lot as the car pulls away from the kerb and into the traffic. 'California Dreamin'' is how I feel, and inside I'm bubbling up like a champagne bottle about to burst its cork. The limo takes us up and through Bel Air, where the mansions are spectacular and the cars out of this world, all of it steeped in movie-star magic. Every once in a while, the driver points out a famous person's house. Hollywood history: not ancient, but oh-so glamorous.

We arrive at a pink confection of a hotel: the famous, fabulous Beverly Hills Hotel. As we drive up the long, slim driveway, I see palm trees and small pink cottages nestled in the dark-green vegetation. I'm breathless. When we pull up outside the main entrance, Leee tells the band to go with him while Zee takes the crew and me into the main hotel. I go up to my room and after my case arrives, I grab my swimsuit and make my way down to the pool, where we agreed to meet.

We have a table and some loungers. Iggy Pop's here, and as soon as I sit down I'm given a menu and a waiter asks for my order. I've never known such luxury. I stretch out and watch Mick dive off the side of the pool into clear aqua water. I close my eyes and hear Woody telling Pete his cottage is right next door to Elton John. It's a dream, or at least it feels like one, and I can't help but think of all the people in my life who could never have imagined this for me, and my family and friends freezing their arses off in London. David's driving here from Kansas, and I can't think of any other place I'd rather be waiting for him than here.

While we wait for David to arrive, we're invited everywhere. Rodney Bingenheimer has a club on the strip – he's a huge fan of David, and we head there as well as the Whisky a Go Go and other clubs. Surprisingly, and to our collective disappointment, everything closes early in LA: it's all over by 11 p.m. We invite people back to the hotel, hang out at the pool, the bars or in our rooms. We're relatively well behaved at first, but LA girls come on strong and it's not long before the band and the crew alike throw caution to the wind and behave as one would expect rock stars and their crew to behave. We've been told by Tony Defries to be as out- rageous as possible, which certainly isn't a problem, and with Leee, Zee and Jamie to show us the way, I let my hair down and become as uninhibited as I've ever been.

The most beautiful people mill about the hotel and the Polo Lounge. They all look like movie stars with perfect suntans, perfect hair and perfectly white teeth, their clothes casual but definitely not the kind of casual I know. I've seen some high-end stuff with David and Angie, costumes mostly, and Freddie taught me a few things too, though he's disparaging about other designers for the most part. He and Angie know the difference between couture and high-street clothes, about the cut, the weight of the fabric, the way it hangs, the colour. I don't have couture clothes: my swimsuit is from Marks and Sparks. I've got on my best Bowie gear, but I still feel out of place.

Zee, seeing my hesitation, steps forward and whispers, 'You're young, Suzi, something any one of these people would give everything they have to be again!'

With this ringing in my ears, I step forward and join my friends in ordering exotic cocktails with outlandish names and exquisite food, eating and drinking under photos of Dean Martin and Frank Sinatra. I order whatever takes my fancy; I'm wining and dining at RCA's expense. Leee is so infatuated by the chocolate soufflés that he has one every morning for breakfast. They take forty-five minutes to make but, according to him, they're well worth the wait.

Our tour has a funny arrangement with cash: we never have any. I have a little for expenses and diligently keep a log of everything I spend, right down to the last dime. Our wages are paid in the UK and we live off per diems and the record company on the road. I'm not sure RCA realise what they've agreed to. According to Zee, we end up spending a quarter of a million dollars on that first American tour and this, in 1972, is a breathtaking amount.

David and Cyrinda arrive the next day and move into another bungalow. With their presence, and with the gigs fast approaching, we become hyperactively involved in LA life. The girls in the clubs are young and pretty, giggling and laughing, shaking with excitement as they wait for the band. I'm feeling in a friendly mood and ask one of them if they want David's autograph.

'No!' she gasps. 'I want to go to his roooom,' rolling her eyes suggestively. 'Can you get me to his room?' I don't know what to say. Her friend chimes in.

'I like David, we both do, but she said so first and Mick's hot as well.'

She wets her lips as if preparing for a good meal. Zee comes over

– he knows them both – and they hug. As we walk to the bar, Zee explains that they're always at the clubs.

'But they look so young.'

'Well, they are,' he answers, 'maybe fourteen.' He laughs at my shocked expression.

'Where are their mothers?'

'I think their mothers dropped them off! They want them to have a good time.'

Now I really don't know what to say. I look over and see that, yes, they seem to be having a great time. They're wearing skimpy outfits and loads of make-up. The blonde has a childlike body and wears a long-sleeved top with a plunging neckline in purple glitter. Even without womanly curves, she's striking. Her arms are full of bracelets and there's a flower in the blonde curls; a lot of necklaces hang around her neck. Her face is radiant.

'Can you tell us their room numbers?'

It's said to Zee almost in unison, and with such innocence, almost as if they're asking the way to the library. David arrives and as he comes in they both jump up and run towards him, shrieking his name, their bare legs and high heels almost comical. They throw themselves at him and he takes it all in his stride and soaks up the attention. After the show, they're backstage; this time, Zee introduces them as Sable Starr and Lori Lightning.

We play two nights at the Santa Monica Civic Auditorium. These are vital gigs; David has to live up to his hype. The British accent alone seems to fascinate everyone, and I use it to my advantage. RCA buzz about, helpful as can be. I have a limo to take me shopping and we can all do whatever we want. I demand and get everything

I want for the dressing rooms; the crew demand and get everything they want for the gigs. I feel as if we're unstoppable, and my confidence soars along with everyone else's. By the time we get to the show, it's as if we're invincible.

The first gig is a solid knockout, a couldn't-be-better gig. The band romp through the set, the audience up from the first notes. After the show we go to a party at Wolfman Jack's house in the Hollywood Hills. I don't know who Wolfman Jack is, but Zee tells me he's a local DJ. He's loud and fun and welcomes David and the rest of us with open arms. The house is huge with its own swimming pool, people moving in and out of it while David, being typical David, stands as still as a statue with one hand on his chin and the other on his hip, surveying the scene. Wolfman talks non-stop to him and is rewarded with a small smile. I go to the bar with the band and make small talk with some of the other guests. The whole thing feels a bit odd, fake and meaningless, and if I get called 'cute' or 'sweet' one more time . . .

I wake up early the next morning to a letter slipped under my door. It's from Defries. We all have to attend a meeting at 10 a.m. in the hotel, where he tells us in no uncertain terms that we're spending too much money. It's hard not to, he reasons, but there has to be some restraint. I look at Leee and think of his early-morning chocolate soufflé and laugh to myself; Leee bats his big baby-blue eyes as if he hasn't a care in the world. Everyone else looks a little bored. I'm giggling as the meeting ends with Defries saying quite forcefully:

'Don't pay for entertainment, cut back on expenses and send the groupies home before breakfast!'

◆

When I met Iggy in London, we barely said 'hello'. Now he's here and I'm not sure if he knows who I am. Seeing him tanned and animated is a revelation, and he chats away with ease to Mick and the band. I'm drinking a lunchtime cocktail, basking in the sun, when a shadow falls over me. When I open my eyes, Iggy's standing there. I'm surprised, and even more so when he sits next to me.

'Hi,' he says, before asking me about his hair. I sit up and have a good look at him. To tell the truth, I like his hair: it's long and shiny, a wonderful messed-up layered do. What can I do to make it better? Iggy's unusual-looking. His body is pretty amazing, a bit twisted here and there with some scars, but still, it's muscular and good.

'I can cut it a bit, and we can play around with colour.' He's interested when I say the word 'colour'.

Mick Rock's scheduled tomorrow to do a photo shoot with David in the grounds of the Beverly Hills Hotel. I make sure David is up for the shoot and when it starts, I'm there. David's on brilliant form in a dark-blue bomber jacket, which looks amazing against his red hair, along with tight black pants and high Pelican shoes. He poses on some steps as Mick shoots roll after roll of film.

After it's finished, I go back to stretching out on a lounger next to the pool and have a proper think about Iggy's hair. I have corn-flower blue, which I use to give Trevor's hair that blue-black sheen; I think I could lighten Iggy's hair and apply that to make it really bright. I relax a little while longer, and as the sun goes down I go up to Iggy's room. I mix up double blonde bleach with 30 volume for maximum lift and apply it. After the bleach comes off it's a bit gold, but I'm confident the blue will cover it. If Iggy's nervous, he doesn't show it, and in the end it works out well. The colour is brilliant.

I finish with a trim and a warning: 'Wait a couple of days before going into the pool, the colour needs time to set.'

The Spiders and I leave the next afternoon, and when we get to San Francisco I hear that Iggy has been asked to leave the Beverly Hills Hotel. He didn't listen, and there's a streak of blue dye that stretches from one end of the pool to the other.

Defries loves it.

19
RACING THROUGH AMERICA

After the heady excitement of LA, we fly on to San Francisco to play at the Winterland. Like many others, I've seen San Francisco on the telly, and I remember a song by The Mamas and the Papas about going to San Francisco with flowers in their hair. I couldn't possibly have imagined when I was younger that I'd end up here.

We have a new addition to the group: Gustl Breuer. I see his name on the room itinerary and wonder who he is. I meet him at the bar and he introduces himself as he buys us all a drink. He's an odd duck from RCA, older than any of us, portly, with a heavy European accent and white hair swept back from his face. He wears a dark suit, an open-collar shirt, no tie, slip-on shoes and black socks.

After a few drinks, he has an audience and becomes frank. He waves his rather short arms in wide gestures and says to me in a heavily accented voice: 'I don't know vy I'm 'ere, I am a- a- a classical man, I am part of ze classical division at RCA. I know nosink about David Bowie or rock and roll.'

Gustl talks about his history with RCA, about the artists he represents, and I feel ignorant as I don't know any of the names. He's an unlikely addition to our crew but he enters the fray with gusto. If RCA thought he was going to keep an eye on things, they chose the wrong bloke.

◆

The second night at the Winterland is a drama for me. I go to the side of the stage to change David during Mick's guitar solo and he comes off a sweaty mess, grabbing the cigarette and wine as I pull down his trousers. The top comes next, and I slip it to one side and slide a jacket on to his sweaty body. He yells at me to ask for more piano in his monitors, to which I nod. I grab the costume trousers for him to step into and he pulls them up over his skinny hips, but as he goes to zip them, it gets stuck. We look at each other in horror. I have three minutes. While he tugs to get them off, I run to the dressing room. Mick looks over his shoulder and sees David trouserless; he stamps to the middle of the stage to stretch out the solo. With the guitar blazing in my ears, I grab another pair of trousers before sprinting back. I hold my breath as David snatches them from me and wriggles into them. My heart is racing but David is cool, and the trousers hold. He gives me a grin, and with a nod to Mick he goes back on. I catch my breath and thank my lucky stars it worked out.

In the dressing room, I look at the broken zipper and it's just as I thought: the zip is corroded with sweat. In fact, it's not just sweat. When the costumes come back from the dry cleaners, the zips are always stiff, and it sometimes takes a product called Zip Ease to make them work smoothly. I know I need replacements, but we're never in one place for long enough – plus I don't have the know-how, nor a sewing machine. I swear to myself that the next time we stop, I'm going to replace all the zips. The costume fabric is delicate, and I don't know how much longer it'll last. I have two costumes for each band member, but even with two each we're cutting it fine. I've started to reinforce underarms, and wherever the fabric is thin. I sew it all by hand, backing it with silky black fabric I found in a local shop. Tonight, I pack in sober silence, and go back to the hotel and on to an after-party.

Gustl is there, holding court at the bar; he whispers in my ear, 'Somevone vants to meets you. He says you look like Ava Gardner. He's somevone in my division in New York.' I can tell he's excited. 'It's Plácido.' I look at him, still not really getting it but liking the compliment all the same. My dad thinks Ava Gardner is beautiful. 'Plácido,' he repeats urgently.

I don't know who Plácido is and when I look over to see a small chubby guy smiling at me – forgive me, readers – I'm not interested. I later learn he's an opera singer, and opera isn't my world, nor has it ever been. Gustl is surprised and bitterly disappointed at my lack of interest; Tony Defries just laughs.

◆

A photo shoot for 'Jean Genie' is scheduled with Mick Rock. Cyrinda Foxe – still the girl of the moment – is with us, and she's going to be in the video. Cyrinda, all peroxide blonde curls and red lipstick, wears impossibly high Pelican shoes, tight jeans and one of David's bomber jackets. David is riveting in a matching jacket of egg-yolk yellow. He stands moodily behind the bar, the yellow fur surrounding his pale face, and with his high cheekbones and bright red hair he looks amazing, but also, I notice, distant and cold.

Mick Rock is set up and ready to shoot. David and Cyrinda rehearse some moves, leaning and posing with a bar stool, dancing around the bar. I think about Angie when I see Cyrinda wriggle around; I wonder if David ever thinks about her. Mick turns the music up and 'Jean Genie' blasts from the speakers. They go over it a few times together and I think it looks marvellous, but when I see the final result, I'm surprised. Cyrinda is not featured as much as I thought she would be – Mick cleverly cut the footage along with some live performance and the studio footage the band did with David.

The fake-fur-lined bomber jacket makes it to the stage but it's too hot to wear for long, so after a song or two David takes it off to reveal a thin sparkly lurex top that clings to his body. His black jeans have a diamante strip sewn down the side of each leg, and that, along with a pair of high Pelican shoes, completes the look he wears onstage. The whole outfit is incredible, but the lurex top proves difficult to get off David's sweaty body without any damage – it's as if you're taking off a pair of tights after you've been dancing all night. I doubt it'll hold up for very long so I make a note to buy them in packets and get as many as I can.

David is a magpie and collects looks and ideas wherever he goes. He's taking his cues from Cyrinda now. In New York she introduced him to the Pelican shoes, and now in LA the bomber jackets are all the rage.

In Seattle, we stay in the somewhat famous Edgewater Inn; The Beatles stayed here when they toured America. You can hire a fishing rod and bait at the front desk and there are photos behind the reception that show The Beatles fishing out of the windows of the hotel! All the roadies get rods and lines, Pete being the ringleader. When I go into their room to have a look, I find a poor, bloody shark in the bathtub. I want them to let it go and leave them in disgust when they won't. I wonder how many dead sharks the cleaners have had to dispose of . . .

Seattle feels a little provincial after the raucous nights in LA and San Francisco. The gig's good but doesn't feel like anything special. After a long flight we get to Phoenix and here, in the desert, we wait for David. I immediately send the costumes out for dry cleaning and zip replacement and bite my nails until they come back. We hear rumours of cancelled gigs, but no one knows for sure. The weather is beautiful, there's a pool, and we can charge food to our rooms. Sunbathing and swimming are just about the only things to do and for British people that's not a problem; it's hot – really hot – and day after day we stretch out in the sunshine, swim in the pool and chat to the other guests. Mick gets a lovely tan, but his bleached hair ends up turning green, and as he continues to swim his hair starts to break off in clumps. He ends up with spikes whether he wants them or not. Woody doesn't fare any better. His hair is coarse and dry, and it sucks up the chlorine; I have a lot of trouble trying to coax the green out of it.

◆

One night, there's a knock at my door. It can only be one person. I grab a robe as David bursts in, nervous and excited.

'Hey.' He leans in close. 'What do you think?' I don't know, I'm half asleep. He looks different – in fact, he looks really different – but I can't put my finger on why. Suddenly it clicks: he has no eyebrows!

God knows why we have eyebrows – and after the gig in Phoenix, so do David and I. With no eyebrows, the sweat, along with a cascade of make-up, flows over David's brows right into his eyes. He runs to the side of the stage, screaming at me, 'I can't see, I can't see!' There's little I can do except wipe his brow and send him back on with a clean towel. I make a mental note to stock up on eye drops.

◆

We continue on to Miami. There's talk about staying by a beach; if we're going to wait for David anywhere, what better place than a beach? We pull up to what looks like a retirement home, the sun blazing down on the long, low building. I can smell food as we come in through the glass doors and, sure enough, attached to the lobby is a coffee shop full of elderly people.

'Are you sure you have the right address?' I whisper to Zee.

'I think so . . .' He walks up to the front desk, and with a laugh turns to me and holds up my key. We check into our rooms and go to the pool for lunch. Mick orders a drink and before long is chatting with one of the residents; he's always so friendly, and they laugh at his accent, wanting to know what we're doing here. The band don't disappoint and before long, out come the guitars. The residents can't get over it and we have a great afternoon.

On my twenty-third birthday we're on a plane for Nashville, and then it's back to Cleveland and the majesty of two sold-out shows at the 10,000-seater entertainment arena. This is what we're waiting for, another step up. The audience are on their feet, holding up lighters and lit matches at the end of the show, and the sight sends a chill up and down my spine, David and the band too – we're all flabbergasted, none of us have seen this before. We are invincible, the band are gods; nothing can stop us and we all ride high in the stratosphere.

After the Pittsburgh show, we go to see Mott the Hoople play at the Tower Theater in Philadelphia. David and the Spiders are playing right afterwards and it's a good chance to see how they might be received. David's driving in with Stuey while I travel in with Defries and Melanie. As a surprise for the audience, David's going to introduce Mott and later be a guest singer as they play their hit 'All the Young Dudes'. I learn that David, a fan of Mott, gave them 'All the Young Dudes' to stop the band breaking up. He and Mick record and produce it with them – it saves them, makes their career really. Now they're on tour in America and tonight are playing at this rock and roll stronghold.

Ian Hunter, their lead singer, is tall with wild, curly red hair. He doesn't say much to anyone and never takes off his sunglasses. His wife, Trudi, is a beautiful girl, dark and petite; she doesn't say much either. Time goes by and there's still no sign of David. I offer to help with the band's hair in the meantime, but all I'm met with is blank stares. Mick Ralphs – Mott's guitar player – giggles and says he'll have a trim later.

Stuey calls from the road. There's a problem with the car, but after a few minutes he calls back and says they've got a yellow cab and will be there in twenty minutes. The tension is thick until they arrive, but it all dissipates soon enough. David goes out to the stage and is met with a huge roar as he introduces Mott. As they start to play, I see what all the fuss is about. They're not David and the Spiders, but they're really good and get an enthusiastic reception from the crowd. David watches the show from the wings and comes out for the encore. The audience go crazy to see him perform with Mott. It feels like a good omen: if this audience like Mott, they're going to love David and the Spiders.

◆

The next day we set up for our last gigs in the USA. We return to New York in a limo and from there onwards to London. And for me, home, to Bromley.

It still hasn't quite ended though, as we have two Christmas shows at the Rainbow, the last being on Christmas Eve. I go home to see Mum and Dad and invite them all to the show; Mum's quite proud now, and I see them in their seats and hope they enjoy it. I love being back at the Rainbow; this old theatre is magic to me. David asks for children's toys, to be donated to Dr Barnardo's homes, and the fans outdo themselves. Great piles of toys are stacked in the foyer waiting for collection. David and the band, maybe knowing it's the last gig for a while, give it their all.

After the show, people come back to say hello and the boys can finally properly relax. Mick's parents are here. His mum tells David how pleased they are that 'our Michael' is working with him.

'I think you're wonderful,' she says, beaming in delight. 'I think it's a wonderful show.' She sighs with pleasure. 'I'm so glad you let Michael play with you, 'e's so glad to be in t'picture.' She can't stop thanking him, over and over again, for being so good to 'our Michael'.

Mick smiles and says to her gently, 'Cum on, Mum,' and he walks her to where Woody and Trev stand.

I'm speechless, and so's David. What is she talking about? 'Glad to be in the picture'? He is the bloody picture! It would have never flown without Mick, it's obvious to me, the crew, and even to David, I think. The fans idolise Mick and David in equal measure, they each have a huge following; girls scream as much for Mick as they do for David, maybe more so – at least they know what they're getting with him, is my opinion!

Mick, apart from being very good-looking, is also the most

exciting player to watch. When he gets a guitar in his hands, his face changes and he looks a bit like an evil little doll, and when he stands on the edge of the stage and holds his guitar out for the fans to touch, girls faint in the front row. His interaction with David and his Les Paul varies every night; sometimes he straddles David, crunching chords over his crouched body, other times there's David using his teeth on Mick's guitar. The contrast between David's pale skin and Mick's muscular tan is bewitching.

Mick offstage is not the same man, though: he's soft, he cares about his fans and is more accessible to them than David.

When it's finally over and guests and band leave, I put the costumes to bed and go home for Christmas.

20
CHRISTMAS

1972

I sleep in my own bed for the first time in ages, and when I wake up on Christmas morning I can hear singing. For a minute I'm confused, until I recognise Mum's voice. She sings when she's happy and she's happy today. The sun shines cheerily through my window, and I can hear birds in the garden. I wrap up the presents – small gifts for Mum I found on the road, a bottle of Scotch for Dad, and for my brother a Bowie T-shirt – and go downstairs to the kitchen to enjoy a full English breakfast with Mum's fresh farm eggs. Dad looks at me from behind his paper and the conversation, for now, revolves around 'Spot the Ball', Dad's job and who's been in the shop.

Mum pours me a cup of tea while we wait for my brother. The smell, along with breakfast bacon, is Paxo sage and onion stuffing that Mum has waiting to stuff the bird. We examine the turkey.

'What a lovely bird,' we say in unison.

It's what we say every year; Dad laughs at us, and Mum doesn't mind. The turkey goes in with bacon on his breast, and I take a small knife and start on the Brussels, Mum standing by me as she peels potatoes. We talk about her job, Dad, her boss, Mr Jutton, and my brother, Mick, who joins us now. My brother and I are not that close, but something binds us. It might only be blood; I hope not. I love my brother and that's never going to change.

We take our tea into the lounge. I'm feeling the Christmas spirit, so I pour Dad a small Scotch and myself a large Harvey's Bristol Cream. As we open our presents, I'm transported back to when I was a child. I got my first bike for Christmas in this room, and my first camera too – not in the same year, of course, but there was always one fab present at Christmas. The TV is on low and the talk turns to David and my time with him. I entertain them with descriptions of America, and tell them how different it is there, making sure to leave out anything that's too risqué or scandalous – they don't need to know everything, after all. Mum says everyone in Beckenham knows about me now and she seems rather pleased.

Christmas Day passes as it usually does: with way too much to eat and drink. The Queen's speech comes and goes and I'm still on the couch, dozing. I never knew how tired I was until I stopped working, and I wonder if anyone else feels the same way.

Later in the afternoon, Mum toasts crumpets to have with celery for tea, and there's mince pies and Christmas cake too, all made by my marvellous mother. In the evening, we attack the turkey again for late-night sandwiches, and I'm full to bursting point as I stagger up the stairs to the attic.

I spend most of Boxing Day slouching about at home, but in the evening my brother and I go down the pub. Over a pint of beer, he tells me about his job. Mick works on a building site, which is hard, and he tells me he's just started something else on the side. He seems awkward talking about it, but I press, and he finally admits he nicks lead from building sites and off roofs.

'It pays well,' he says. 'I just toss it down to the truck.'

It sounds dodgy, but he shrugs it off. He has an optimistic view about life and doesn't complain. He drinks more than I remember and becomes loud with his friends at the bar. I look at him, my handsome brother, and I just wish I could get him on the road with me. He doesn't seem unhappy, but he looks tired, and I know he can do more. He'd fit right in with the crew; he's a lot of fun and a hard worker. I'm sure he'd like to be part of something artistic and see a bit of the world; it certainly beats nicking lead off roofs! I resolve to try harder to get him a job.

I'm home for a few days but soon enough I pack my case and go to Haddon Hall to prep the wardrobe cases for Manchester Hard Rock. I love my family dearly, and we had a great Christmas, but this isn't my life. I know Dad can sense it, and Mum too, I think. It makes her sad – she misses me – but me, the horrible girl that I am, I just want to get back out there.

21
HERE WE GO AGAIN

A couple of days later we're in Manchester, loading in and comparing Christmases as we set up. These are great gigs – the fans are in a holiday mood and the band go down a storm. We do two nights in Manchester and then head home for the New Year.

David is changing costumes more and more, so Tony Defries asks me to find an assistant to help me. I call Judy and we pick her up for the rest of the UK dates. Judy's just as I remember her, fun and always in a good mood. She helps me with the band, which gives me more time to concentrate on David.

The American press from the Ziggy tour filters across the Atlantic. It exaggerates the success of the tour: David did make a huge splash in major cities in America, but other gigs were only half full, and a lot of the South and Midwest never saw David Bowie and still don't know his name.

Next stop, *Top of the Pops*. This is David's second time, and this time I get to go too. We arrive late in the afternoon, and when the band rehearse they're so loud that everyone complains. David is unapologetic and in true star form goes and waits in his dressing room. Everyone looks old-fashioned compared to Ziggy and the Spiders.

I go out and grin at the audience; I'm as excited as they are to be here. I take it all in: the cameras, the lights, the multiple stages. Freddie Burretti's girlfriend, Daniella, is here with her friend

Maxine, dancing at the back of the stage. The band are quietly confident as they wait to be introduced before they deliver a gritty, high-energy performance of 'Jean Genie'. The next day it's transported into millions of living rooms, and on this high we go to Scotland.

It's a long drive from London to Glasgow. Green's Playhouse is a huge venue and 3,000 people have bought tickets. It has an enormous stage, about twelve feet high – most stages are nowhere near this height. At sound check, David's concerned he won't be able to relate to his fans from this distance, but he need not worry; the Scots are formidable and try to breach the stage by climbing up it as if it's Hadrian's Wall. It's a raucous do right from the get-go, the kids more like a football crowd than a rock audience. During the second half, I go out to the sound desk. Robin Mayhew, safe in his booth, smiles at me. The hall smells of cigarettes and beer, but oooohhhh the excitement of this crowd, the raw energy of these Glasgow fans is out of this world. We barely get away from them in one piece.

We make our way south through Newcastle and end in Preston. The English dates are nearly over, and everyone's talking about what's coming up next. Zee, who has Defries's ear, fills me in, and I'm thrilled to hear that we'll be going back to the States.

When we get back to London, David's invited on the telly for *The Russell Harty Show*. It's a relatively new show and seems very cool, its finger on the pulse of what's hot in London; Marc Bolan's been on and so have other luminaries. On the screen, David looks very young and earnest, and he sounds so sincere. It's not the David I know, whose caustic wit and devilish sense of humour contradict the person I'm watching now. Russell does his best to get him to say something controversial, but David doesn't bite. Instead, he takes it right to the edge, teasing Russell about his oh-so naughty fan letters, and then takes it back, telling us how sweet his fans are when they write to ask about his wife and baby. I thought it was very clever.

They play 'Drive-In Saturday'. The performance is David's, and he does it so well. He's dressed in a Freddie suit with all the reds in it, and a silver tie. David wears a lot of Freddie suits now, some creations made in thick uncrushable fabric and others perfectly cut in shades of pastel, lilac and ice-blue. Some have a simple wash of colour, and others have bright contrasting patterns that shouldn't go together but somehow do. On one ear is a huge chandelier earring of diamonds that twinkles in the light. The band wear suits too, but on the telly it's all about David. His hair is as red as ever.

◆

I'm called back to Haddon Hall and arrive to a maelstrom of activity. Everyone's here and all of us have something to do. Hutch – a guitar player from Yorkshire who played with David years ago in Feathers – is joining us. I'm asked to do his hair, and when I sit him down I find he isn't brave and begs me not to go too wild. His hair is strawberry blond, long and straight. I take some off the length, shape it up and layer the top. Freddie's making him a costume in green satin. Hutch looks a bit bewildered at all the attention.

''e says I'm fat!' he says, tossing his head at the wall. 'When 'e measured me, said I should get in shape.'

Hutch isn't fat, but he is a different shape from the rest of the band. David, Mick and Woody are greyhound-thin. I sympathise:

I always want to be as thin as Angie, but it's never going to happen. I'm simply not the same shape. I reassure him, tell him he looks fine. He likes his hair and the colour of his costume.

There are two other players I haven't met yet. I ask about them but Hutch isn't sure and neither is here today. I see their suits, big-shouldered jackets marked with their names. I suppose I'll meet them in New York.

David – who still won't fly – departs ahead of us from Southampton on the SS *Canberra*. He's with another childhood friend, Geoff MacCormack, who'll be singing background vocals on the tour. A few days later the band follow, and that leaves me waiting for the costumes and Robin waiting for a motherboard. Before the band depart, I go and do their hair in Beckenham. As they leave, they call out:

'See you in New York, Suzi!'

How glamorous we all sound: 'See you in New York!' We say it as if it's nothing.

◆

While I wait for the costumes and my time to fly to New York, I explore my old life. I drive to Beckenham and park by St George's Church, just like I used to. I slowly walk down the High Street, pass the police station and cross the street at the traffic lights by Furley and Baker sports shop. The windows of Evelyn Paget are dark but I see Doris's reception desk and the swing doors that lead to the salon. I can see myself there too, in my blue nylon uniform, scissors in hand, waiting to snip off a grey-haired pensioner's curls. It looks smaller than I remember, and it feels like a lifetime since I was last here – even though it's only been a few months.

I leave the ghosts of Evelyn Paget behind me and go home to spend time with my parents. I try to take an interest in their lives – I marvel with Mum over the cut-price Christmas ornaments on sale for next year, shop with her in Bromley and take her for lunch in the new Bromley Mall. I get a book my father recommends – but I feel like I'm playing at my old life. I see Judy and Wendy and pretend everything's the same. Judy isn't coming to America, and I know she's sorry about it.

A couple of days before I'm due to fly to New York, I go to Haddon Hall. It feels empty without Angie and David there. As I walk in, sunlight follows me into the hall. Sue Frost is in the kitchen, looking nervous. I ask her where the costumes are, and as we walk back to the sewing machines, my mouth goes dry. Rather than being presented with complete costumes, all I can see are swathes of gold and silver fabric lying limp on the table. I don't know what to say.

'It's not my fault,' starts Sue peevishly. 'Freddie hasn't been here. I've had Zowie to look after, and I can't do this alone.' She's right.

In a panic, I call MainMan. Someone gives me Freddie's number; I call but there's no answer. By some miracle, though, he does call me back, promising to come down that night. I make an inventory of everything that's complete while Sue cranks up her machine and starts on a jacket. When Freddie gets to Haddon Hall, he throws a fit. It seems he's been left with too much to do and not enough time to do it.

I'm back the next morning to find them hard at work, and between the two of them they manage to pull the rest of the costumes together. Late in the afternoon, I cram everything into the suitcase, grab my own case and take a Clockhouse minicab to the airport. Robin's in the lounge with his motherboard. We have a quick drink in the bar before boarding the plane, and to our surprise and delight it's virtually empty! What a relief – we both stretch out across five seats and sleep.

22
BACK IN THE USA

In New York, the band come to me for a fitting. It's early evening and they're about to go out for dinner. Neither Woody's nor Mick's trousers fit properly, Mick's jacket needs taking in at the back and Trev's collar won't stand – the stiff backing part is missing.

I remain calm and with a mouthful of pins I pin the seams of the trousers and pull in darts in the back of the jacket.

When they leave, I cry. We've got Radio City Music Hall the next day and I have neither help nor a sewing machine. Everything has to be done by hand. I silently curse Freddie through my tears of frustration. I'm tired, jet-lagged and my nerves are fried. I almost wish I was home watching the telly with Mum and Dad.

After a minute or two I pull myself together, smoke a cigarette and start sewing. I scold myself for being so stupid, for not checking on Freddie and Sue earlier. I try and see the bright side: I only need one costume for each band member, the rest can wait until I have more time. I stay up, flashing my needle through the fabric, and hold my breath as they try them on the next day. To my relief, everything fits.

The next morning, I pack the case with the altered costumes and get a cab to the venue. The theatre has an art-deco front with 'DAVID BOWIE: SOLD OUT' plastered on the marquee outside. It's such an iconic venue and I can't help but feel a thrill. Someone tells me it's the largest indoor theatre in the world, though I take that with a pinch of salt – 'everything is bigger in America', after all. Inside, the period details are stunning, the walls and ceiling forming a series of sweeping arches that define a huge, curved space.

David, Defries and the band come to the theatre mid-morning with a man from RCA. A theatre representative is here to tell them what this venue can do. He's proud – and rightly so – as he gives a brief, colourful history of Radio City. After the speech, he and his assistant show us the ropes. The stage itself has moving parts, genie traps and risers that move in different directions; there are lighting effects, dry ice and a silver sphere that lives up with the lights, above the stage. David is immediately drawn to the sphere. It's an obvious choice, Starman arriving from the heavens, and it'd be a great way to kick off the show. I watch as it comes down. It wobbles a bit onstage, but David, looking as if he hasn't a care in the world, steps in. We all know David doesn't like heights, but it seems as if he's determined to try and overcome his fear. They signal to hoist him up. David doesn't say a word.

As they're rehearsing with the sphere, I welcome Yacco, Kansai Yamamoto's assistant, and take her to the dressing room, where she hangs new costumes from Japan on the clothing rail next to David's stage suits. The design and quality of these Japanese costumes is completely different to what he has at the moment. The Freddie space suits are relatively easy to look after and have stood up well to the rigours of touring, despite the problems with zips. The Kansai costumes, on the other hand, are really delicate, the fabric varying from piece to piece: one is fine silk with intricate embroidery; another is knitted in metallic wool, with a matching anklet and bracelet; and there's also a cape of white satin with red and black lettering on it.

front row. I'm glad Angie made it to New York; I wasn't sure if she'd come, but seeing her here, I'm happy. I know David likes to play the rock star, but when Angie drops in, he's always pleased to see her. She's his biggest fan.

During the intermission, David and the band are in great spirits. There is another new costume to get him into – knitted, with one arm and one leg bare, adorned with anklets and bracelets; over the whole ensemble goes the beautiful cape. David says the writing on it has something to do with spitting fire. I hope he's right; it could say anything. The cape is also held together with snaps and I'm going to repeat my kabuki move after the first number.

The band's entrance for the second half is spectacular, rising up through the genie trap. It's a tight fit with all four of them, and I hear a roar as they appear. Mick lets loose on one of his fantastic solos, and I run to the side of the stage to do my bit. We rip the cape off with a flourish, a wide arc over our heads. Everything's going to plan when, without warning, the drum riser starts to move forward. A roadie goes white as he sees Mick's guitar cord get trapped underneath the stage. I look on in astonishment. Mick feels the tug and glances over his shoulder. He steps back, the cord gets shorter; he's still playing his heart out, but there's a desperate look on his face. David looks at Mick quizzically as he drops to his knees in an attempt to keep the guitar cord from coming out. He's almost on his back before the number ends, and darkness covers the stage like a blanket.

He comes off, laughing. 'Fur fuck's sake, what was that?' Somehow, he managed to make it work.

The evening ends dramatically with David collapsing onstage at the end of 'Suffragette City'. It's a glamorous fall, and he's carried off with shrieks from the fans ringing throughout the theatre. None of us is sure whether it's a ruse or the real thing, but he recovers quickly and we head back to the hotel to celebrate. The next night runs smoothly, and we leave the New York audiences on a high.

Our next stop is the Tower Theater in Philadelphia, where we are welcomed as friends. When I shop in Philadelphia, I see a peacock feather necklace that stops me in my tracks. It's just the sort of thing David would like . . . I think? I take a chance and buy it, along with some gold hand jewellery. I hand them over, praying that he likes them; he doesn't say much, but he wears them here and there, and at one point I see the necklace in a photo.

We sell out in Philly, day after day. Tony adds matinees to the last three days: seven shows in four days. It's more like a residence. David's tired, the tension shows, and as for me, I'm worried. David changes costumes many times. I iron the sweat out of them during the break between shows but I'm always anxious something will give. It's the seventh show on the fourth day when it finally happens. David comes offstage into the dressing room at the intermission. I pour him some wine and take the costume he's been wearing and put it to one side. He's sweaty, his face pale under his make-up. He takes a gulp and sends Stuey to get Robin. For some reason, he seems irritable – Defries is in the dressing room, maybe that's it. The calmer Defries is, the angrier David becomes. I hand him black jeans with diamantes along the leg and a sheer glitter top. The glitter top slips on, but as he zips the trousers, the zip breaks.

I bring out the second pair and watch him wrestle them on, and as he zips them up the seam at the back rips. My heart goes cold.

'Another pair!' he snaps, but that's it: I don't have another pair.

They both watch me as I reach into the back of the case, praying for a miracle, but I know I only have two pairs. I have to come up with something, he's back onstage in five minutes . . . He finally struggles into a pair of red trousers, nicked from another costume, and runs back to the stage.

This is the first time David has been annoyed with me. I feel crestfallen, but upon reflection I think he's more annoyed with Tony Defries than me. I wonder why Tony is here: he rarely comes on the road, and we just saw him in New York. Maybe it's to discuss adding more shows – the more popular David and the Spiders become, the more dates Tony wants to add and the more exhausted David and the band become, and that's without mentioning all the press, TV and photo shoots. As a star you might bask in some well-deserved glory, but the basking doesn't last for long, and before you know where you are the record company starts asking for another record and the whole cycle begins again. Becoming the new hot property is one thing, staying there is quite another. Fame is fickle, that much I know.

◆

The Grand Ole Opry in Nashville is a revelation. It looks like someone's front room: the artists sit on couches or chairs right onstage, taking turns singing and playing, ready to perform whenever they're called upon. The songs I hear are about wild women and fast cars, cheatin' hearts and beers and bars. They're sung by men with dark voices and cowboy hats, women with huge hair and cowboy boots. I love the look. It's amazing to me that people who look like me, who speak the same language as me, can have such a different life. It makes me feel homesick, as if I don't belong here – and truly I don't – but it doesn't last for long, and after two gigs in Detroit we're off to LA.

In Detroit, we board a jumbo jet. The band are travelling first class; Mick Ronson has a word with Zee and suddenly I'm upgraded. I marvel at the size of my seat, and I lean back and look out at the runway until it disappears. After the plane levels off, we're invited to visit the lounge upstairs. I follow Mick and Trev up a narrow spiral staircase to the lounge, which has a piano, and a bar with bar stools . . . this is beyond belief! We order drinks from the bar, and as I sip mine I think of David driving beneath us. Mike jumps on the piano and after a minute or two Mick and Hutch pull out guitars. We're at 40,000 feet and there's music in the clouds. It's a fantastic flight, and as it comes to an end and we take our seats, we hear applause from the other passengers floating up the stairs. The musicians are thanked by the captain over the loudspeaker as we fasten our seat belts for the descent into LA.

We get to LA in great spirits. This time, there are station wagons waiting to collect us rather than limos, and instead of the Beverly Hills Hotel we're taken to the gritty Hyatt 'Riot House' on Hollywood Boulevard. This hotel has some history – not quite the same as the Beverly Hills Hotel, but history nonetheless. Keith Moon famously threw his telly out of the window here, into the swimming pool; the rest of The Who trashed their rooms. We arrive right after Led Zeppelin – they too have left remnants of themselves everywhere, including groupies at the bar. It's all a bit seedy, really – part of the charm, I suppose.

There's a new MainMan residence in LA, in Hollywood Hills. Leee Black Childers is living here with Iggy and the Stooges. Defries asks me to take my scissors, go visit and see what's going on. When I walk in, I see Iggy and say hello, but this is a different man from the one I met at the Beverly Hills Hotel. He's sullen and withdrawn, barely responding before disappearing outside. The kitchen's a dreadful mess, with dirty counters and a sink full of dishes. Leee is cheerful, rallying the band for haircuts. I set a chair up in front of a mirror and under a chandelier. One of the Stooges comes out and sits down. I'm not sure if it's Scott or Ron Asheton – no one says, and I doubt it matters. Whoever it is, he looks sleepy and smells bad. I try to make conversation, with little luck. He sways softly on the chair and can hardly sit up straight. His eyes are closed, and when he finally opens them, they are an unfocused, brilliant blue.

Leee gets increasingly nervous as I ask, 'What's wrong with this lot?' He doesn't say anything in return. I think he's pretending everything's all right. I don't stay long, don't see Iggy again, and report their exhaustion back to Defries.

David's different these days too. He doesn't socialise with the band and the rest of the crew as much as he used to. He isn't staying with us at the Hyatt; instead, he goes with Geoff to a different, more expensive hotel; he only sees us at the gigs. I go to give him a touch-up before the LA gig. He doesn't say much, and seems very tired, worryingly so. He looks skinnier than ever; his face is pale and exhausted. I try to make him laugh but he doesn't seem to have the energy. Maybe he misses us. I hope so. I miss him and the way it used to be.

David might have changed, but not with me. I'm as close with him at shows as I have ever been. Before the show, in the dressing room, it's usually just him and me. Stuey is close by and when it's showtime, I lead him to the stage. When he comes off to change his costume, we might have a word about the audience, but whatever other confidences he shared with me will remain that: confidences.

23
JAPAN

How exotic the word 'Japan' sounds on my tongue. My parents can't believe I'm going, neither can I. It's a long flight, and when we land to refuel in Russia, I look out of the window to see armed guards standing in hard sleet beside a metal staircase. They board, bringing the cold with them. I imagine they want our passports or some other paperwork but they walk directly to our group and order us off the plane. Some passengers give us sympathetic looks as we pass by, others avert their eyes altogether. The wind bites my cheeks as I take a tentative step into Mother Russia. The guards follow us to the terminal.

The airport is like nothing I've seen before. It's all grey. No shops, no restaurants, just lines and lines of empty counters with plain black clocks above them. There isn't another soul in sight. The guards are wordless and serious. I feel flamboyant in my blue Bowie T-shirt, white bomber jacket and glitter high heels; the boys look even more outrageous than I do. Should we be worried? It's not a warm and fuzzy greeting, to say the least, but it doesn't feel that dangerous either. We wait in silence, and after about half an hour we're escorted back to the plane without another word. The passengers look visibly relieved to see us, and a few of them smile as we pass by. The plane takes off a few minutes later. Moscow fades behind us.

◆

The record company meets us at Tokyo airport with smiles and bows. We are hustled through customs straight into waiting limos, with assurances that our cases will follow. Bright-pink cherry blossom seems to be everywhere. My mum would love it.

The Imperial Hotel, with its enormous portico facing a leafy park, is very classy, on a par with the hotels on Park Lane or in Beverly Hills. The hotel staff greet us with more bows and smiles, which we gladly return, but underneath their welcoming smiles I sense silent questions. How will this fêted band from the UK behave? I'm not sure how the Japanese feel about bisexuality or homosexuality, but we haven't been told to tone anything down. When I first met Kansai Yamamoto, the designer, I wondered if he might be gay, but now, as I see him in David's suite with his wife and child, he obviously isn't. David also looks quite the family man with Angie and Zowie, and I'm glad to see it, I'm glad for Angie. Angie seems to give David a normality that might be beneficial while in a new, more traditional country, and I for one celebrate the family togetherness.

We all receive detailed itineraries that leave us in no doubt as to what we are doing, when we are doing it and how it will be done. It's clear they're concerned about tardiness and are expecting us to adhere tightly to the schedule. Trains run on time and everyone has an assigned, paid-for seat. Zee echoes the memo, saying something about dire consequences if anyone fails to turn up.

David, the band and I are invited to dinner with RCA to celebrate our arrival in Japan. I'm sure this will be something special, something to remember, and I'm not disappointed.

We're ushered into a private room of a restaurant, and we take off our shoes as we step down to a long, low table surrounded by soft cushions. I sit cross-legged next to Mick, while David sits at the other end of the table with the RCA people and Angie. They are both laughing along with their Japanese hosts. The band tell me that the fans they have met, even the girls, are more interested in the music than trying to get into their bedrooms. It's refreshing.

Warm sake is poured from china flasks. We take delicate sips, and the sake slips down with ease. The atmosphere is light and fun and the table itself is beautifully set, decorated with flowers and intricately folded napkins at every place setting. Women in traditional dress smile and bob as they offer us scented water in ornamental porcelain bowls to rinse our fingers. There are no menus – not that we would have understood them – but soon dishes begin to arrive at the table. Little seaweed things are served alongside offerings of radish and pickled vegetables. All of it tastes wonderful. The sake keeps flowing, and after these dishes are taken away, servers with large platters enter the room, parading the centrepiece of the meal above their heads with great fanfare.

A huge, fat, glistening fish is placed right in front of me, and there's another by David. The fish itself is beautiful, head and tail still on, scored into thin pieces, ready to be picked up and eaten with the provided chopsticks. It's adorned with intricately carved carrots and surrounded by little pats of mustard and small bowls of soy sauce. The Japanese men applaud. I try to smile, and then, yes, I see it move! A tiny, tiny shiver crosses its skin. I take a gulp of my sake and turn to Trev.

'I think that fish is still alive . . .'

Trev goes pale and we both sit and stare at it. The Japanese men start with gusto pulling the flesh from its bones. I can't bring myself to eat it, and maybe because I'm a woman, it's not noticed.

153

We eat little and drink a lot. We lose Mick somewhere between a club and a bar. Robin, the sound guy, goes back to find him asleep, his head on a kerbstone. *Can't hold his sake* is what I think.

We're scheduled to do three shows in four days in Tokyo. Two are at Shinjuku Kōsei Nenkin Kaikan Hall, split by a day off, and then the third is at the Kōsei Nenkin Kaikan.

Shinjuku Kōsei Nenkin Kaikan Hall, from the outside at least, is not what I imagine. It almost looks like a car park. The crew and I get in early. I'm part of a skeleton crew while the remainder of us are cooling their heels in London or America. Robin and Bob See, the lighting designer, are understandably nervous without their regular team, but they need not worry as the Japanese union workers are amazing. They work together with an easy efficiency, setting up quickly and quietly. They make it look like nothing and Robin and Bob laugh, relieved that these men know what they are doing.

The audience at the first gig are passionate and scream a lot but don't move off their seats.

'Why aren't they dancing?' David asks as I'm changing his costume.

'Security, Dave, it's really tight here. I've been in the audience, and they are jumping up and down in their seats!'

David isn't having any of that, and when he goes back to the stage he engages with the crowd even more, making gestures to the security guards to stand back and the audience to dance. At the end, as I peel off his costume, he decides he's going back on for the encore in just his jockstrap.

'What do you think?' he asks me as he looks in the mirror.

With his long thin white body and dancer's legs, he looks incomparable. The strap matches his hair! All of a sudden, I have a brainwave.

'Just a minute, David.'

I go over to my case and bring out one of the diamond earrings he's been wearing, holding it up at the front of the jockstrap. He doesn't need persuading, so I sew it on with a few stitches. It looks great, and in the wings the diamonds glitter and catch the light.

As soon as he hits the stage, the crowd explodes.

Tomorrow's a day off and I can't wait to explore this extraordinary city. In the morning I go out with Robin and Ron, crew members, to explore.

In Tokyo, you step into the crowd and walk. It's like Oxford Street on Christmas Eve. A sea of black heads surrounds me, and as if I'm in a river I bob along. As a trio, we're head and shoulders above everyone else. There's a massive photo of David hanging outside a large department store, and inside the shop it's the same: David is everywhere. I shop as best I can, buying myself a kimono, some trinkets and a few small presents for my family, and, without understanding the language, I seem to do okay.

It's not until I go to pay that I realise I'm the only European person at the counter. Other customers are staring at me and the salesgirls giggle, but it doesn't feel malicious – they seem amused more than anything else. I've been to America and Europe now, but this is nothing like that. The East is another world altogether. Everywhere is crowded and yet, like I've heard, everything is so orderly and neat. There's no pushing and shoving in shops or in the street, no overflowing rubbish bins, no homeless people (that I can see, at least), and everyone is charming. All in all, I have to say it makes for a nice atmosphere.

Later that day, I get a message from David to come to his suite. He and Angie are still playing the happy family, flipping through books on Japanese culture and fashion, and Kansai's young daughter plays with Zowie. Zee asks me to pick up costumes from Kansai at his studio, handing me a handwritten address. Brimming with confidence, I ask for a taxi at the front desk. The Imperial Hotel doorman opens the door to the taxi, and with a bow and a smile we pull into traffic. The driver says something, and I hand him the piece of paper with the address. He turns the paper every which way until it becomes clear he doesn't understand it, and why would he? The Japanese alphabet isn't the same, and I think they read right to left. I sigh in frustration. He pulls over and gestures to a phone. I call the studio and tell them my predicament.

'Where are you now?' the voice asks.

I look around: I can see a roundabout, that doesn't help; the billboards are in Japanese, so are the street signs. I can't even hazard a guess! I motion to the driver to come to the phone. He reluctantly agrees, and after a few minutes the word 'Harajuku' is said several times, and the driver, all smiles now, drives me to the studio.

The studio is most welcoming, light and airy, full of activity. The costumes are ready on a rail. They're beautiful, labelled with their individual names: 'Spring Rain' is one of them, a silver short-legged suit with a deep V-neck outlined in black. Dripping down from the sleeves are rows and rows of crystal droplets. They look like a beaded curtain. It feels heavy, and as I watch them pack it carefully in tissue paper I can't help but wonder how it'll hold up after being shoved in a case every night.

◆

The second and third shows are like the first, they sell out and both the excited fans and the band are marvellous. If Robin thought the Japanese crew were fast at loading in, he's shaken by the speed with which they load out. I've only just closed my wardrobe trunks when they're at the door asking for them.

We will return to Tokyo to do more shows, but today we're going to Nagoya on the bullet train. I wait with everyone else on the platform, giggling and laughing as I find the place that's indicated on my ticket. David and Angie are here with Zowie. Zee whispers to me that we have two carriages to ourselves. I know nothing about the bullet train other than the fact that it travels really fast – hence the name, I suppose. When it pulls into the station, I gasp in admiration. This train is beautiful. Funnily enough, it is actually shaped like a bullet, with a long sleek nose and clean lines of carriages. It stops silently, the doors open with a whoosh, and directly in front of me is my seat. There's no pushing or shoving, everyone gets on calmly and goes to their allocated seat, and as I sit down I chuckle to myself in delight. I can't help but think British Rail could learn a thing or two from the Japanese.

The train departs the station without a sound, it's a marvel. There's no noise at all except our chatter. David and Angie seem as relaxed and happy as I've ever seen them. Neither one of them has a lover in tow, and they hold hands and gaze into each other's eyes. *Long may it last*, I find myself thinking. Soon we're whipping through the country at a breathtaking speed. I sit and look out in awe. This is like something out of *National Geographic*. There are fields and fields of rice tended by people who wear huge hats to protect themselves from both sun and rain. They prod horned cattle

157

with long wooden poles to encourage them to pull farm equipment through the long grass. The scene is picturesque, stretching on for miles. After passing through villages, we come out to a flat stretch, and in the distance the famous Mount Fuji rises up in the sun. What a sight, the snow-capped mountain. I take a few photos and hope they'll come out.

We play the show in Nagoya and hop back on the bullet train the next day, this time bound for Hiroshima. I have mixed feelings about Hiroshima and joke with the American crew about keeping my distance from them. In Hiroshima we stay at a hotel overlooking Peace Park. The Hiroshima Peace Memorial is a shattered building, the only one left standing after the atomic bomb was dropped here in 1945. It's a sobering thought, but nothing prepares me for the overwhelming sense of despair and regret I feel when I go into the museum. No one's laughing now. The city still visibly carries the scars from that bomb, and I can't imagine what the mental trauma must have been like. The photos in the museum of the dead and dying are almost incomprehensible, as are the before and after photos of the city and the utter devastation. In the space of just a few minutes, this once vibrant city turned to dust. It's hard to take in. How can the Japanese even entertain Americans? Or us, for that matter? We are all struck dumb with disbelief and horror. War is one thing; the aftermath is something else.

There are men on Bob See's crew, Ronnie Meadows and Tony Massochi, who served in Vietnam. Ron has a scar on his neck to show for it; he won a medal for bravery. I hear his nightmares on the bus sometimes. He doesn't talk about it. I think how lucky I am that my generation didn't have to fight a war, my brother and I the first generation in three that didn't have to go kill anyone. Instead, we got The Beatles and the pill.

We play in Kobe and Osaka before returning to the capital for our final shows in Japan. The shows have been a bit more sedate out of town and David can't wait to get in front of a Tokyo audience again. Tokyo is ready. Tokyo is mad for this band.

◆

It's in Tokyo where I hear the news. Tony talking to David and Mick about breaking up the band. My mouth goes dry as he says it, and a pit forms in my stomach; I can't quite take this in. He reassures Mick, tells him he'll be fine, that he'll have a solo career, but he isn't saying anything about Woody and Trev. After David and Mick leave the room, Tony asks me to stay. I don't think he meant to be so open in front of me and now swears me to secrecy. I must keep my mouth shut if I want to continue to work with them. It's a tall order. These people are my friends. I'm shaking and the shadow is with me for the rest of my time with them.

The final show is a mixture of artful performance and near disaster. From the start of the show, the audience are up and dancing – Zee had a word with the promoter about the over-the-top security. Leee, Zee and Angie are sitting a few rows from the front having a great time with the Japanese fans when, without warning, the seats in the first few rows collapse. Immediately, the fans from further back swarm over the broken seats and whoever is underneath them. They're desperate to get to the band, to clamber up on the stage. Stuey hasn't got a chance, there's just too many of them, fans on top of fans, all trying to get to the band, and they won't be held back.

David, the band, and Stuey make a run for it, leaving carnage in their wake, and I follow quickly behind them.

Later, I learn the scary news that people are really hurt. Damage to the theatre is extensive and the press are all over it; the next day in the papers, David is vilified. Defries has to deal with the promoter and the outraged press. None of us likes to hear people were hurt. Angie and Leee are blamed and might be arrested for inciting a riot, but the reality is that they were trying to help fans trapped under the seats. An arrest warrant is issued all the same, and they get hustled to the airport and put on the first plane anywhere. They escape to Hawaii.

24

A ROCKY START

12 May 1973

When the Japan dates are over, David leaves as David does – on a boat and train, travelling with Geoff through Russia – while we fly home. I sleep a lot of the flight back, arriving in London feeling completely disorientated and drained.

Bromley and Beckenham feel like a time warp. I'm lost in them. After the initial rush of excitement and gift-giving, my time at home grows boring almost immediately. Dad is still sitting in front of the telly and my mother's mantra hasn't changed a bit, the constant complaints about Dad and her life. My brother's out every night at the pub and I'm feeling increasingly worried about him; he seems lost. I've asked everyone if they need help on the crew, with no luck so far.

Before long, thankfully, I'm relieved of the boredom of home by rehearsals for the forthcoming UK tour that will run into spring and summer, followed by what promises to be the mother of all tours in the US next autumn. No further mention has been made of the band breaking up, and I'm hoping it was just a passing phase. Maybe they've changed their minds.

Aladdin Sane is in the charts at number one. The pre-orders reached over 150,000 copies, which, according to the *NME*, hasn't happened since The Beatles. The country aches for David and the upcoming tour sells out in a flash. I go to the London MainMan office and look at the schedule: day after day, week after week, all booked solid with shows. A matinee performance has been added to a lot of the evening shows, and as soon as any tickets go on sale they're gone in an instant. It's hysteria at the office, too, with demands for photos, interviews and TV appearances coming through thick and fast. What is it that makes David Bowie so special? What is that magic?

Our first date on this triumphant comeback tour is in London at the Earl's Court Arena. We're coming off a wonderful American and Japanese tour, and we have new costumes and make-up – what will they think of us now? When I walk in, I can only stand and stare at the empty arena and its cavernous concrete space.

'They're never going to hear him in here!' Robin says in frustration. 'We don't have enough speakers to fill this hall, plus, with the concrete, the sound will bounce all over the place.'

Bob looks disheartened as well: he knows the lights will be lost in the space, the follow spots not powerful enough. The equipment comes in, goes up and it's laughable. Our towers and speakers look like toys in this place. The mood of the crew is despondent. There are calls to Defries and Zee, but the only thing suggested is to hang huge parachutes from the ceiling to try and hold the sound down. It's grasping at straws, and we all pray. Eighteen thousand fans are attending this gig, it's been sold out for weeks, and there's nothing to be done. 'When the kids get in it'll help fill the empty space, that might help with the sound,' Robin says hopefully.

Another problem: the stage, even with risers, is too low. It's a jerry-rigged piece of rubbish, just scaffolding with planks on top. Unless you're in the first few rows you won't see much, and if you're halfway back you won't see anything at all. David arrives for a sound check and it's utterly hopeless. He's silent. I try to be cheerful but we're running towards a cliff and there's no way to stop us from jumping off. With trembling fingers I do up David's costume, and wish them all luck as I lead them to the stage.

I wish I could say our fears were groundless, that the gig, against all odds, worked better than we ever thought it could, but it just isn't the case. As soon as they start, people call out saying they can't hear; the sound comes off the stage and drops into oblivion. David walks off in frustration, then comes back on, but there's nothing to be done. He tries, they all do, but this time there's no pulling it out of the bag. The hall is simply too big. David tries for intimacy but there isn't any, just a lot of pissed-off screaming fans. They drown whatever sound there is with catcalls and boos of frustration.

When the band finally come off, they're devastated. They've never been booed before. David is furious. This is not the homecoming he imagined. The fans are beyond upset, fights breaking out as they take out their anger on each other and anything else they can find. When David and the band leave, I follow them to the hotel and return with wet costumes and an earful of woe from David. I walk out into the hall to sympathise with Robin, and we both marvel at the amount of damage people can do with a few chairs and some bottles and cans.

The only positive thing of the night comes when Bob calls to me from the stage, 'Is your brother still looking for a gig?'

'Yes!' I gasp.

'Tell him to be at the hotel by 10 o'clock tomorrow morning.'

'Okay,' I say, and try to imagine how I can get my brother out of bed before then. I call home, but it's late and no one answers. I call again at eight o'clock the following morning. This time, Mick answers.

'I've just got in,' he giggles. He sounds really drunk.

'Sober up,' I hiss. 'Do you want to come on the road? I've got you an interview at 10 a.m. with Bob See, the lighting designer. I told him you could work a follow spot.' Silence. 'Come on, Mick, it can't be that hard.'

'Okay,' he breathes, and I tell him that we're at the Hertford Hotel.

'It's on Bayswater Road. Get ready, sober up and come on up here,' and with that I put down the phone.

I find Bob and tell him that my brother's coming for the interview. My phone rings just after eleven o'clock: it's reception, with Michael Fussey looking for me. As I walk to the lobby, I catch a glimpse of him in the mirror . . . I can't believe it, he's come in a suit and tie for his interview!

He's laughing as he hugs me and says, 'I've seen Bob See, great bloke. They're going to try me out. I've got to go and get my stuff, I'm leaving with you tomorrow!'

I've rarely seen him so excited. I hope he'll be okay.

25
A BUMP IN THE ROAD

Fortunately, the brutal reviews from the Earl's Court gig don't keep the tour from becoming its usual explosive self. We go to Scotland and play sold-out shows in Aberdeen, Dundee, Glasgow and Edinburgh. From there we travel south, and everywhere we go we sell out. I'm loving it but I'm tired, and the band and David are exhausted beyond belief. After weeks of shows we settle into a routine, and it all seems to be working well, but there's a bigger problem: the costumes. They're literally hanging on by a thread.

It's the middle of June and we're in Birmingham for two back-to-back shows. It's a bit of a relief as when we're in the same place for two days I can leave the dressing rooms intact for the next day's performance. Granted, I still have to do the costumes, but at least I can dry clean and repair them at a local place, and I don't have to iron out the sweat from them for the evening show. By now, the sweat's so thick they almost stand up by themselves. There's always a bit of a party atmosphere at the hotel when we have shows scheduled like this. The band and crew have some time together and we all get a little legless at the hotel bar.

David spots a beautiful girl in the audience at the first show. He points her out to me before he goes onstage for the last encore. I follow his finger to a young girl with long blonde messy hair, a large pale-pink mouth and huge dark eyes. I can see the attraction;

165

she looks really good. After they've come offstage, I go out into the audience to find her. I tell her David wants to meet her at the hotel, that the bus is in the car park and she needs to meet me there in ten minutes. Her eyes widen in disbelief.

'Me?' she gasps. I nod my head.

My new job: tour madam. After the demise of the Elvis exit, my role has expanded. I now wait with the rest of the band for the bus. It's less glamorous, but I can pick up fans who want to meet the band. Other fans follow us in cars. I leave them at the hotel bar, promising that David and the band are coming down soon. Playing a gig with mass adoration is as addictive as any drug and it takes the band time to come down after the high.

I stand on the bus steps, waving aboard the prettiest girls and boys to come to the hotel. The blonde finds me in the car park; I get her giggling self on to the bus and we're off. At the hotel I take her to the bar where David's chatting away, and as he flashes a smile at her she suddenly seems a little shy. He welcomes her into his circle and slides his arm around her shoulder. I wander off and join the crew as they come in, boisterous as they order drinks. I'm sitting chatting to Robin when a very pale roadie, Willie Palin, finds me.

'There's a mum in reception, looking for her sixteen-year-old daughter.'

My stomach drops and my mouth goes dry as I hear raised voices at reception, and yes, here comes trouble. There's a blonde, good-looking woman in her forties with a red face and a determined attitude walking into the bar. She looks like an older version of the girl with David. They're pointing her in my direction.

'I'm looking for my daughter. She's tall and slim with long blonde hair.' I glance across to where David was sitting but he's gone, and so is the girl. I stammer that I haven't seen her but she's having none of it. 'She was seen getting on your bus,' she says sharply. 'She's only sixteen years old and I'm not leaving without her.'

'Well, you're welcome to look around the bar.'

'She's not meant to be in a bar, she's too young,' and with that, she storms further into the bar and starts to ask everyone where her daughter is.

'Stay with her, Willie,' I call out as I make a beeline for the lifts.

I get myself upstairs to David's room and curse when I see Stuey isn't here to let me in. I tap at David's door. There's no answer. I tap louder and call his name, and finally I hear, 'Fuck off, Suzi.'

'David,' I say in my best stage whisper, 'that girl you've got in there is sixteen. Her mother's downstairs looking for her.'

Silence, and then: 'Me mother?'

'Yes, your mother.'

'Oh, trust her to cum and spoil my fun.' There's still not a dicky-bird from David.

'She's got to leave, David.' No reply. 'Her mother knows she's here, she's searching the bar for her downstairs and kicking up a hell of a fuss.'

This gets some action. The girl is deposited out the door on the end of David's arm. He kisses her and tells her to come back next year. *She won't be legal then either* is my first thought, but now I need to do some damage control.

'Now calm down,' I say as she sobs. 'David thinks you are amazing, but you're too young. I promise I'll get you tickets to any gig you want. Give me your telephone number, I know David will call you, but you're sixteen, you can't stay.'

'I don't care, I luv him.' More tears.

'If your mum makes a stink about this, you'll never see him again.' She goes quiet, and we walk into a lift and ride the three flights down in silence.

'Me mum's going to be really cross,' she says, sniffing. I know that, but I'm banking on the fact that when she sees her daughter unharmed, some of the heat might go away. There's a bathroom off the lobby and we go in there so she can wash her face, then together we walk casually back to the bar.

'She was in the bathroom,' I say calmly, 'here she is.'

'What were you doing in the bathroom all this time?' her mother demands, but I'm right: the heat has gone out of her voice, and she seems genuinely pleased to see her daughter safe and sound. It was a close call.

As I escort them out of the hotel, the mother now directs her anger towards her daughter, who once again bursts into floods of tears. I wearily return to the bar for a much-needed drink. It's hard to tell with girls, and even though I could see she was really young after she cried her make-up off, at the gig she looked amazing and could easily have passed for twenty. *I might have to start asking for proof of age before they get on the bus*, I think to myself.

We leave for London the following day.

26
CURTAIN CALL

3 July 1973

The last two shows of the tour at the Hammersmith Odeon are being filmed. The film crew are all over the theatre and there are extra lights backstage, along with a lot of cameras and other equipment. We've been told the Pennebaker film crew are to be given any and all help from us, including access to the dressing rooms and backstage areas. They run a direct feed from our sound board to a truck outside the stage door.

I can't believe this is the last show. The secret I heard in Japan weighs heavily on my mind. Is it possible Mick and I are the only ones who know what's about to happen? Mick's never mentioned it again. I wonder if anyone's told Trev and Woody yet. Everyone else thinks we're running off to America in a few weeks. My heart feels like ice. I'm selfish: I don't want to go back to Beckenham, and Tony said that if I keep quiet I might not have to. The whole thing feels biblical – to break up the Spiders when it's all going so well seems crazy. I want to talk to someone about it, but I don't know who knows what! I can't say anything to Mick and Zee invites no conversation; it's as if it never happened. Maybe David will change his mind? I've thought about that possibility so much I almost believe it.

This might be the last time I'll be ironing these costumes, I think mournfully as I'm pressing the creases out of the Spring Rain outfit.

I leave the dressing room and go to the sound booth.

'Hey Robin, what about the States then?' I look up at him as he wires up the sound board.

Robin looks down and says with a grin, 'Yeah, coming right up, can't wait!'

'No, me either!' I reply. I look at his face. It's guileless, he doesn't have a clue. I try again. 'When are we going? I've heard there might be some sort of delay.'

'Really? Well, no one's told me anything for certain. It's in the middle of September, I think.'

Throughout the day I fish, but no one seems to know a thing. I know MainMan isn't going to die. There are other artists – Mick Ronson, for one. If there was ever a prince-in-waiting, it's him.

Everyone arrives for the sound check at around 4 p.m. I scour the band's faces, but nothing's written there. There's lots of laughter in the dressing room and everyone seems quite relaxed. We've been out on tour for such a long time and the band, understandably, seem happy for some time off. Woody's getting married, everyone's family's here. Mick seems a bit nervous, but he's always nervous before a show. There's that pre-showtime buzz in the air that comes while the audience fill up the theatre. I can smell pot mixed with that certain smell of anticipation and excitement.

Showtime. I walk with David and the band to the side of the stage, watch the band go on behind the curtain. The rumble of the London crowd turns into a roar as the lights go down and 'Ode to Joy' starts to play. I stand in the dark with David. He's dancing like a boxer warming up, his face a concentrated mask of make-up and readiness. I'm holding his wine, and he's got a Gauloise in his mouth. I wonder what he's thinking; he gives nothing away. Surely it must be strange for him too, no? Mick struts out, guitar howling, into the spotlight. David takes the last drag from his cigarette and makes his entrance. I take the tab end and his wine, stand back and watch. The fans roar as he goes on.

Will this be the last time I work with David? The last time I see this band? I try to drink in every moment. I've become someone else, caught up in a crazy existence that is David Bowie and the Spiders from Mars. This is my life now, and I'm not sure if I'll like my life afterwards.

At the first costume change, I hand David the prerequisite glass of wine and cig as he comes off. Once he's in the dressing room, he wriggles into the new outfit I've laid out, drinks a little, adjusts his hair, slicks some lipstick on and walks back to the stage in the pool of light from my torch; we're as smooth as silk. Mick is possessed, strutting around with his guitar above his head and a snarl on his face. He's fantastic to look at. David waits for the moment when Mick strikes a pose, nods to the band and runs out to join them.

Back in the dressing room, I prepare for the next change. We're halfway through the show and everyone's laughing and joking about, just the same as any other gig. I close the Kansai white flowing cloak over David's silk leggings; his long, pale throat and scarlet hair make him look like an exotic bird. To the audience's surprise and delight, Jeff Beck comes onstage, Mick welcoming him with a flourish. Backstage we treat him like royalty. I know he loves his guitar-playing. Jeff looks a bit of a relic next to the band, in his T-shirt and flared jeans, but he plays beautifully.

At the last encore David goes to the mic, quiets the audience with his hands and speaks:

'Everybody . . . this has been one of the greatest tours of our lives. I would like to thank the band. I would like to thank our road crew. I would like to thank our lighting people. Of all of the shows on this tour, this particular show will remain with us the longest' – cheers rise up from the audience – 'because not only is it – not only is it the last show of the tour, but it's the last show that we'll ever do. Thank you.'

They move into 'Rock 'n' Roll Suicide' and as I look around, everybody's still smiling and laughing. They don't seem to understand; maybe they're still processing what has just been said. It's not the reaction I was expecting.

The band leave the stage. No one says a thing to me, and I don't say anything to anyone either. The audience seem puzzled, and some are crying, but that's normal – it was an emotional gig.

'Did he just say what I thought he did?' one of the crew members asks.

'Yeah,' I answer numbly.

I go to the dressing room to find David and Mick gone. Only Woody and Trevor remain. 'What do you think?' I say to Woody.

'About what?'

I take a glass of wine. 'About the "last show".'

'He means the "last show" of this tour,' says Trevor.

I drop it. I can't believe he didn't tell them. How could he publicly humiliate them like this? Why didn't Mick say anything? There's a million questions running through my mind. The band and David have been through so much together, been on such a journey. They've had some ups and downs, but all in all it's been a huge success, due in no small part to the band. I see how ruthless David can be and feel horrible for the band.

I don't go to the party at the Café Royal, getting drunk in my room with some of the roadies instead. Tony Defries is furious, but I couldn't face it. The Spiders from Mars disappear, never to be seen again. The end of Ziggy is swift and brutal.

27

AFTERMATH

'BOWIE'S LAST SHOW' scream the headlines from a shell-shocked press. 'FANS IN TEARS AS THEY LEAVE THE HAMMERSMITH ODEON.'

They even call the house; Mum's impressed they found our number. I don't see Woody and Trevor and I'm not sure I want to. In the days after the gig, I wait for contact from anyone, but none comes. Everyone's gone to ground.

Woody and Trevor must be the most crushed out of anyone – they didn't know a thing before David's announcement. I put myself in their position: how would I feel if I was one of them? *Foolish* goes without saying; then angry and disbelieving, upon realising that others knew; maybe surprise at the disloyalty from supposed friends; then I suppose gradual acceptance, followed by sadness, anxiety and fear. The MainMan mentality is to trample on anyone that gets in your way, and this is that, in spades.

Although the Spiders are well established as a band, if you take away David and Mick, how well known are the rest? The band never did interviews: it was forbidden. Mick had tried but the things he said didn't resonate well with Tony Defries or David, so any other interview requests were denied. The Spiders tried for a record deal and got one with CBS until Tony blew it all away with just a single phone call. He told CBS if there was a deal to be done with the Spiders, *he* would be the one to do it.

Tony has David under contract, one that gives him half of whatever he makes. Mick is under the same contract (though Mick didn't know it at the time), but Tony didn't have Woody or Trev signed to anything. If they get a record deal, Tony won't be in the picture, won't make any money, won't have any control – he can't allow that to happen.

Pin Ups was about to be recorded without either one of them until Jack Bruce – the bass player who's been asked to replace Trevor – said he couldn't make it. It puts MainMan in a sticky position, and without a thought they ask Trev to come and play on the album. It's bloody cheeky but Trev's caught between a rock and a hard place – he has a family to support – so he accepts and comes to France to play. I wonder if he talked to Woody about it.

The final blow comes for Woody, however, on his wedding day. Defries calls and fires him on the telephone, telling him he won't be recording the new album with David. Woody, confused, asks to speak to David: request denied. He then asks to speak to Mick: also denied. This leaves Woody, shocked and pale, stuttering down the phone searching for an answer. Defries enlightens him, reminds him of his 'disloyalty'. Woody thought that was all behind them and says so; but not for David and Defries. They have an axe to grind, and they intend to grind it.

Defries is referring to a confrontation that occurred in America during the second US tour, months ago now. Mike Garson and Woody were talking, the conversation turned to wages and Woody discovered that Mike was being paid a lot more than the band. 'But surely you get points* off the record?' asked Mike.

---

* Points are a percentage of a royalty.

'No,' replied Woody, seething inside.

He couldn't wait to tell Trevor and Mick. Even the two brass players were getting paid more than the band. It was a bitter blow and Woody, in a fury, demanded an explanation from David. David, never one for confrontation, consulted with Defries, and they called a band meeting. God knows what Mick was thinking as he walked into the room: he'd been offered a different deal if he promised to keep quiet. Woody argued that they deserved at least the same and possibly more money than the new musicians. David and Defries cut him down as they dealt out crushing blows. They insulted the band, dismissed them as nothing more than backing musicians and refused to pay more money. Woody, hurt and incandescent with rage, walked out, followed by Mick and Trev. As Woody explained later, it wasn't all about the money: it was the way David treated them, and the way he allowed Defries to treat them. He swore that, for him, the tour was over. There was a gig that night and he had David and Defries over a barrel. Eventually, they had to capitulate. David never forgot that and considered the band disloyal; in my opinion, he was the one that was disloyal, no matter his later excuses.

'I know I really pissed off Woody [Woodmansey, drums] and Trevor [Bolder, bass],' David conceded in a 1993 interview with *Select*. 'They were so angry, I think, because I hadn't told them that I was splitting the band up. But that's what Ziggy did – so I had to do it, too.'

He also blamed cocaine for his bad behaviour. I laugh when I read this and don't believe it for a second. It was raw, naked ambition, and a bloody-mindedness that is particular to a few people. I never saw cocaine in the dressing room during the last tour, never saw any sign of it. Even looking back after becoming familiar with the drug myself, I never saw any reason to believe this was what influenced David. It was revenge and control. David was an undeniable creative force and a blazing talent, but he couldn't do it alone.

Mick was the one who put the band together and the band he found were brilliant. He brought them down from Hull, along with Stuey and Pete Hunsley, their roadie. He led the band, wrote arrangements, played multiple instruments onstage and in the studio. He was a powerhouse performer. He produced Lou Reed's album with David, another example of his genius; the piano he plays on 'Perfect Day' is sublime. He got a credit for that album but no royalty, no money. All of that for fifty quid a week. It was criminal – hell, I was on twenty quid.

David and Defries were both equally guilty in this exploitation. You might ask why Mick put up with it, and I can only say it was ignorance. He was brought up as a Mormon, living by the motto 'do as you would be done to'. He had no idea of his own worth, no idea how talented he was. He was just grateful not to be a school gardener any more. Heartbreakingly, he thought David and Defries were his friends, people who would look out for him, and they milked this naivety for all it was worth.

David was forced to change as he got older. I've met other musicians with whom he worked, and they all had to fight for credit and payment. They weren't Mick Ronson, they were professional and experienced musicians – they'd cut their teeth in other bands. They both demanded and got payment and credit. There was no other way really, as they wouldn't put up with David's shenanigans. These musicians were not the Spiders from Mars.

◆

The day after Hammersmith, I wake up with a hangover and a heavy heart. The hotel kicks us out at noon; the American crew go to the airport and I go home. I don't see my brother until I get there and when I do, he's all fired up about going to America with Bob See. He'd been promised a job, but for now it's back to the building site. The David and the Spiders era is over, and I've come to accept that. I have to say goodbye to people I've shared so much of my life with, but soon enough self-preservation kicks in, and no one likes a sad girl, so I go to the office to see what the future might bring.

When I walk into MainMan, Tony Defries is at his desk talking to Mott the Hoople's lead singer, Ian Hunter, and his wife, Trudi. The atmosphere is decidedly unpleasant. Trudi's face is like thunder. Tony sighs as they walk out the door. He makes tea for us before we sit down. Tony likes to talk, and I like to listen. Despite everything, Tony has always been good to me – he's been a mentor, in fact. I'm fascinated by the way his mind works.

'Mick will be the next MainMan star,' he tells me grandly, accentuated by a wave of his cigar. It seems the most natural thing in the world for Mick to pick up the mantle of superstardom. When I'm asked to work on the project, I pause to think. David hasn't called me, and neither has Angie. Everything feels discombobulated and strange. Mick sounds like an exciting project. Tony asks me to think about it while I'm in Paris at the Château d'Hérouville, where David is recording a new album. It's an iconic recording studio in France. With a sense of relief, I pick up my itinerary on the way out and clasp it to my chest.

I have to tell Mum I'm leaving again, but it gets easier and easier each time if I'm honest. Mum's vision for the future is for me to come home, settle down, get a regular job, find a boyfriend, get married, have babies and live around the corner. I'm sorry to disappoint her, but I'm not giving up this life until it kicks me out.

◆

After the emotional drain of the past few weeks, the idea of going to Paris brightens me up no end. On the journey, Trev's silent for the most part, Mick his usual bonny self. I don't mention Woody, no one does, and even though I'm dying of curiosity I stay quiet. It's late in the afternoon when we're picked up by a limo from Orly airport and driven through iron gates into the courtyard of Château d'Hérouville. It's the beginning of July, the sun is warm and the sky bright blue. The villa is romantic and gorgeous with pale-gold stone walls and tall chimneys. It's a little unkempt but nothing detracts from its beauty. I walk across the gravel courtyard and look at a relic of a swimming pool that has lilies growing in it, home to ducks and frogs, it seems.

We are welcomed by the château staff and shown to our rooms before gathering at a long wooden table next to the kitchen. I see David and we all welcome Aynsley Dunbar, our new drummer. He's light-hearted and fun and if he knows anything about the drama preceding him, he chooses to ignore it. David, sitting with Mick and Ken Scott, the producer, looks peaceful, younger even. His friend Geoff MacCormack is here too, as well as Stuey. It's as if the weight of the world has been lifted off his shoulders. He catches my eye and gives me a smile. It's hard to stay angry at him. Without him, none of us would be here. I hate the way he's dealt with the band, but at the same time I can't imagine the stress he's been under.

I think Trev misses Woody the most. They were the closest. He's quiet and withdrawn and without him doesn't join in the banter that echoes between us. Maybe he feels guilty. I wonder if he knows he's only been asked because Jack Bruce couldn't make it. Whether he does or doesn't, he sees the writing on the wall. Whatever he thought before, he now knows that they're not a band: he works for David, just as we all do. As unfair as the whole situation is, I can't imagine he didn't understand that it was always just David Bowie.

The studio itself is across the courtyard from the main house, and after dinner we go to listen to some tracks they started at Trident Studios. The day ends drinking wine in the control room. After everything that's gone down, I'm just relieved to still be here.

As the sun rises the next day, I open my eyes in a narrow bed covered with white linen smelling of lavender. I can hear men laughing and talking outside; their language sounds so romantic. Downstairs I find fruit, toast and milky coffee for breakfast. I want another look at the lounge underneath the studio, and when I walk out into the sun I gasp at the sheer beauty of my surroundings. The smell of country air with flowers blooming in full summer glory is potent. The lounge itself is large, clean and comfortable with couches, cushions and chairs. There's a TV in one corner and speakers dotted around the room. A fireplace takes up most of another wall and stone steps lead up to the studio. Mick's already here and working with an engineer, bouncing tracks. He rolls a ciggy as he drinks tea and smiles at me as he listens to the music.

After a communal lunch, David and the others go over and work on the tracks in earnest. Trev plays well enough but is quiet and disappears whenever he isn't needed. Other than that, the chemistry feels good, and everyone pitches in with suggestions. It's the first time David hasn't written any tracks for the album – they'll all be covers. The chosen songs are part of my teenage years too, and though I'm nostalgic as I listen to the originals, I have to admit their versions are dazzling.

To my surprise, Lulu arrives at the château; she's here to do some tracks with David. I remember the first time I saw Lulu, on *Top of the Pops*. At fifteen years old, she had a fantastic hit, 'Shout', and her powerhouse voice gave her a lasting career. 'Watch That Man' and 'The Man Who Sold the World' are the two tracks that have been chosen. I'm not sure about 'The Man Who Sold the World' as a choice but I'm interested watching it play out. I'm a little starstruck with Lulu but she's a great girl, easy-going and looking wholesome in her red roll-neck and denim overalls. Ken Scott gets an unexpected emergency call: his wife is having their baby. He leaves in a hurry, followed by Trevor, who has finished laying down his bass. As they continue to work, it becomes clear to me that Lulu has her eye on Mick. He's oblivious to this, but David isn't, and I feel sure she and David fool around at the château. Before I know it, she's come and gone. The backing tracks for both the songs are finished and the energy is infectious. David plays sax and lays down some harmonies over Lulu's voice; it all sounds golden.

A few days later, David and I leave for Paris to do a photo shoot for *Vogue* with the iconic Twiggy. I'm going to take care of David and do his hair. I've idolised Twiggy since I was a teenager and I can't wait to meet her in person. At the studio I'm introduced to Justin de Villeneuve, her manager, who also doubles as the photographer and is in charge of the session. Twiggy herself isn't that tall but as thin as a pin, with a beautiful face and flawless skin.

Pierre LaRoche joins us again, this time painting masks on David and Twiggy's faces. David looks quite masculine next to her. He stares directly into the camera, her head soft on his shoulder, his milk-white skin in sharp contrast to her golden tan. It makes for a brilliant photo.

When David sees the end result, he immediately wants the photo for his album cover. Pierre says I should get a credit for his hair and I want to ask, but think about Woody and dare not say anything.

28
FALLING IN LOVE

After recording *Pin Ups* at the château, I'm invited on holiday to a villa in Rome with David, Angie and some friends. We go straight from Paris to Rome and meet David's guests, who fly in with Angie from London. The villa is magnificent, with landscaped gardens that surround a pool with life-size marble statues. Attached to the house is a shady terrace, scattered with pots of fragrant flowers and herbs. We dine under brilliant bougainvillea then sink on to long, low couches to relax; the weather is perfect. Mick asks me why I didn't make it to the party at the Café Royal after Hammersmith. I tell him I got drunk with the roadies instead. He laughs, and when our eyes meet he doesn't look away, and neither do I.

For whatever reason, Mick starts to seek me out, and as we begin to spend time together, I begin to feel like the leading lady in a movie who's about to win the leading man.

One night Mick and I are having dinner out on the terrace; the air is black velvet and the perfume of night-time jasmine floats over us. He smiles as he leans towards me. I don't expect it but I close my eyes as he gets closer. I briefly think about the first time I met him at Haddon Hall, how handsome I thought him, how attracted I was and how hard I fought the attraction. Kissing Mick is easy, passionate and perfect. I don't know how he feels but for me, it's a shocking, melt-in-your-mouth, heart-stopping moment. If this is a dream I don't want to wake up.

We spend the night in his room and when I wake up, I don't know where I am. I look across the pillow and see him asleep. He's the most beautiful man I've ever seen. Leee Black Childers once said Mick looks like a Greek god, and he's not far wrong.

We make tea and take it back to bed and talk and talk. Mick is a shy man by nature, but today he's eloquent, animated and very funny. He's such wonderful company. He tells me about his family – his parents, his sister, Maggi, and his younger brother, David. He tells me he's always been musical, picking out tunes on his toy piano when he was five years old. His mother tried to help him, finding him piano lessons with Trevor's grandmother, no less. His dad fails to understand Mick's passion for music and advised Mick to get a regular job, maybe alongside him at the BP factory. Mick refused and fought hard to make it in music, moving to London and living on baked beans before going on to Europe. On his way back from France, he was arrested at Hyde Park Corner for driving without a licence or insurance. Mick had reached his breaking point: he was broke, hungry and homeless, and the resistance he felt before faded. Moving back to Hull, he escaped the BP factory and got a job as a school gardener, seemingly resigned to his fate.

This is where David found him, thanks to John Cambridge. John, also from Hull, had played in the Rats with Mick. He left to seek fame and fortune in London and joined David, who was in the process of revamping his band and needed a guitar player. John remembered his talented friend and went to Hull to persuade him, finding Mick marking out a football pitch. Initially, he was resistant – he had tried this before and he quite liked gardening – but John was persistent and by some miracle coaxed him into meeting David. Mick's lucky break was meeting David, but it was a lucky break for David as well.

At the time, he too was struggling to find a way forward. He had a hit, 'Space Oddity', and some wonderful people helping him – Tony Visconti, Lindsay Kemp – but it seemed as though he had exhausted his options. Then he met Angie, Tony Defries and the final part of the puzzle: Mick Ronson. The rest is history.

David and Angie seem to be hiding away most of the time we're here, and even when they do appear David doesn't say much to anyone. Sitting by a swimming pool was never David's thing. He's a workaholic and I imagine he doesn't find Italy as relaxing as he thought he would. He's just let go of the most successful thing England's seen for years and he might be suffering from withdrawal symptoms. After a few days they end up leaving the villa, and the tension disappears along with their limo. Mick and I spend all our time together and do things that people do when they first get together. It's a romantic place, an easy place to fall in love. He looks happy in a straw hat, colourful shirt and black speedos, and when he calls me 'Suzi, baby', with that soft Yorkshire accent, I melt.

This is an idyllic time and a new beginning for both of us. The thrill for Mick is going into the studio to record his own album; the thrill for me is being with him. He plays me the title track, a Richard Rodgers piece called *Slaughter on Tenth Avenue*. The original track sounds old-fashioned, but Mick has a million ideas for it. We spend another few days in Italy before going back to the Château d'Hérouville to record with Trevor Bolder, Mike Garson and Aynsley Dunbar. When we arrive, I go with Mick to his room and nobody says anything. Mick tells me not to worry, so I don't.

After they finish recording the backing tracks at the château, we return to London.

Mick and I go to the flat in Beckenham; it feels large and empty without anyone else there. I stay with him for a wonderful week before going back to my parents' house. I've told Mick a bit about my mum, so he smiles and wishes me luck as he leaves for rehearsals at the Marquee Club.

I walk into 96 Cumberland Road to an enthusiastic welcome. Mum's happy to see me, and although I'm scared of upsetting her, I want to jump right in and get this over with.

'I came back from Paris last week.'

I don't think she hears at first, but suddenly a steely look comes into her eyes. She repeats my own words back to me.

'. . . what did you say, back for a week? Where were you staying?'

'Beckenham.'

Then, as it sinks in, her face changes and her voice goes up an octave: 'Do you mean to tell me you've been home for a week, staying in Beckenham, and not even called!' There's a dangerous edge in her tone.

'Yes,' I say in a whisper. I feel awful but there's no turning back. 'I'm not coming home . . . I'm moving in with Mick.' There, I've said it.

'When did this happen? . . . But your bedroom, I've just redecorated your bedroom!'

I feel bad. I look at the bedroom with her then try to tell her what a wonderful man Mick is, but she's having none of it and runs from the room in tears. It's no great surprise, I expected this from her. I know she's unhappy, that she misses me, that she's scared of my independence. My dad is more relaxed and tells me to give it some time, that she'll come round. I wait a few days and call again. Mick and I go round to meet them. Everyone likes Mick, and my parents are no exception.

29

THE 1980 FLOOR SHOW

18–20 October 1973

The Midnight Special is being filmed for broadcast in America at the Marquee Club in London. It's October and there's a slight chill in the air. Mick and I take a Clockhouse minicab up to the club and when we arrive together no one says anything. It's an anticlimax and – for both of us, I think – a relief.

David's dressing room is small and dark, with bright lights surrounding a mirror. I work on his hair while he gets his make-up done by Barbara Daly. There's a beautiful woman walking around backstage as the band rehearse, tall, slim and curvy, with wavy blonde hair, razor cheekbones and dark-brown eyes. She moves as if in her own world. David seems as in awe of her as we all do. Angie tells me it's Amanda Lear, the model posing in all black, holding a panther, on the cover of Roxy Music's album *For Your Pleasure*.

Amanda is the compere for the show as well as the object of desire in David's song 'Sorrow'. I see a different David onstage – he's relaxed and smiling, and sounds so normal talking to the audience between takes. It makes him seem softer, more accessible; the fans lap it up. A lot of the audience are invited members of his fan club, and these die-hard fans are enthusiastic and patient. David's in an extraordinary mood, joking around in and out of the dressing room. I've rarely seen him more laid-back at a show. The Troggs are the warm-up band and when they go on, they get the whole place up and shaking. Outside the Marquee is a crush of fans trying to get in, the line winding all the way down Wardour Street.

David has two new backing singers who join Geoff MacCormack: Jason Guess and David's new girl of the moment, Ava Cherry. Ava is a great-looking African American girl with short blonde hair and a fabulous figure. She always has an adoring look for David. I see her take my place, along with Jason, to enact the kabuki move I used to do onstage for David, peeling away one costume to reveal another. David's costumes, including a patent-leather feather thing with a stiletto boot, don't really appeal to me; they feel like a parody of before. Ava, Geoff and Jason are christened the new Astronettes and take centre stage along with David. The focal point of the show has changed, and now the band are pushed into the background, except for Mick, who shines like an angel on the front of the stage in an all-white suit. On the second day of filming, *Pin Ups* is released. With advance orders of 150,000, it goes right in the charts at number one. Perhaps that's why David's smiling.

Wayne County is here too, a recent MainMan artist who was introduced to Defries by Leee Black Childers. He'd previously been involved with Andy Warhol and tonight he's resplendent in red chiffon as he chats up people who walk by. Everyone loves his shocking behaviour. Cherry Vanilla in true Cherry Vanilla style aids and abets him, throwing suggestive remarks to anyone who looks their way. Together with Leee, they shriek and carry on while we wait for the American roadies and crew to get things ready. I haven't seen Wayne perform but I hear he uses a toilet bowl onstage, which doesn't sound like my cup of tea. The American crew from *The Midnight Special* seem a little uptight in the face of it all, and their equipment isn't working well . . . they're embarrassed, as everyone's ready but them. I know Robin Mayhew controls the sound out front, and Ken Scott is recording it all in a sound truck on the street, so it's bound to sound good despite the mistakes. David takes it all in his stride.

Another 1960s star in attendance: Marianne Faithfull. A former girlfriend of both Brian Jones and Mick Jagger, she had a whimsical hit with 'As Tears Go By' in the 1960s. Tonight she is doing two numbers, one with David – 'I Got You Babe' – and the other her teenage hit, 'As Tears Go By'. The costume she is wearing to sing with David is a nun's habit with wimple. I attach the white wimple while she puffs on a cigarette. She tells me, 'I can't raise my arms above my elbows, that's what addiction will do to you,' and, laughing, she blows out a huge cloud of smoke.

Ava watches as David sings 'Sorrow' to Amanda, who is posed high on the side of the stage on scaffolding. Amanda gives David a sultry look and I wonder what Ava thinks. She can't imagine she's the only one. I look at both David's girls: an innocent young American and a sophisticated older European woman whose sexuality is a mystery. David can't resist either, and Angie's laugh is way too loud as she struggles to find a place between his two mistresses.

Amanda is followed by rumours that she used to be a guy, but who cares? She looks incredible. The crew tease and laugh as I walk towards Amanda's dressing room. She doesn't need help changing from me, she's a very private person, delightful and polite.

The show as a whole feels a little flat to me, nothing like it was before. We leave in a crush and that's that.

30
A CHANGE IN DIRECTION

'Love Me Tender' is the choice for a single off *Slaughter on 10th Avenue*. It was Tony's decision; he has a Colonel Tom Parker fantasy and a hard-on for Elvis. I think it's a mistake, but what do I know? Mick doesn't know what to think.

While Mick is mixing *Slaughter* at Trident Studios, I look for a place for us in London. We find an enormous flat in Hyde Park Gate, close to the Albert Hall and on the same street Winston Churchill used to live on. It's truly beautiful and well beyond our means and needs. The entrance leads to a long hallway with a chocolate-brown carpet and two chandeliers. Mick and I have a master suite at the end of the hall, with our own wonderful blue-tiled bathroom. I love it, even if I feel dwarfed by the space. The whole place is decorated and fully kitted out, no expense spared. All our bills go to the office. Our only role models are David and Angie, so we move in and run around London in limos, spend money and enjoy life. I'm under the illusion Mick has a lot of money, and I think his family thinks the same thing. I'm congratulating myself. I'm living with a pop star I love and I'm really happy.

Mick's mum calls and says his sister, Maggi, is having a hard time in Hull. She asks if she can stay with us. Mick looks at me; neither one of us is sure, we've only just moved in with each other, but I want to be nice to Maggi, and I want Mick's family to like me. She comes at the weekend and is given a room. Pete, the roadie who lived with Mick in Beckenham, takes a room too, and a girl called Cezuire moves in for the weekend and never leaves. I don't even remember where we met her, but she says she'll make costumes. We think we're doing the normal thing, gathering our group. I feel sure Mick knows what he's doing, and he seems happy these days, working on his album and upcoming tour.

I hear rumours that things are not going well between David and Defries, but the MainMan machine grinds on with Mick in the spotlight. We fly to New York to shoot a *Slaughter* promo film that Cherry Vanilla and Macs McAree have written. MainMan books us a suite at the Park Lane hotel. I feel like David and Angie, and with uncharacteristic carelessness I order something different from the room service menu: quail. When it comes, it looks like a sparrow and I can't eat it.

Mick calls David but he never gets an answer. We know David's in New York, he's staying at The Sherry-Netherland – I can see the hotel across the park from our window. For all the help he is, he might as well be on the moon. I wish he'd get in touch; I wish I knew what was going on with him and Angie. I miss them both, their undeniable style, their instinct of what to do next and how to do it. I hear stories about parties at the Sherry supplied with enough cocaine to support Bolivia. Huge Courvoisier bottles, once full of cognac, are now filled with cigarette butts. I'm surprised he isn't dead already.

At MainMan, they tell me David's recording songs for himself and for the Astronettes. His interest in the Astronettes isn't surprising, given that Ava and his friend Geoff are both in the group. Still, even with David putting his time into them, those songs never make it out of the studio. I can't help but think Mick's the missing piece.

We arrive at the shoot the next evening. I haven't seen Cherry Vanilla for a while and barely recognise her when I do. I first met Cherry in New York when David was playing at Carnegie Hall. She was introduced to me as Kathy Dorritie, office manager for MainMan. Kathy Dorritie was refined, with little make-up and dark, shiny bobbed hair. I never thought much about her until she started to show up at gigs on the Bowie tour. Her appearance changed, along with her attitude. Cherry turned out to be as loud and crazy as Leee and Zee, and just as much fun. I had some great nights with all of them.

Cherry's in charge of the shoot. She and I are both cast as hookers, me in a tight red skirt with a purple sequined top and her in a low-cut silk dress, high heels and full make-up. Mick, the hero, is the man we're both in love with. His character promises me a better life and we plan to run away together. I'm saying goodbye to my friends when Cherry, in a jealous rage, tells my pimp I'm leaving. We walk out of the door, there's a shout and a shot, and I throw myself in front of Mick and die tragically in his arms. It's so much fun. Mick cries glycerin tears, and Leee – the photographer for the shoot – gets the cover shot for the album.

While the promo is in production, MainMan continues to work with their other artists. Tony Ingrassia – who is relatively new to MainMan; he directed *Pork* – has written a play about Marilyn Monroe called *Fame*. It opens on my twenty-fifth birthday at the John Golden Theatre on 45th Street and Broadway. In true Broadway style, we stay up for the reviews. They are dire. The lavish production, which costs MainMan a fortune, opens and closes the same night. I look at Tony Defries for his reaction. He doesn't bat an eyelid and just takes it all in his stride. The man's got balls of steel.

◆

Once we're back in London, Mick starts to put his show together in earnest and the PR continues. He does a great interview with Bob Harris on *The Old Grey Whistle Test*. Bob is a fan of Mick's and his soft-spoken style suits Mick, the interview showing him to his best advantage.

Defries suggests bringing the London Philharmonic Orchestra in to play with Mick at his first solo shows. It's a huge offer and Mick's understandably floored at first, but then he jumps right in and starts to write parts for them. He also has to rehearse the band and prepare himself to be the front man of his own show. Defries tells us the show will be filmed, which adds even more pressure. I don't know how to help him, and neither does his sister: it's all on Mick and we both feel helpless. I wait for the album to come out, but I wait in vain. The only thing out in time for the show is the single 'Love Me Tender'. The clock ticks down and here we are, back at the Rainbow.

I set up the dressing rooms and nostalgia washes over me: I remember the success we had here with Ziggy and it feels like a good omen. On the night of the show Mick and I stand together side by side, waiting for the orchestra to settle and the band to take their places. I feel the familiar tension start to build as Mick slips on his guitar, then with a few words to me and a smile he goes on to a roar. Mick's in top form, the orchestra and band are wonderful. I look around me and everyone is cheering and loving it. I get swept away; I want to believe it. David arrives – and stands opposite me on the stage. I only half expected him to come. I heard stories about him wanting to go on, but if he was tempted, I didn't see it. He doesn't stay long and doesn't come to the after-party.

Mick takes his time and after the show, illuminated by lights for Cherry's film, we chat and laugh easily with the band in the dressing room. Defries is here and is all smiles, telling Mick what a wonderful show it was. Mick grins and, with a cigarette clamped in his mouth, changes his clothes for the party. We pop champagne to celebrate and then the two of us leave together. We walk down the long corridor towards the stage door, lights and cameras in our faces. It's all wonderful – until we step outside, then all hell breaks loose.

The lights and cameras are upended and disappear into the crowd as the crew are knocked to the ground by fans. Mick and I are surrounded, with no time to react. Mick grabs my hand; I catch a glimpse of an open limo door, it's tantalisingly close, but a wall of people push us down the street away from it. More and more fans throw themselves into the fray and I hang on to Mick as we fight to stand up. Bits of his coat and chunks of his hair get pulled out in the process. Someone is trying to drag my coat off and I feel nails rake my arm. It's scary and dark, and it seems as though it takes forever before a couple of blokes come to rescue us. They grab on to Mick and I'm mistaken for a fan, pulled off to one side. I scream and Mick hears me, and I'm thrown into the car battered and bruised. It shakes me. Mick laughs.

'You all right, Suzi baby?' he says tenderly as I inspect the state of my coat. Soon enough, though, we catch our breath and laugh on the way to the after-party. Everyone's here: celebrities, fans and friends alike. We're the guests of honour – well, Mick is, and I, as his girlfriend along for the ride, relish my new role. Both our families are here, as well as Mick Rock, who floats about snapping photos, same as always. Cherry simulates sex with a champagne bottle in her mouth, the footage of which, with my parents watching, is priceless.

◆

MainMan send Cherry and Macs to film casual home footage in our flat to publicise the release of Mick's album.

'It'll be fabuuulloous,' purrs Cherry over the phone.

They arrive early one morning with cameras rolling. I've been told to open the door and act surprised, but there is no need to act: I am surprised. Cherry's in full make-up with pink hair straight from the salon, wearing a very sexy dress. She walks in looking like a movie star. This is not what I was expecting. I'm in a sludge-green candlewick dressing gown with no make-up on. I've been told to run down the hall and wake Mick up – it's meant to look as if we have both overslept. I'm waiting for direction but there is no direction, no second takes, no script, no ideas. Mick and I are painfully inadequate. It goes from bad to worse. They set up in the kitchen and film as I, still in my dressing gown, pretend to make phone calls. Mick makes tea and rolls one endless cigarette after another. We both smoke incessantly.

I think about David and Angie, how they'd never be in this situation; they would never do anything that hadn't been carefully planned and rehearsed. They know what they're doing and they surround themselves with people who are creative and artistic. Mick's been caught up with the Rainbow shows, I have too, and neither one of us has given this much thought. Now we're at the mercy of MainMan and Cherry Vanilla.

Cherry casts herself as an interviewer and has come well prepared with questions. Mick struggles – he's a shy man. Cherry laughs at everything, bats her eyelashes at Mick and the camera, and when the doorbell rings again, I leave them and run to change. When I return, Trevor and his family are crowded into the kitchen along with Mick's sister, Maggi. Trevor isn't exactly star material either and, despite her best efforts, the only things animated are the cherries on Cherry's bosom, which shake and bounce with every toss of her pink head. Afterwards I wonder why they chose to film in the kitchen, the smallest, least glamorous part of the flat.

After an hour or so, they pack up before filming us in a limo on our way to the train station. I want to look cool and glamorous, but I feel underdressed and dull.

'Just be yourselves,' says Cherry with a bright smile as she poses for photos in the corridor of the train. 'Ourselves' aren't that captivating, Mick pretends to read the paper, and I struggle to see anything of interest out of the window. Cows in wet fields is all that's there. In Hull, we skip around a graveyard, hiding behind headstones. Why? No one we know is buried there. We eat fish and chips at the local chippy, which are delicious, but to what end? The only good part is when Mick walks alone at the docks. The weather is lovely, and he looks wonderful.

When I see it later, I cringe at how awful it is. The *Slaughter* video Cherry did was fantastic; she came up with a clear plot, picked a great location and it came out really well. The filming at the Rainbow show didn't come out too badly, but this, Mick and I in the flat, is truly horrible. Maybe Cherry didn't realise how much help we needed. I think we should have had a rehearsal, or at least a discussion about what to say and how to look . . . David and Angie always made it look so easy.

◆

In New York, Tony's been busy buying out two huge billboards in preparation for Mick's success, one on Sunset Strip and the other in Times Square. The one in Times Square is so enormous that it covers two buildings; and as luck would have it, the painters go on strike right afterwards, so it stays up for months. There's a slew of paraphernalia for the fans: photos, *Slaughter* stickers, a flexi disc. Both of us are drowning in the expectations of MainMan. We say we're all for it – well, I say I am, I'm not sure what Mick thinks. He's still under the impression he hasn't signed a contract with MainMan, but the truth is that he has. Leee admits years later that Tony told him to get Mick to sign something no matter what, so Leee got him drunk and made him sign a ten-year contract with the same terms as David: half of everything.

It's laughable how naive we both are, how stupid. We go along with all of it, led like lambs to the slaughter, our eyes open but not seeing a thing. It seems okay . . . good . . . is it? . . . maybe . . . but it really isn't. A career in music is so much more than just music.

31
WHERE DO WE GO FROM HERE?

Slaughter on 10th Avenue is finally released and charts, and after endless rehearsals we go on the road thinking it's all going to be okay – and for the most part it is. The band are great, but there's no big hit and the reviews are mediocre, with more than one saying that it's Bowie without Bowie.

David has an uncanny knack of being able to change completely and move on. He's now another person. Mick isn't made that way, and I'm no better. It takes a certain talent. I can't blame anyone, but I think to throw Mick out there so soon after the Spiders' break-up was a foolish idea. Mick should have been allowed some time to find himself, to find his own way, his own path. He doesn't want to be a sex symbol or a teen idol, but he doesn't know how to say no and he doesn't have a better alternative.

Michael Watts writes in *Melody Maker* after the Rainbow gigs: 'Ronno is the victim of massive hype.' He's right, but what does he expect? Mick was half of David, both in the studio and on the stage. Live, Mick has no one to play off. It's just him, and I think it's proving difficult for him to lead the band and hold down both the vocals and the guitar work. Meanwhile, David's riding high in the charts. His 'retirement' only fuels the fire that was set. He releases 'Rebel Rebel' and it sounds fresh and new; Lulu releases 'The Man Who Sold the World', and it ends up charting. There's a reception for her, which Mick and I attend. I'm hoping to see David but he isn't there.

Mick still has his share of screaming fans. Three young lads attach themselves to us while we're on tour, following us around the country. One night, we pass them on the bus as they're dejectedly walking home in the rain. Mick stops the bus and brings them on board; this is the kind of man he is. They're wearing striped *Slaughter* T-shirts and muddy white trousers, with spiky Ziggy hair. Not one of them has a coat and they're all soaked through. Mick gets them a hotel room and gives them money to go home in the morning. They're back again after a couple of days.

Despite the gigs going well, Mick doesn't seem as happy as he should be – I don't know why and I'm not sure he does either. Maybe he's just not cut out to be the centre of attention. After the tour ends, we go back to London and Mick's parents come from Yorkshire to stay. While they're with us, a burglar comes in through our kitchen window and quietly robs us while we sleep. He doesn't take a lot, but what he does take are Mick's favourite albums. Mick's upset, and even more so when we discover that the burglar left *Slaughter on 10th Avenue* on the floor. He looks at me and we both burst out laughing.

After his parents leave, we find ourselves unsure of a way forward. David is in the studio recording what will become *Diamond Dogs* while we just sit about. My mum drips poison in my ear about who's paying for what and asking why we live with so many people, and all of a sudden, I'm over it. The people in the flat don't feel like a team. There's no scintillating conversation, or great ideas – we're just a bunch of people living together. I don't include Maggi in this – she's Mick's sister, after all – but I feel stuck and frustrated. Mick has another record to deliver, he must find songs and musicians, and he needs to surround himself with people who inspire him, not people to have a cup of tea with.

Mick's a fabulous musician, a talented arranger, and a great producer – these are the talents he should be pursuing. Unfortunately, I only realise this later: isn't that what a manager is meant to do?

32

PLAY DON'T WORRY

Mick starts to put the tracks together for the second record. He's never been a great lyricist and this time I decide to give it a go. As a teenager, I fancied myself as a singer-songwriter à la Julie Driscoll; I loved her song 'Wheels on Fire'. I'd taken some guitar lessons too, from my friend Chris, but my heart was more set on writing lyrics. I wrote pages and pages of songs about love and life and thought they were just as good as anything I heard on the radio. Then I met David. His songs were so good, so different, and he could say things I could only dream about saying, and soon enough my confidence disappeared. It's only now, seeing Mick struggling to find words, that I feel confident enough to offer some help. 'Billy Porter' is my first attempt, and then 'Empty Bed'.

Strawberry Studios in the South of France, a few miles from Grasse, is booked for Mick and the band to record the album. When we arrive, our bedroom is cool and dark. I throw open the shutters and windows and the overwhelming smell of oranges rolls into the room. In the morning, I look out to see nets full of orange blossoms being harvested in the garden. We have coffee and croissants on an open stone terrace overlooking the pool. The sun is warm and I'm once again full of hope.

Mick and the band go to the studio to start laying down tracks while I explore the local market. It's an open-air affair, with stalls of vegetables, and cold marble halls full of meat and fish. Other dusty, dark establishments have delicacies and very inexpensive wine, of which I buy crates. Flowers are everywhere and brightly coloured bougainvillea climbs the pale-pink walls and cascades over into the street.

The husband-and-wife team who own the studio invite us for dinner at their home. Their villa overlooks a terraced garden and a verdant valley. We eat a delicious meal of roast lamb punctured with garlic and garnished with rosemary. I'm used to English lamb with mint sauce; this has a completely different flavour. I ask about the orange blossoms, and learn the locals rent their land to factories in Grasse, who use the blossoms for perfume. I know my mum would love it here and ask Mick if she can come down. To my surprise he says I can invite her, so I do and she comes on the train.

The music isn't going well, and Mick seems overwhelmed and kind of stuck. He's often in the swimming pool for a good portion of the day, deepening his tan and sleeping off the night before. When I ask about the album, I get a noncommittal answer. We both drink too much and take mandies, the drug of choice in London. It's a deadly combination that has Mick comatose and me crying for my father. When Mick's found asleep under the piano during a session, I know we're in trouble. It continues, one beautiful day after the other. I never see my mum; she's running around the South of France with a woman called Tilly, having the time of her life. She asks me to go with her but I can't leave Mick. I'm really worried.

Finally, Mick and the band get some serious work done. It seems to coincide with when we run out of mandies. They're in the studio day and night and the tracks are sounding great. I'm so relieved, and after a particularly good day we take the band out for dinner in Grasse. We drive back to the villa in high spirits, but as we pull in, Ritchie, our drummer, calls out, 'There's a man climbing out your bedroom window!'

I see a silhouette jump down from the balcony; he's in our headlights for a second before ducking and weaving through the orange-blossom bushes. The boys pile out of the car to give chase while I run into the house to see what's gone. He'd taken all the cash I had for our time here; it was no small amount, and a cold stillness settles in my stomach. I'm sure Tony is going to be furious. We call the police but there is little sympathy and no help. Why didn't we have a safe? Why did we leave money in the house? Both valid questions, and I curse myself for being so stupid.

I make the call to Tony and the silence from New York tells me everything. Later that week, Jamie Andrews, as Defries's representative, arrives. As expected, the robbery hasn't gone down well, but what overshadows everything is the enormous expense and drama that is *Diamond Dogs*; David's incessant demands are driving Defries and MainMan up the wall. We play Jamie Mick's tracks, and he listens without much comment before leaving for New York. Defries calls a day or so later and tells us that we're leaving and not to tell anyone. He'll deal with the studio later.

Mum doesn't want to leave; she's fallen in love with the South of France and never wants to go home. I can see the allure of living here and am sympathetic about going back to rainy Bromley, but I can't deal with her disappointment in the way life turned out. I take her to the station and put her on the next train to London.

The band leave first, and then it's us. The way we sneak out is horrible. The people who rented us the studio are so nice and we both feel dreadful skipping out on the bill. Mick wants to make a fuss, but his hands are tied – what can he say or do? I help slide our cases into a limo that arrives – without lights – at 11 p.m., and we disappear into the perfumed air. Mick swears he'll pay them back when he makes it, and it's at this moment I realise that Mick hasn't got any money, that he doesn't have any say, it's all Defries. No one can talk to Defries about money, it's impossible. He thinks it's his money and we have no right to ask. He tells us that Mick should just focus on making music and leave the money for him to take care of. Alarm bells go off and all the red lights are flashing, but we are in too deep.

Mick and I aren't sophisticated people, and I'm as foolish as he is. I wish Mick could talk to David, but David is embroiled in his own bitter battle with Tony, and his own career.

In London, Mick seems happier and books time at Trident Studios and Scorpio Sound to finish the overdubs. There are a lot of people around, including Ian Hunter, who helps Mick with vocals on 'Girl Can't Help It'. It's while we're at Scorpio Sound that Mick gets a call out of the blue from Jack Bruce saying he and Ginger Baker of Cream want to play with him. Shocked, he can only say yes. They swear him to secrecy and arrange to come to the studio. Ginger arrives looking as if he's been in a fight or a traffic accident, his face all busted up, and Jack follows shortly afterwards. The three of them go into the studio and fool around but there's no magic, and when they leave a few hours later we never hear from them again. I wonder what happened to those tapes.

The end result of Mick's time in the studio recording is *Play Don't Worry*, and it's wonderful. The guitars are brilliant on 'Angel

Number Nine', 'Seven Days' is a masterpiece and I love the lush arrangement on 'This Is for You'. Despite our troubles, Mick now has a great record to deliver to RCA.

The new album cover is shot by Clive Arrowsmith and it's an inspiring session. Mick looks wonderful and, though he's clearly still shy, with encouragement he loses his inhibitions and pulls off some incredible moves. After all's said and done, Mick and I lurch in the dark, unsure of what to do next.

Glen Matlock comes into our lives. He's a big fan of Mick's and remembers him browsing for shoes in a shop called SEX on the King's Road; Glen used to work there and is now in a runaway hit band called The Sex Pistols. He invites us to a club in London; we are thrilled to be asked out. After stumbling down some dark steps, we find ourselves in a dank basement somewhere on Wardour Street. We're surrounded by young people staring daggers at us, and for the first time in my life, I feel out of step. It's as if my time has come and gone and I didn't even see it pass. Mick and I are in our mid-twenties, but I for one feel as old as my mum! I glance at Mick and he seems okay, but he looks so clean and fresh with his bright blond hair and lightly mascaraed eyelashes. We're in a crowd of people with tattoos and face piercings: punks. With black eyes and crazy hair, they stare Mick's smile down.

Glen fights his way to the bar to get drinks and we're left alone. There's a band onstage, and when they start playing . . . well, it's hard to describe. To me, it's a bunch of blokes thrashing around making a hell of a row, and again, I feel like my mother. The audience gather and jump up and down, spitting at the band. I've heard about this phenomenon, I've read about it in the papers, but to see it in front of my face is shocking. What does it mean? Why are they spitting at a band they like?

People look at us with hard, blank stares. Their shaved mohawks tremble with the heavy music as they pogo dance and smash into each other. Mick tries to talk to Glen but it's impossible. Someone shoves him as he's dancing, and again Mick's good-natured smile only gets him a glower in return. I want to leave, but I'm not sure if Mick feels the same so I grab his hand. He doesn't take much persuading. We catch a cab and drive home in silence.

'Guess I've got the wrong image,' Mick says, and we both laugh, but it's a sobering thought. He's right – things have done a 180-degree turn and glam feels as if it's over. I think of David's 'Rebel Rebel'. He knew what was happening. Mick and I feel more lost than ever.

33
MOTT THE HOOPLE

Ian Hunter and his wife, Trudi, visit us at our flat. They admire it and ask how much we pay for it. I'm not sure, and Mick isn't either. I roll my eyes. They must think we're mad. They're down-to-earth people with down-to-earth values and we get along with them. I find Ian a little scary. I feel uncomfortable talking to someone who wears sunglasses when there's no sun. Trudi looks a bit like Natalie Wood with her huge brown eyes. She doesn't drink or smoke and talks with a soft American accent. They're both deadly serious, though I privately think she's a bit of a goody-goody and wonder what she's doing with a rocker like Ian.

Mick puts on some music and we talk about Bowie, Mott, 'All the Young Dudes' and what's coming up next. Ian says Ariel Bender's leaving the band and that they're looking for a new guitar player to perform on their European tour.

'Do you want to join Mott the Hoople?'

The question hangs in the air. We look at each other, and I'm not sure what to think. Ian, seeing our hesitation, laughs and with a grand gesture says, 'Well, what are you doing sitting here with all this?' It's a good question. We look at each other again, and I'm sure we're thinking the same thing: this might not be a bad idea. We talk for hours, Ian being his persuasive self, and as we are weighing it up, he says, 'You can play your own songs. The band will learn the songs.'

Mott are a good band, Ian a good lead singer. It might be the answer to our problems. It feels like a win-win situation, so we take the idea to Defries, but with him a simple solution is never simple. Defries being Defries, he wants complete control, a different deal to the one being offered. He's unsure of Mott.

'I've dealt with them before, they're a democratic band,' he tells me with a strange smile. I'm not quite sure what he means. He suggests Mick should not get involved in the financials with Mott and instead play the tour for expenses. The record company will cover hotels, food and transportation and won't have to pay him. This sounds good to us. On paper, it sounds good.

Mick does a single with them, 'Saturday Gigs'. It's a great song and sounds like a hit but doesn't end up being one. The tour rehearsals go well but as we get ready to leave, there's a problem: I'm going on the road and Mott don't allow girls on the road.

'Suzi's going, she works for me. And she's looking after Mick, a MainMan interest,' Defries says.

Well, that puts the cat among the pigeons, because not only do I work for MainMan, I also live with Mick. Trudi and the other Mott girls kick up a fuss. They want to go too, but there's 'concerns' that the band won't have the freedom to be the rock stars they like to be. The girls stand alone. I'm covered under the MainMan deal, but I see both sides of the coin. It's the same as always: wives and girlfriends get the rough end of the deal.

Suddenly and out of the blue comes a press release, a headline in the *New Musical Express* that holds a promise of something really different for Mick: 'IS IT RONNIE OR RONSON?' Mick Taylor is leaving the Stones. We both gasp with excitement. What an offer this could be! Defries calls us to ask if the Stones have been in contact.

'No,' says Mick, and, of course, it's Ronnie Wood who joins them.

◆

We all agree Mott needs an update, but how do we do it? David can change his look in an instant, he always makes it seem so easy, but we find it impossible to think of something new and so do Mott.

My hairdresser friend Billy cuts Ian's long red curls off at our flat. When it's done, it's shocking and I'm not sure I love it, but positive energy is needed here and you can't stick it back on. Trudi stays silent. The rest of the band get their hair cut too, but in the end they just look like Mott with shorter hair. We try an all-in-one suit on Pete, the bass player, but without his long boots and hairy chest on display he seems to lose confidence. Morgan, the keyboard player, is the one who comes out best; Buffin, the drummer, doesn't change much, but he's behind the drums, not in full view.

Truth be told, the changes that have been made take a lot away from the boys. They look uncomfortable. We take photos in our flat's hallway for the new album cover. Mick, who's had a perm, laughs and says that he feels a lot like his mum. I didn't want to say it, but I have to agree . . .

The tour begins in Sweden. Trudi *is* coming, and the other wives and girlfriends will visit too. It's a decision they've come to themselves. I'm grateful when we arrive to an enthusiastic welcome from fans at the airport. This hasn't happened to Mott before and it gives them a much-needed jolt of confidence. David didn't tour in Europe, so I'm gratified to be somewhere other than the US or England.

When we arrive in Stockholm, I'm eager to get out and explore the city. Sweden is a country of islands and soon enough I'm by the water, breathing in fresh air and marvelling at the northern light. Everywhere is so clean, there's no rubbish in the streets, everything feels in perfect order. There are a lot of parks and green areas, with water views all around me. The shops and houses are colourful, not Mediterranean bright but painted with soft yellow and burnt oranges, with contrasting teal shutters in the windows. London buildings suddenly seem grey in comparison. I buy a couple of shirts for Mick and myself before going back to the hotel.

The evening sound check goes smoothly. Mick seems to have fitted right in; he's always funny and he doesn't disappoint tonight. The show is phenomenal, Stockholm really loves Mott, but the warm fuzzy feeling of the night before disappears the next morning. Mick and I are eating breakfast in the hotel restaurant, as per our agreement, when we see Pete and Buffin. They walk past us and, without a word, exit the hotel. The way they walk spells trouble. Mick laughs at them, but the day continues with a distinctly chilly atmosphere. According to Ian, the band don't like the deal they've agreed to. RCA sends limos for Mick and pay for both the hotels and our expenses. It's true, some of the hotels cost a lot, but this is our deal. Mott want Mick to be the same as them, 'in the band', but he isn't, and he doesn't want to be. He's just come off the most successful thing in England since The Beatles. He is valued by the record company and may well be one of the reasons Mott are doing so well in Europe. They're being childish, and it's a shame, but that's the way it is.

Blonde! Eighteen years old and looking for adventure – 1967.

What a shock to the world this was . . .
– Oxford Town Hall, 1972.

Listening to advice from Angie, with Iggy Pop, Trevor Bolder and Lou Reed
– Plaza Hotel, New York, 1972.

Looking on as David speaks to Robin Mayhew (sound technician)
– Plaza Hotel, New York, 1972.

Standing in the wings watching David and the Spiders perform – 1972.

Face to face as I snap David into his silk Kansai costume – 1973.

Trevor's collar gets an adjustment as David touches up his make-up
– London, 1973.

David quaffing some wine before he heads onstage – 1973.

Mick Rock and me bubbling with excitement in the dressing room,
along with Stuey George (David's bodyguard) and
Pete Hunsley (guitar technician) – 1973.

Mick and me at the press conference announcing him joining
Mott the Hoople – 1974.

Our wedding day – Bearsville, New York, 23 March 1977.

Lisa and her dad as he fluffs her tutu – *c.*1979.

I see how Defries operates: he's engineered an impossible situation. He knows Mott aren't going to just play and be glad they have one of the top musicians in the world to work with. He understands Mott, and seems to delight in antagonising them.

Ian is as puzzled as we are. He wants to be loyal to the band, he can see what Mick brings to the band, he doesn't know what to do. I've never seen Mick get cross with anyone, but he becomes so frustrated with the attitude of Mott that he starts to order room service wherever we go, telling the band on the bus how good it is. He stands outside his hotel room with a drink, saying hello as they pass by. It winds them up no end. Buffin throws a wobbly nearly every night over some perceived wrongdoing, and Pete isn't handling it any better . . . it's a nightmare.

Mick and I have never toured like this before. It was always hard work, of that there is no doubt, but it was also fun. We carry on regardless, and the saving grace is the shows. I would understand Mott's attitude if the shows were rough, but they sell out night after night and the audience constantly scream for more. With David and the Spiders, everyone would hang out together at the hotel bar after a show, there'd be adoring fans to talk to, and everyone would generally be in a good mood. Any comments or criticism about the show would be saved for the next day. It's not like that with Mott.

Fred Heller, Ian's manager, lobs questions to me about Defries at the gigs, but his curiosity is quickly replaced with incredulity and despair. I'm in a tough spot as I happen to agree with some things that Defries is saying and that doesn't make me popular with anyone, including Mick. I'm rapidly becoming disenchanted with Mott, Europe, both the managers and the whole shebang.

From here we go to Denmark and then on to Germany, where we meet the Baroness Francesca von Thyssen, a very attractive girl with a posh English accent. All the band fancy their chances with her but she's only got eyes for Mick. I'm not sure where she came from or why she's here, but she acts as if hanging out with rock musicians is definitely her thing. After the show I find her backstage talking to Mick, telling him how wonderful he is. I don't worry, given that Mick is idolised by a lot of women. I watch as they walk out together and get on the bus. They take seats towards the back of the bus, laughing softly. It isn't far to the hotel, so I take a seat in the front.

'Suzi,' Mick calls out, 'where's me 'airbrush?'

I don't say anything, but he goes on, 'Suzi, did you forget me 'airbrush?'

Silence, then he continues, 'Did you leave it be'ind? It must be in t'dressing room. I like that 'airbrush.' He moans, there's more noise as he searches his bag, then: 'It's not 'ere, you better go back and get it.'

Mick has never talked to me like this before and I'm about to tell him to go and look for his own bloody hairbrush when I glance around the bus. The band are staring at me, waiting to see what I'll do. I'm here as Mick's assistant, that's what they've been told, so I bite my tongue and get off the bus. I find the hairbrush where he left it and resist the temptation to throw it at him as I get back on. There are pitying looks from everyone – except the Baroness von Thyssen, who takes it all in her stride. I feel frustrated, and humiliated. Very quickly, the novelty of being the girlfriend-slash-assistant wears off. It's not the role I want to play – I want to be someone who is wanted and needed, not a bit of fluff who has to run and get a hairbrush. I'd rather be with the crew, working and having fun once the prima donna pop stars have left the building. I sit and fume for the short journey to the hotel and leave everyone at the bar when we get there.

We breeze across borders in Europe with no effort until we get to Switzerland. As we collect our bags before customs, I'm pulled out of line by a policeman with a dog . . . ! I'm the only one being pulled out of line, the only one being taken away. I'm wearing an Afghan coat, patched jeans, my hair is long and wild. I'm a rock chick with a rock band and an attitude: what do I expect? I'm a prime target.

I catch Mick's eye as they walk me away. This single glance speaks volumes; we both know my future is in jeopardy. They take me to a small room and when I see an officer pulling on plastic gloves, I know they're going to search me. I have a tiny piece of hash tucked inside my Gossard push-up bra, courtesy of Manu, one of the roadies. The bloody dog is salivating at my side, and my instinct is to cover the guilty breast! I feel as if I'm going to have a heart attack. I'm panicking, thinking about what my life will be like if I'm found out: no work, no touring, and maybe even no Mick. I strip to my underwear and indicate that I don't want to strip any further. I tell them I'm shy, that I don't want to take off my bra or knickers. The officer calmly feels my breasts through the bra and finds . . . nothing. Thank God for padded bras.

The rest of the tour is uneventful, but it's a sad affair. In the end Mick can't take it, and Ian can't take it either. He and Trudi go to America and Ian ends up in hospital suffering from stress. That's it:

Ian's out and a week after that so are we. It's ironic that Ian leaves Mott before Mick does. The rest of the band are understandably angry. We give them a wide berth, as they do us, and quickly follow Ian and Trudi to the States.

34
MICK AND IAN

We hole up in Bobby Colomby's house in Nyack, NY; he's the drummer with Blood, Sweat & Tears, and a friend of Ian's. It's lovely here. I first fell in love with the wide-open spaces that are America while I was on tour with David. Now I'm in a big woodsy house with an open fire burning and a studio attached.

A bass player, Jaco Pastorius, is staying at the house too. He tells us that he met Bobby in Florida, and when Bobby heard him play, he offered to bring him to New York. It's easy to see why. I've never heard a bass played the way Jaco plays his; he plays it as if it's a guitar, and the melodies he creates are one of a kind, so unusual and moving. His bass is with us all the time, from breakfast and lunch through to dinner, and nearly every moment in between.

He's a good-looking bloke, tall and slim with wide-set eyes, an expressive mouth and long hair worn with a red bandana. He looks about my age and has a soft southern accent. He seems shy, but I can't really tell as he doesn't say much. He's here, like us, trying to make it. We sit and talk, and he tells me about his wife back home in Florida. He asks how Mick and I do it.

'Do what?'

'When he goes on the road? How do you survive all that time apart?'

'Well, I've always gone on the road. I work in one role or another.'

He looks at me in surprise but doesn't say more. There's an air of innocence about him, and it reminds me of Mick, but it's not just the innocence. He plays bass with the same intensity that Mick plays guitar, he's completely immersed in it. It's as if they only live for the moment.

Ian and Mick talk about making a record, a solo record for Ian. Ian wants them to form a band, a joint venture, but Mick doesn't want to be in a band. I don't know why. It could be something to do with Tony Defries and RCA, or maybe it was the memories of that tour with Mott. But even if he doesn't want to be in a band, he is adamant about Ian making a record with him. Ian thinks he's mad, but listens. Ian's a man who operates on instinct, and he trusts Mick, so they go ahead.

When emotions run high, the music is energised, Mick knows that. As they start to put songs together, the electricity between them sparks, the dynamics of their playing and the quality of Ian's songs shining through. Ian is a prolific writer, and after about ten days we fly back to London to put together a band for the album.

Ian and Mick put their heads together and with Mick's little drum machine Ian writes 'Once Bitten Twice Shy' in our flat. Ian's on fire and the energy is buzzing. They start to record at a studio in West London and when Mick brings home tapes of the songs they're working on, I'm impressed. After they are knocked into shape, they bring them to AIR London Studios, high above Oxford Circus. It's right after Christmas and we all pile into the studio to witness the making of an undeniably amazing record.

They call in a fantastic drummer, Simon Phillips, who plays with Dana Gillespie, but he's too young to come on tour in America. Ian wants a band to tour with as well as record so instead he recruits

Dennis Elliott, who, after playing with Ian, goes on to great fame and fortune playing with Foreigner.

While they're in the studio, Marc Bolan comes to visit. I barely recognise him until he's introduced: he's far from the curly-headed angel he used to be, looking a little overweight and dejected. He comes by more than once and after listening to 'Once Bitten Twice Shy', he tells Ian he's underestimated him. I'm glad for Ian – Marc's a huge star and his admiration must give Ian a lot of confidence. Ian looks to Mick for most of the production and all the arrangements. They're both at the top of their game and the end result is aptly named *Ian Hunter*.

Ian's album is released in the spring, entering the charts to our collective delight.

◆

Ian and Trudi have bought a place in Chappaqua, NY. We all think the US is the place to be so, with Defries's support and Ian and Trudi's invitation, we leave our glamorous flat and move. I'm not sorry to leave London – it's time for our flatmates to live their own lives and pay their own bills. I know Mum's upset, but we have to try something new. In Chappaqua, Ian and Mick rehearse day and night with the band. Fred has organised a short tour for them while Defries is on the sidelines, somewhere he doesn't like to be. Ian and Mick are well received.

After these few dates we go back to Chappaqua, hoping this might work out. We know it won't be easy with two managers and two record companies, but I think the record is wonderful and the band are great. Mick seems happy working with Ian. We're invited to visit Defries in his mansion in Greenwich and we're anxious to share our plans for the future. Defries listens quietly for a minute or two then tells us in no uncertain terms that he doesn't like Fred or his ideas, that he's not dealing with him or Ian's record company and thinks we should move out and move on. He offers us an apartment on East 58th Street and a fresh start. He sits back, having thrown the bomb.

Mick and I look at each other. New York City. We can't help but find it appealing . . . Both of us are sick of fighting for this band. Tony is offering us a way out of a situation that is frankly exhausting. When we get back, Ian and Trudi can see it in our eyes. We talk it out but the writing is on the wall. Without Defries's support, Mick can't go on. A couple of days later, we pack our Cadillac Sedan de Ville and float like a boat down the Saw Mill River Parkway to New York City. We're all sorry it didn't work out, but it wasn't as if we didn't try.

As soon as we are on the road, I feel a huge weight lift off my chest, and when I glance at Mick I can see he feels it too. We look at each other and I can't help but smile. The horizon is clear, and I feel a freedom that I haven't felt in a long time. By the time we get to our new apartment on East 58th Street, it's getting dark. We unload our cases and leave them inside the double doors of our new building. Everything's in plain sight, but we think it'll be okay for a couple of minutes while we park the car.

Somehow, we miss the garage on Second Avenue and end up on the 59th Street Bridge on our way to Queens. Mick's a bit of a nervous driver at the best of times and shoots me a glance before getting off at the first exit over the bridge. We eventually find our way back to the city, driving over the wooden boards that are Second Avenue and 135th Street. At every red light people surround the car, desperate faces at the windows pleading for money. One man drags a greasy rag across the windscreen. I'd like to give them something but I'm too terrified to open the window; I can't believe how many homeless people there are. Mick swerves around fires that burn in large metal cans in the middle of the street. New York City is not what I expected.

It takes forever for us to get back to 58th Street but when we finally do, by some miracle all our stuff is still there. I hop out; Mick finds the garage and comes back with a bottle of wine under his arm.

The apartment is one flight up and has two floors. According to Jamie, there's a couple of working girls who live opposite. We open the front door to a green metal spiral staircase that leads upstairs. The living room beyond is spacious, with an open-plan kitchen at the back of it. A loft looks over the living room; it's typical Defries, everything operating below him while he lords it from above.

What really catches my eye is an enormous stain on the beige shag carpet at the bottom of the spiral staircase. I call Leee the next morning and he tells me it's the stain of a suicide, whereas Jamie says it's wine. I'm not sure who to believe but don't worry too much; we're not destined to stay long, just a month or so until the end of MainMan's lease.

35
BOB DYLAN

A few weeks go by before Ian calls saying he's heard that Bob Dylan's in New York and he's coming to see what's going on. Mick and I laugh: Ian's a *big* Dylan fan. Mick isn't enamoured by him, nor me really – we're glam rockers – but it's Bob Dylan so we thought we'd go and have a look.

We meet Ian downtown at The Bitter End on Bleecker Street; Ian knows Paul Colby, the owner, and we all say hello. We order a couple of drinks at the bar and decide to get a table, and while we're chatting Ian suddenly goes silent as he looks over my shoulder. I turn and see Dylan with some people walking down the street, guitar case in hand. They turn into the bar and sit a couple of tables away from us. It's hard not to stare but they're blissfully unaware, all laughing and carrying on.

Out of nowhere, Dylan whips out his guitar and starts to play and sing, and what a revelation. He's mesmerising, dipping and swaying on his chair as he sings 'Hurricane', 'One More Cup of Coffee' and a sweet, sad song for someone called 'Sara'. His feet tap gently as he leans into the songs. The emotions pouring out of him are unbelievably raw; Mick and I are silent as we listen. His music is so simple, so unique, with no fanfare or glitter; it's just a man with his guitar, and a voice that gives me the shivers. He hasn't got a great voice, but he doesn't sing like anyone else I know. Mick has jokingly said in the past that he sings like Yogi Bear, but as I look at

Mick now, he's motionless. Dylan's charisma is overwhelming. It's nothing you can put your finger on. I mean, Bowie has it in spades, but even David would be equalled or surpassed in this presence. Ian sits quietly, smoking, as he listens to Dylan and smiles at us.

We're all caught up in the musical storm, and before we know it, word's out on the street. Within seconds people start to pour in, a crush builds up in the bar and there's pointing and whispering as faces appear and disappear around the corners of where we're sitting. Paul isn't sure what to do, but he needn't have worried; these guys are used to this kind of attention. As they get up to move to a less conspicuous table, I get up and motion to Ian and Mick, who follow me into the dark recesses of the club where the smell of beer and cigarettes lingers on everything. I get a table between Dylan and the stage, and as we sit down I motion to the bartender for drinks. I act as if we belong here, and with Ian and Mick we surely do. If Dylan doesn't know who Mick and Ian are, it seems as if a lot of other people do, and drinks are shared with us freely.

A band wheel their equipment in: a rack of monitors, guitar cases, amps and drums. As they start to set up on the small stage in front of us, I can see a look of surprise on their faces as they begin to whisper among themselves. The place is packed, and I don't think they expected it, but when they look in the direction of Bob Dylan, their shoulders collectively sag. These people aren't here to hear them play, they're here because of Bob. Privately, though, I think they're also in the presence of the great Ian Hunter and Mick Ronson.

I keep my eye on Dylan's table and when one of them – a tall, dark, good-looking man – goes to talk to Paul, I quickly go to the loo so I can pass by and eavesdrop.

'I've got a band this week, Bobby,' Paul says to the man, shaking his head. 'I can't pay two bands.'

'We'll play for drinks,' says Bobby immediately. Paul screws up his eyes as he considers this. I miss the rest but Bobby smiles at me and as I pass by, I smile back. After a quick look at myself in the mirror, I'm back, and I talk to him as he stands by Paul. He's a flirt, so am I, and as we chat away he says he's going to play later and asks if I'll be staying. I lay on the English accent thick.

'Yes, I'm here with Ian Hunter and Mick Ronson.'

'Who?' he asks, and it's not until I mention 'All the Young Dudes' and David Bowie that it seems to register.

The band play a somewhat anaemic set – there's no spring in their step, the audience talk the entire time they're playing – and now, to cheers, Bobby and his friends set up to play; then he asks for a bottle of tequila to be sent to the stage. He passes it around the band then, when it comes back, he passes it out to the audience.

'Bobby?!' Paul calls out. His shoulders rise and his hands open in disbelief, his eyes wide, but Bobby just laughs and asks for another bottle. I glance at Paul, who shakes his head then finally motions to the bartender to send up another bottle. There's certainly a buzz now. An assortment of musicians set up on the small stage and start to play. It's country music, heavy on the heartbreak and lonesome songs. Bobby sings and someone else steps up to another mic to sing harmony. I don't know a lot about country music so it's all new to me. Singers and musicians come and go, each playing a couple of songs, and the whole thing is held together by Bobby. It's a glorious mess, one song after another in seamless disarray. The room buzzes and after a while Bobby asks for yet another bottle of tequila to come to the stage.

While it's being delivered, he calls out, 'Is there a spider in the house?'

'A spider?' someone calls back. 'We need more tequila!' We all laugh, and the tequila goes around.

'Yes,' shouts Bobby, 'a Spider from Mars!' This elicits more laughter. Bobby walks over and looks down at Mick. 'Hey, spider, you gettin' up here?' I'm pushing Mick as he protests that he hasn't got his guitar, but one gets put in his hands and with a little encouragement from Ian and me, he gets up.

He fiddles around at first but soon begins to play soft notes over the songs. If it was good before, what Mick brings to it is magic. It's as if Mozart dropped in. The simple country melodies give him a lot of space to play some beautiful lines over the top. What a sound. The audience are quiet at first, but soon enough they begin clapping loudly at the end of each number, calling out for Mick. I steal a glance at Dylan, but he's hidden in deep shadows at his table, impossible to read.

The phone at The Bitter End rings off the hook. Paul's smile is as wide as a mile as he surveys the crowded club. What good fortune this is for him; the club's full, he has to be pleased that this is where Bob Dylan chose to stop by. The night wears on, the tequila does not stop flowing and no one leaves. Mick has always liked a drink or two, which puts him in good company here. He sometimes gets a little rowdy, as he does tonight. He's been playing onstage and drinking along with everyone else, and now during a break he's at the bar weaving and getting loud.

I'm trying to keep the peace, but eventually Mick gets thrown out. He talks his way back in, but Mick is never easy to handle when he's like this. He starts up again and after a few minutes gets thrown out again. Ian and I follow him outside, thinking it's time to go home, but Mick isn't giving up. We stand and watch him threaten Paul and his bouncer, with a promise:

'One more time . . . I'll cum back thru that fuckin' window.'

His nostrils flare as he sways. I flash a look at Ian as Mick staggers. Mick's a little bloke, especially compared to the bouncer, who doesn't look amused.

'Oh my God,' I whisper to Ian, 'what are we going to do?'

'He'll be all right, it usually works out,' he says with a shrug of his shoulders and drag on his fag.

We both watch Mick as Bobby and Dylan walk out of the club, followed by most of the band and some of the audience. Bobby looks at Mick and grins:

'What you doin'?'

'They keep throwing me out,' Mick complains, with a steely look at the bouncer and Paul, who just shrug their shoulders. Bobby looks at Dylan and they both laugh at this skinny, irate English rocker who's shouting in the street.

Bobby puts his arm around Mick and says, 'Come with us,' and together they walk him down the street, away from the club.

I follow them down Bleecker Street. There's quite a few of us, but Dylan, a master at disappearing suddenly, does just that: one minute we're on the street, the next we're not. A quick turn, down some steep dark steps, and we disappear into a small, smelly underground bar. One of Dylan's security blokes mans the door. It must be around 2 a.m., and the bartender holds up his hands in disbelief, annoyed at the sudden crowd. He calls out that he's closed before spotting Bob Dylan, then he changes his tune, rushing around to get drinks.

Dylan and Bobby waste no time securing themselves a place at the bar. Everyone is in close proximity. I nab myself a seat and talk to a girl sitting next to me and watch them as they nod in the general direction of Mick, who's chatting with Rob Stoner, the bass player of the night. They leave the bar area, walk over and join the conversation. The conversation flows but I can't read lips and I'm just praying Mick's okay. I see them laugh at something he says, and I relax. Mick looks at Dylan and Bobby, perplexed, then surprised. He chuckles as he answers them and Bobby claps him on the back as they walk away to catch up with the drummer. Mick glances over at me; I subtly beckon him over. Whatever was said has sobered him up a bit, and he whispers in my ear with breath that smells like a brewery:

'Eh,' he says, 'they just asked me to go on the road with 'em.' He laughs in disbelief.

◆

Bobby Neuwirth calls the next night and so it starts. Unbeknown to us, the Rolling Thunder Revue is auditioning for a tour Bob Dylan wants to do across America. Mick goes, and he tells me it looks as though he's in.

Bobby runs the show. He gets his own way with Paul and we end up at The Bitter End the next evening. Mick brings in his guitar and amp and sets up with everyone else. More people are here the second night, it's completely jammed. I think Bob Dylan's here but I'm not sure and I'm not going to ask; the man's a magician, here one minute and gone the next. A pretty girl with long curly hair is talking to Bobby as I go over to say hello to him. She smiles but doesn't stop talking, determined to make her point.

'You need him,' she insists. 'He plays wonderful fiddle as well as guitar and pedal steel.' She's young and earnest, talking up her man, whoever he is. Bobby's taken in.

'Tell him to come down then,' he says to her with a smile, 'we need a fiddle player.'

She walks away, calling out, 'You won't be disappointed.'

Someone whispers that Allen Ginsberg is here. I don't know who Allen Ginsberg is, but I sense he's someone. He's holding court at a table in the middle of it all. Bobby goes to the bar and sits by a small scruffy bloke with dark hair and paint on his clothes. It seems as if they know each other well. The band starts to play and when Roger McGuinn from The Byrds steps up, the crowd applaud before he even sings a note. He has a unique voice, very unlike anyone else's here tonight, and he plays a little harder than the others too.

After the show is over, Bobby tells me to bring Mick to this address, somewhere downtown. It's late already but for these people the night has just begun. The loft we go to is huge, the floor covered in green-as-grass flat-weave carpet. The walls are white and serve as the background to huge pieces of art, the smell of paint and turpentine overpowering. The guy with the paint on his clothes is introduced as Larry Poons; it's his place. There's not much furniture and what is there is arranged tightly together, an island in a sea of green carpet. The rest of the place is empty except for the art and a basketball net; the space is so big that a girl shoots hoops at the other end of the main room.

Tequila is passed around, along with joints that are being rolled on a stainless-steel counter. T Bone Burnett – a tall, slim Texan who is part of the scene at The Bitter End – plays a song, Roger McGuinn plays another, and then Bobby Neuwirth plays 'Annabel

Lee', a sweet, sad southern song that I don't know. Mick's right there, playing with everyone.

I get up to have a closer look at the paintings. Larry's work is extraordinary. The huge pieces take my breath away. I'm not sophisticated, I don't understand art at all, but as I look at them it's overwhelming, piece after piece of abstract beauty.

People come and go, and soon enough Mick passes out on the couch, so I cuddle up to him and we both fall asleep. Bobby and Larry leave us there until the morning. I wake up to see lumps of people all over the floor. It's what I think might be called a 'happening'.

For the next two weeks, we sleep most of the day and go to The Bitter End every night. Afterwards, we go on to Larry's place, where they play for the rest of the night. This is a new existence for me; I've never changed my hours like this. I feel like a shift worker.

There's a core set of players who stay onstage, Mick being one of them. He wears a Manny's Schlepper T-shirt and some old jeans. Mick, always a spare player, doesn't know a lot of the songs and has only heard of some of the artists, but when he stretches out with a solo or a random guitar line, it's so beautiful; everyone looks at him and I can't help but feel proud. The girl with the long curly hair brings her boyfriend down: he's an angelic, Botticelli-like boy, no more than seventeen, his face framed by huge curls. Jenny, as I find out, is right: the boy plays beautifully and can play anything. His name is David Mansfield.

All sorts of people roll into the club but it's a real surprise when Bette Midler jumps up onstage one night. She quips that she was dragged out of bed to come, and I have to say that it does look a little like that. She sings a song and goes straight to the bar after raucous applause; I never see her again.

Another night Patti Smith is here, looking cool and vulnerable, and a lot like Keith Richards. I instantly want to look like her: she's rail-thin and pale with a black scarecrow hairdo, wearing black drainpipe jeans and a man's jacket. If it felt like English glam rock was old when we were with the punks, it definitely feels like it's properly over now. She performs a poem and then a Stones number, and the way she does it is so violent and intense. The audience and I love it.

People are flying in from all over the country, and out of this mayhem comes a band. It seems so right, so perfect: an artist, Bob Dylan; a cause, Hurricane Carter; and a great name, the Rolling Thunder Revue. I don't know who Hurricane Carter is, but I learn he's a boxer from New Jersey who, it's said, has been wrongly convicted of murder. He's serving thirty years for the crime. Dylan is passionate about his innocence. Mick and I are a bit in the dark about the whole thing, but everyone involved seems convinced.

Tony calls, asking what Mick's doing, and we're happy to say Mick might be joining Bob Dylan and going on tour. Tony doesn't show it, but I know he has to be pleased. This could mean a lot for him as well as Mick.

But just as things turned around for Mick so quickly, things shift again as Bobby Neuwirth tells us he's leaving for LA the very next day. He says he'll be in touch but doesn't say when, and we're left gasping like fish on the shore when the tide goes out. Tony asks us for details about the tour, but there's nothing we can tell him.

36

STUCK IN TORONTO

We're called to the office, where the usual mayhem of MainMan is in full swing.

'You two are going to Canada next week to keep the authorities in the US happy,' says Tony Defries. I understand what he means, it's an immigration thing. We've done it before; you have to leave the country and then come back so they don't accuse you of sticking around for too long without the proper documents. 'Let's do it now in case anything with Dylan comes up.'

We arrive in Toronto in the late morning and check into the hotel, which seems nice enough, though it pales in comparison to the places we've stayed before. After dropping off our cases in the room, we go downstairs to look for lunch. It's a lovely day and I suggest eating by the pool. We get a table and look around, and sitting on the other side of the room is a pale-faced man dressed in black with mirror sunglasses, smoking a cigarette: it's Lou Reed! Mick makes his way over, and though Lou doesn't recognise him at first, when he hears Mick's accent his face breaks into a smile. He tells us he's 'hiding out' from his manager, Fred Heller, here.

'Oh,' I say, 'Fred Heller, we know him.'

We sit down and order some lunch, then begin to disparage Fred. Lou looks over my shoulder and calls out to a girl in the pool, 'Rachel!'

Rachel turns towards us, and I see a beautiful girl with high cheekbones and long dark curly hair floating on the surface of the pool. As she emerges from the water, she's a contradiction of what I'm expecting: instead of a bikini top, she's naked except for a black speedo, her long black hair curling against her white skin. She laughs at Lou as she makes her way up the steps and quickly kisses him on the forehead before turning to us to say hello in a high falsetto voice.

In the evening, Lou invites us to a club where George McCrae is playing. The place is small and sweaty, people spilling out of the door. After a few songs, Lou starts to call out for George to play 'Rock Your Baby'. George looks over at him and smiles: it's his hit, so he gives us what we want. The opening notes start, and when he begins to sing the club goes wild. George has them in the palm of his hand. After he's sung it for some time, he takes it down really low. George sweats as he keeps singing the same line over and over until it's nearly a whisper, swaying to the music as he croons and sighs:

'Rock your baby, rock your baby.'

Lou shouts out over the crowd: 'Why don't you tell us what you really want to do, George?' I look at Mick, he's laughing; Lou's on a tear. 'C'mon, George, you don't want to rock her, do you? No, I think you mean something else, why don't you tell us what you really want to do?' By now, the crowd is egging both Lou and George on. George doesn't know what to do and Lou isn't stopping. 'What do you really want to do, George?'

It's a late-night rowdy crowd and he resists for a while, but in the end he cracks and sings:

'Fuck you baby.'

Lou's triumphant, and the crowd goes wild.

The next morning, I remind Mick of what he must say at the border: that he's on his way to the UK and is passing through New York; he has a plane ticket for London in his hand.

'I know, I know, Suzi, it'll be fine.' He flashes me his lovely smile.

We go and check in. I say a goodbye to Canada, walk to the US desk and get through without trouble. Mick is delayed: 'I don't know,' I hear him say, 'me manager tol' me that if I cum up here for a couple a days, I can cum back in to America.' He looks indignant. Mick's an innocent, pure person, he doesn't know how to lie, and I love him for it – except at times like this. I try to save the situation by saying we're just passing through but it's not working, and they promptly send us back to the Canadian side.

'Why are you back here?' one border guard asks me. 'Can't get into the US?' He looks at a co-worker and flashes a wry smile.

Mick is often harassed at airports, he sticks out like a sore thumb: blond-streaked hair, flashy clothes, a suggestion of make-up. Even without the guitar, the way he looks alone is enough, and today is no exception. We're taken to a room and told to wait. After about an hour, our luggage is unceremoniously dumped beside us. We are interviewed separately, and I'm told that if we cannot get into the States we will have to go home to London. We are allowed one phone call. I call Defries, who sighs and tells us to sit tight, that he'll get on to it. After a miserable five hours we're finally allowed to leave, though they tell us to go back to Canada.

We wearily go back to the hotel, only to find there are no rooms available. Mick calls Lou and he and Rachel offer to share their room with us.

'We have two beds,' says Rachel with a smile. Mick and I are grateful that we have somewhere to sleep. The next morning our flights are booked, our visas amended; Defries has worked his magic and we're able to return to New York, though he's not pleased with Mick and the time and money that the delay has cost him.

37

ALLEN GINSBERG

We get back to New York, go to our flat and wait to hear from Bob Dylan and his people. I've nearly given up hope by the time Mick gets an invitation from Allen Ginsberg to come to an afternoon party at his house. At last, some connection with Bob. We invite Shane – another Brit, who's been playing with Mick – to come with us.

Allen's a mysterious figure to me. He's a man people whisper about, a preacher, or a poet. I don't really know what he is, but when he speaks, people listen. Allen lives on Avenue A and East 12th Street, way downtown. The heat bounces off the pavement as we get into a cab and glide down Second Avenue. The apartment buildings change as we drive, becoming lower, closer together, not as pretty as their uptown neighbours. There are more people on the streets, men hanging around street corners and spilling out from local bars. They drink out of bottles wrapped in paper bags; some look a little worse for wear, and there are panhandlers* at every traffic light. There's a ton of liquor stores, and pawn shops that have signs outside: 'CASH FOR GOLD!' or 'SELL YOUR SILVER HERE'. Most of the shops are protected with steel gates and huge men whose muscles bulge under their shirts.

The driver pulls over at a light and grunts: 'This is as far as I'll go.'

---

* Panhandlers: beggars.

We don't ask why. We're British and polite, so we say nothing and obediently step out of the cab. Mick smiles as he pays.

'Which way should I go then?'

The driver looks puzzled before indicating a street with a nod of his head, and as we look across the road he leaves in a rush of hot air.

The street we walk down is full of people sitting outside on their stoops, staring at us; mothers clutch children on their hips, teenagers loiter and watch us, old people on rickety chairs murmur as we go by. Shane has long black curly hair, parted in the middle and flowing past his shoulders; he wears a chest-baring T-shirt, tight blue jeans and big boots. I'm in platform shoes and tight jeans, with wild hair, and Mick looks as he usually does, long blond hair and a touch of mascara. The situation reminds me of when Mick and I got lost in Harlem on our way to our new apartment, when we were fresh from the suburbs. The difference? This time we're not in a car, we're on foot. It's hot and humid; I feel sweat running down my spine. The streets are heaving and the noisy hum from the crowd lowers to a whisper as we go by.

'Are you all right, Suzi?' whispers Mick, moving closer to me.

'Sure. I think so.' Mick reaches for my hand as we move towards the centre of the road.

We make it to Allen's house, which is situated across the street from a church with a copper roof. My hopes are dashed when I walk in: there's no Rob Stoner, no T Bone Burnett, or Roger McGuinn. I hope to see Bobby Neuwirth, or Patti Smith, but they aren't here either. The place is full of people congregating around Allen, who's sitting cross-legged in the middle of the living-room floor, talking and chanting with a group who hang on his every word.

His partner, Peter, welcomes us with a smile and offers us a drink. There's a crowded kitchen leading to an unremarkable living room. The men look scruffy and there aren't many girls, and definitely no one who looks like us. The place is full, people spilling out to the hallway and up the stairs. The kitchen doesn't smell good, so the three of us move to the back of the living room and stand and sip our boxed wine. It tastes dreadful.

Allen is dressed in a shabby jacket and baggy trousers. His long hair and bushy beard are unkempt. He pauses as he sees Mick, and, peering at him myopically through his large glasses, beckons him over. Denise, a girl I met at The Bitter End, is here and I'm glad to see someone I can talk to. She lives here with Allen and Peter. It seems quite small for all of them, until she tells me she lives upstairs in a separate apartment that Allen keeps for his friends. This is what I imagine a commune would be like and now I know I'm not the commune type of girl! But with that thought, a wave of shame washes over me – just because the kitchen smells and odd people live together, who am I to judge? Allen is a famous poet, but apart from that he is a protester, he leads a movement against the war in Vietnam, he champions gay rights, and he's a friend of Bob Dylan's; he's someone I'll never be. I might think about how unfair things are in this world, but I never speak up, never say anything.

I lean up against the wall and Denise introduces me to a couple of people. As I greet them, I'm told to 'shhh' by a large man with stringy grey hair who's straining to hear Allen. I retreat further, while keeping my eye on Mick. He looks settled. Someone refills his glass and, thinking we might be here for a while, I take another glass of wine myself, smoke a cigarette, and listen to the people around me. The Vietnam War is discussed with outright contempt;

everyone there feels it is a lost war that should never have started and should end immediately. There's a lively discussion about Jack Kerouac's book *On the Road*, which seems to be a bible to people who've read it. I'm at a loss – I don't know about the war or Jack Kerouac, so I don't say a word. To talk about glitter and Bowie in this company would sound so foreign. I start to feel inadequate, less serious than the people who surround me. They look for the meaning of life and I'm just living it without a thought. They seem confident in who they are, and go with the flow and live wherever the wind pushes them. Is this the way life should be? I don't want to appear shallow, but I like a bed, a place to call my own. Mick and I are pretty footloose, but it's not the same. Frankly, I'm relieved when we finally leave and drive back uptown.

38

FIRE ISLAND

All of us melt in the heat of this New York summer. The movie theatre is the only place where it's cool. Mick and I go during the afternoons and see *Dog Day Afternoon* and *Jaws*, among others. Day by day it gets hotter and hotter, until it's declared: the summer of 1975 is the hottest on record.

It's taken a while, but I begin to realise that I'm missing England. I write to my mum asking for photos of the garden and my dog, Ringo. I miss home, and I miss her; I miss the fragrant roses she grows, the soft cool rain that waters her green beans, bright strawberries and red tomatoes. Mum makes pies with shortcrust pastry and fills them with delicious blackcurrants from the garden, served and topped with Bird's custard and whipped double cream. I've enjoyed the literal fruits of her labour all my life without a thought about how much work it took to grow them. It makes my mouth water to think of them now and suddenly I'm over this concrete jungle. I'm over it and tired of waiting, waiting, and waiting. For what? The long days are spent trying to keep cool in our apartment with its single noisy air conditioner. At night we go to the Village to eat in cafés under brightly coloured awnings, drinking too much in the dark recesses of clubs before staggering home in the cool of early-morning light and sleeping until the sun hits our window.

Tony Defries is getting impatient. Mick hasn't got a plan; it's all riding on Bob Dylan. I can sense frustration and worry in the air, but suddenly there's a reprieve: out of the blue, Cherry Vanilla invites us to Fire Island for the weekend. We haven't heard from her in ages but I'm glad to be invited somewhere out of the city.

We take the ferry from Long Island and before long we pull into a dock. Cherry leads the way to her pink house, nestled, rather aptly, in Cherry Grove, and it's perfect: the breeze blows lightly, the air smells clean and fresh; I look up at the sky and feel the sunshine on my skin. We have lunch with wine before walking to the beach.

I can't wait to get into the water, and after I slather on sun lotion I wiggle my way down to the surf. I turn, laughing, to say something to Mick, but he's not with me. He's still sitting on his towel. I walk back to him.

'Come on, Mick, the water's lovely.' I smile as I say it.

'Nah, I'm all right, I want to get a bit of a tan first.' He looks away and takes a drag on his roll-up.

'Are you thinking about *Jaws* . . . ?' I'm laughing inside.

'Well,' he says defensively, 'it was in America, an' there's no life-guards 'ere!' I can't help but giggle.

The rest of the afternoon passes peacefully and eventually I do persuade him to swim. Afterwards, while we're sunbathing, I feel Mick tense up beside me.

'I can see a shark!' he says quietly.

'Oh, come on,' I say, thinking it's his imagination. A shriek from the water proves me wrong. People are screaming:

'SHARK, SHARK!'

I can't believe it. I sit up to watch everyone struggling to get out of the water. There's a tall fin silently gliding through the water not twenty feet from shore. Someone calls the coastguard and it turns out to be a sailfish – nothing dangerous. I guess we weren't the only ones to have seen *Jaws* that summer.

◆

New York and MainMan are no more welcoming than the 'shark'-infested waters off Fire Island. Tony is less and less generous with money and more and more concerned with David and his cocaine habit. When I see David on *The Dick Cavett Show*, he sings '1984' and 'Young Americans'. Both Geoff MacCormack and Ava Cherry are still with him. He looks so thin, it's painful for me to watch. He's so high and edgy, fooling around with his cane, unable to sit still, and yet despite all of this he comes across as witty and elegant. He wears a beautiful suit and somehow makes sense when he speaks.

The lease on the New York office on East 58th Street where we live is coming to an end and we have to move somewhere. Danny, who we made friends with at Larry Poons's house, calls us. We meet him at a bar downtown and he invites us to stay at his house on the Hudson in Nyack. I like Danny: he's generous with his time and there's always music in the house. It's here that Mick finally gets the call from the Dylan camp. When he puts down the phone, he turns to me and says:

'I'm startin' rehearsals next week!'

We grab each other and laugh, both of us relieved and delighted: the Rolling Thunder Revue is on. Mick calls Tony, who eagerly welcomes the news. Now we have to find somewhere to live as we can't stay with Danny long-term: his lease is up and he wants to find a house in the city. He asks Mick and me if we want to be room-mates. I can see the sense in this: we don't want to move into our own apartment as who knows how long we'll be there. I'm hoping to be invited on the Dylan tour myself, but we do need a place to put our stuff if nothing else. We talk about it and agree; we tell Danny to start looking.

39

TIME APART

I wait in our half-packed flat for Mick to come home from rehearsals. I'm nervous for him; this is a big deal. It's past 11 p.m.
when I hear his key in the door, and he comes in surprisingly sober.

'How did it go?'

'I don't know,' he starts, 'it's not like I thought. We play fer a
bit, then chat fer a bit, then play some more. It's not like regular rehearsal, and I don't know the songs. I'm a bit lost really.' He
scratches his head as he considers exactly what it is that he's finding difficult. 'There's this bloke called Jacques, 'e's not French,' he
says, laughing, ''e's a really nice bloke and 'e seems to be in charge,
but even 'e don't know what's goin' on. There's so many people
and so many songs, they're not jus' for Bob but fer other people
too. Joan Baez and Ramblin' Jack Elliott, Roger McGuinn, there's
loadsa songs to learn, I don't know any of 'em. Everyone else seems
to know 'em but I don't.'

'Isn't there a sheet with chords? Or the titles at least?'

'No. Bob jus' starts up and calls out the key an' sometimes the
title and we all start playin'. There's no set place for solos, they just
nod at yer and off you go. When I ask what song it is they look at
me as if I'm mad, but I can't 'elp it if I don't recognise "Blowin' in
the Wind" when it's played fast with a reggae beat!' We both laugh
at this.

'Did they like the way you played at least?'

241

'I 'ope so, no one says aught. I don't know where I am, and . . . I don't know the songs.' He says it again, with emphasis.

The next night, Mick comes home a bit more cheerful and says he's got a good couple of solos down. He's brought some records home: Bob Dylan, Joan Baez, The Byrds, plus others. He sits and listens to them while eating his dinner, and afterwards he strums along with them and writes a few charts. It's late before he comes to bed and as we cuddle up, I tell him how proud I am he's able to do this. It can't be easy with the music being so different.

Mick tells me that he and Bobby Neuwirth have become friends. Bobby helps him, standing close so Mick can see his hands and recognise the chords he's playing. They're at it all day and every day for a week or so, until I finally ask, 'Can I come on tour with you?' It's a half-hearted question, really.

'Oh Suzi, I don't think so. I'll try but let's see how things go first.'

He gives me a hug and I have to be happy with that. I'm now the pathetic girlfriend, clinging on to my man, a position I never thought I'd find myself in. I try to be understanding, but truthfully I'm infuriated at being left out. I know I'm not working on this tour – that's the difference – and it pains me to say but I think Mick wants to experience this alone. I don't blame him, but it cuts me like a knife. He's the only Englishman on the road, the only true rock god guitar player, and he's travelling with amazing songwriters. Mick's a wonderful musician but he's never been good with lyrics, and this is his chance to reinvent himself. Reinvention is usually easier done alone.

It's a bitter pill to swallow. Mick and I have always been together. They leave for Massachusetts for the first show.

◆

I decide to go up to the MainMan offices to see what's going on; maybe there'll be something for me to do with Mick gone. While I wait for Tony, I pick up a copy of the *NME* and smile at the cover: it's a photo of Keith Moon in a policeman's helmet and with a limp wrist. There's a small red banner on the bottom, too: 'Bowie's Ma spills the beanz!!'

Inside is an unhappy interview with Mrs Jones. She still lives in Beckenham in what the journalist says is a nice flat, but she's sad and lonely. David's cocaine addiction puts his mum, along with everything else, in second place. Mrs Jones reveals how much she detests Tony Defries and labels him unsympathetic, unwilling to tell her where David is or how she can reach him. Tony pushes her concerns aside, telling her David has no legal obligation to support her and that she should make sure she accounts for what she spends; he even snidely suggests she gets a job. David might not want his mum around all the time but he never hated her, and I can't imagine he'd have been so unkind.

This sounds like Defries's voice to me. Defries never speaks about his own parents. I know he suffered chronic asthma when he was a kid and lived in a foster home for a while during the war. Asthma put him in the hospital for some time, which is where he studied law. I don't think he had a lot of parental love; he seems to get on well with his sister Di, but in many ways he's a cold man who only cares about a few people – I used to be one of them, but now he's too busy to have sympathy for me and my situation. It makes me feel sad and alone, too.

I decide to call my mum.

'Why don't you come home?' she asks me after hearing that Mick has left me alone in New York. In a way I want to go, but what about Mick? If I leave, will he follow me? What would I do in London? What's better: living in New York waiting for Mick or going back to 96 Cumberland Road? For now, New York wins.

I want to be close to Mick. Maybe he'll ask me to go on the road, and I hold on to that ridiculous thought as I try to make the best of it and move into our new place on Spring and Greenwich with Danny. October arrives and it's beautiful, the sun losing its sting and brightening up the house. The ground floor, which was once a shop front, is boarded up to the street. Upstairs on the first floor is a large square kitchen, complete with a fireplace, leading directly into the living room, which boasts another fireplace. Both fireplaces are bricked up and painted white, like the rest of the interior. Everything seems to be in good shape.

Danny has some furniture and I bring the couch from East 58th Street. The kitchen gets filled with a table and a few chairs and Danny has some nice art: some posters and a Poons piece, a deal he made during the halcyon days of last spring. There are two bedrooms upstairs. Mine's a bit small but certainly big enough for both Mick and me; there aren't any cupboards, so I buy a clothing rail and a small chest, which do just fine.

The house is always full of people, mostly Danny's friends: some musicians, some girlfriends, and others who just seem to tag along. Danny likes to cook for them and is constantly cleaning, and nearly every morning I hear him banging the vacuum cleaner into my door and calling out, 'Clean the house, Suzi, clean the house!'

I'm furious that he thinks he can tell me what to do so I ignore him. I'll do my bit, but he's not telling me what to do or how to do it.

The real trouble begins when the hot water goes off. Danny takes up the issue with the landlord, Gotlieb, who promises to fix it but fails to deliver. While we wait, we boil pots of water to wash and are forced to go to Danny's friend's house to shower. The novelty of living alone in New York soon wears off. The hot-water promises keep coming and going, and when the temperature dips the heat doesn't go on.

I've had enough. I'm not used to sitting around doing nothing, so I leave Danny to his building and cruise around in my Cadillac during the day and sleep in my fur coat at night. I complain bitterly to Mick and he invites me to Boston to visit him for my twenty-sixth birthday. As I'm preparing to leave, I tell Danny to stop paying the rent until they fix the flat. Danny doesn't say a word.

The next time I'm at the offices, all I hear about is David, David, David. He's making a movie, *The Man Who Fell to Earth*, with Nick Roeg, and living in Bel Air, and I hear his hit 'Fame' all over the radio, but all in all it seems as though the relationship between him and Defries is difficult at best and fading fast. I hear Angie is having a lot of problems with David too. There's bad behaviour on both sides: her desperate need for attention, his cocaine-fuelled indifference.

David's way too involved with his own life and his own career to care about anyone and turns Corinne from MainMan into his gatekeeper. Corinne became David's assistant after Ziggy and the Spiders broke up. As David sinks into the world of drugs and paranoia, Corinne becomes his only access to the outside world and sees him through difficult times. I think it scares Angie when she's unable to talk to David without going through her first. Corinne's in love with David – she has to be, to do what she does for him. I think she also loves the power. I first met Corinne when she worked as a temp for Defries at Gunter Grove. I liked her: she was small, neat and efficient. I felt, instinctively, that she'd have preferred to be on the road with us instead of in the office, and I was right. After she became David's personal assistant, she spent years on the road with him.

David changed a lot after he killed off Ziggy. Mick and I didn't see him, but we heard about him from people at MainMan. When I worked on the Ziggy tours there were no drugs, and David, Angie and Defries were supportive and liked each other. It was a magical time. It didn't last – well, nothing lasts forever, but before it all went south it was very successful, we were all part of that. In retrospect, Ziggy Stardust and the Spiders from Mars was an innocent time. None of us – including David – had done anything like it before. But I don't include Defries in this; I can't imagine him as ever being innocent.

The rising of Ziggy was magical and looking at where we're at now, no matter what the future holds for Mick, I can't imagine we'll ever live those glory days again.

40
ODD ONE OUT

I fly up to Boston to meet Mick, and after I've checked in at the hotel I go to the rehearsal hall, where I'm welcomed by Jenny, David Mansfield's girlfriend. I look around; a girlfriend of Bobby Neuwirth's, Aviva, is here, along with another girl called Lola – have they just come for the gig? Boston isn't that far from New York, after all. As we get on the tour bus after rehearsals, I'm introduced to Howie, the drummer, and his wife, Rona. As Jenny chatters on about how great the tour is and what fun everyone is having, she asks me where I've been. I don't want to say I wasn't invited, but that's the truth of it. I feel like crying; all the wives and girlfriends are here, and I feel sick as the realisation hits me. Why doesn't Mick want me here? How could he leave me stuck in a flat with no heat or hot water, with a bloke we barely know? I don't know what to think. I've become the very girl I never thought I'd be: the one who hangs on, the one who's unwanted, the one trying to keep up.

The tour has its own fashion: cowboy boots and hats worn with plaid shirts and jeans. Mick's relaxed, laughing along at jokes that I don't understand, and he seems especially easy with the beautiful Ronee Blakley. Ronee has soft white skin and dark shiny hair that she wears tucked under a bright red beret. She has that 'damsel in distress' kind of look and gravitates towards Mick. They laugh together onstage as he asks her something, and when she answers he seems to hang on her every word.

I try to put on a happy face, but inside I'm scared. My heart's in my mouth, and in my very unfashionable boots. After sound check we go to grab dinner, and I put on a bright smile and say hello to everyone I know. I'm usually a confident person and I want to feel that way, but right now I just feel out of place. Mick hardly acknowledges that I'm here. My insides feel like jelly.

The gig is at the famous Boston Music Hall. The stage is set up like a living room, similar to the Grand Ole Opry in Nashville, which we visited when we were on tour with David. There's a large square carpet surrounded by armchairs and sofas; amps and guitars are set up next to small coffee tables, while the rest of the equipment – monitors, microphones, pedal steel, drums and keyboards – is scattered about the stage. As I wait for the band to go on, I watch the road crew work. The feeling, the pre-show nerves, the excitement, the buzzzzzz: I miss it so much I want to cry. Defries arrives with his very pregnant girlfriend, Melanie; he wants to be part of this too.

The theatre smells intimate and warm, the rumble of the audience easy to hear. The band walk on, Mick with them, plugging in behind a makeshift circus-style curtain designed by a young man called Tom Meleck. It has a crazy painting on the front and 'Rolling Thunder Revue' written above it. Bobby Neuwirth is at the mic and for the first few numbers the band play behind him. The backing band all have a song to perform of their own, and Mick plays 'Is There Life on Mars'. It fools me for a minute – it's not the Bowie song but a song written by Roscoe West. I'm sure Defries is disappointed. Ronee Blakley comes to the mic soon after and sings beautifully, followed by Joni Mitchell – she's incredible, I think the world of her songs and performance. I love this new kind of music, it's such a change from glam and Bowie.

When Bob Dylan comes on, it's as if God has arrived. He has a pale made-up face and large dark eyes, his head covered by a fedora adorned with flowers. I might have felt his presence at The Bitter End but here it's magnified a million times. He walks on unannounced and starts to play 'A Hard Rain's A-Gonna Fall'. The band pick it up and the audience, after a roar, settle down to listen. Bob weaves his magic; he's a wonderful storyteller. I steal a look at Defries, who smiles back at me. I know he feels it too. Bob has an enchantment that I've rarely felt. He sings 'Isis' as a duet with a violin played by Scarlet Rivera. His voice is raspy and emotional, while her gypsy violin accentuates the story. Scarlet is slim and tall with thick waist-length dark hair; she and Bob look good together, dipping and swaying in the spotlight. I can sense the feeling between them is close and when they play it's almost lover-like, but Scarlet has a lover – he's on the road with them and jealously guards her.

After an intermission, the second half begins. It's dark onstage as the curtain rises up, then a spotlight illuminates Bob and Joan Baez standing together with acoustic guitars. They start to play 'Blowin' in the Wind' and the crowd go wild. They stand so close that his hat shades her face. I'm mesmerised, not just by them but by the reaction from the audience. The next song has Joan's voice ringing out like a church bell, in harmony with him. I can feel their power and can only imagine how potent they were in the 1960s.

Mick plays beautifully throughout. His guitar lines are spare but extraordinary, complementing and uplifting whoever he is playing with. Dylan shoots him a look here and there and I think he's surprised that this English rocker is now so at home with his music. Mick's come a long way since rehearsals.

Defries and I chat a bit after the show. He tells me Angie bought a house in Switzerland, hoping David would go and live with her and Zowie. David visits briefly, but the idyllic situation doesn't last and he tells her he'd rather live with Iggy in Berlin instead.

41
New York Winter

I arrive back at Spring Street to a distinctly chilly atmosphere. The heat still isn't on, and I ask Danny about the rent. Danny, crest-fallen, admits that he's not had any luck with Gotlieb.

'But he must want the rent?'

'Well, I, err, I wanted a good deal and I paid him in cash.'

'So, when are you due to pay him again?'

'I paid him a year's rent in cash.' He looks at me with downcast eyes.

I'm incredulous. Without the leverage of the rent, there's no way Gotlieb will fix the heat. Why would he? We likely won't get heat for the entire winter, and with this tragic thought I wrap myself in my fur coat and cry. This is not what I had planned. Am I to sit and freeze in New York City while Mick gallivants around the country on a magnificent tour? I feel pathetic, useless and scared. Is this my future? I want to work, but without papers I can't get a job and MainMan hasn't offered any help in this department.

I wonder how Danny had enough cash to pay the rent for a year. He doesn't look or act like a wealthy man, and though he says he sells guitars there's no evidence of it. The truth is soon revealed: one night when it's too cold to sleep I quietly walk down the hall, intending to fill my hot-water bottle in the kitchen. I get to the top of the stairs and hear voices from below. I peer around the corner into the kitchen and see Danny giving wads of cash to two blokes: it's

Dominic and Bobby, I know them from the house. Several garbage bags rest against their legs and the smell of pot is overwhelming. I creep back the way I came, and in the morning the bags are gone. Needless to say, the comings and goings of the house now fascinate me. I fight the cold and depression by smoking a joint for breakfast alongside strong coffee.

A few more freezing days go by before Danny has an idea.

'I think I'm going to break in them there fireplaces,' he says as he sips red wine. 'They must have worked once, so why not now? I'll get George round and a couple of others, we'll start tomorro'.'

The next morning, true to his word, Danny takes a sledgehammer and starts to whack the kitchen chimney in. He's strong, and before long we can see and smell what's behind the bricks . . . more bricks.

Matty, a neighbour, gives an opinion: 'Looks like the chimney collapsed, fell in on itself.'

Danny looks up with a face grey with dust and begins to see just how much brick he has in the kitchen. He straightens his back and calls George on the phone:

'Come on down here, George, bring your wheelbarrow and some help – we need to move some brick.'

George, a small Puerto Rican man with a happy smile and a long scar on his face, arrives late in the afternoon. He brings a couple of big boys with him who don't speak English and stare darkly in the kitchen. We all stand and look at the bricks. Danny rolls a joint, gets them stoned and gives them each a beer.

'I've se'ed a dumpster sittin' on Washington Street, they're knockin' summat down there. Let's dump it after dark. Rick, go get the truck.'

They load the truck up one painful wheelbarrow at a time. The floor is a mess and the whole place covered with fine cement dust, but they stick with it until late in the evening.

Danny starts again in the morning and finally they break through. A fierce wind whips down the gaping hole and into the kitchen. Danny starts a fire with some wooden slats he found on Greenwich Street. Anything that's flammable gets thrown in. It smells awful but I can't complain, it's giving out some heat! 'Living room tomorrow,' he breathes as he downs a large glass of red. The others tiredly agree.

I go and visit Ian and Trudi and by the time I get back both fireplaces are burning brightly, and the smell seems to have dissipated. God knows what they're burning, but it's definitely warm in these two rooms. As I wait for Mick to come back to New York, I hear on the radio that David's going to be on *Soul Train*. It's a big deal: he's the only other white artist to be on after Elton John.

The Rolling Thunder Revue comes into New York at the beginning of December. They're playing Madison Square Garden in a few days; it's a huge gig and Mick's thrilled. Muhammad Ali will be there to speak to the audience in support of Dylan's effort to release Hurricane Carter. The show is titled 'The Night of The Hurricane'.

Maybe it's because it's New York, maybe it's because it's Madison Square Garden or maybe it's because it's the last show of this tour, but this time a Spider steps out on to the stage. Mick spins and struts and shakes the hell out of the guitar while he's playing, and his playing is magnificent. Mick's transformed; he's used to large stages and every solo takes him higher, every move he makes screams 'rock star'. I see the band looking at him, Bob too – no one expected this.

◆

It's hard to take him home after all he's seen, after all he's accomplished. We're living in a cold-water flat, but he takes it in his stride and seems glad to be back. It's too cold to stay long in New York, so soon enough we go back home to Bromley for Christmas.

Mum and Dad welcome us with open arms; I've never been happier to see them. I'm glad to be out of my frosty New York house and hope to get closer to Mick now we're home. We all love Christmas, no one more so than Mick.

Mum tells us she saw David Bowie on *The Russell Harty Show*: 'He was beamed in from LA!' She says it as if it's a joke, and I have to smile. My mum is being hip – or at least trying to be. 'His hair looks greasy and an odd gold colour. I like your haircut better.'

We spend Christmas Day with my family and go up to Hull for Boxing Day. I think Mick's family are a little shocked at how well their boy is doing, and Mick, in turn, is grateful to be here with money to spend and a future to talk about, something for us all to look forward to. We live two lives – one here, close and normal, and the other full of excitement and a little danger.

42
THE ROLLING THUNDER REVUE

1976

The Rolling Thunder Revue don't meet again until the next Hurricane Carter benefit in January at the Astrodome in Houston, Texas. Mick gets me a ticket without any fuss and we fly down. The Astrodome is a huge place, but the sold-out crowd's energy gets everyone going, as do the guest stars: Ringo Starr, Stevie Wonder and Carlos Santana, to name a few. Back at the hotel, everyone's already talking about the next tour.

Mick and I fly back to New York. We're both despondent at the state of our flat, and after a day or so we drive to Connecticut to see Ian and Trudi. We explain the situation, the year's rent upfront, the fact that there's no heat. They think we're mad, I can see it in their eyes, and I think they're right. Ian can't wait to hear about Mick's time with Bob and I'm looking forward to confiding in a friend. It's comfortable and warm here, and we eat and drink as if we haven't been apart at all. It's a miracle we're still friends after the horrors of Mott and managers. I trust the two of them – they're truly decent people and have always been fair to us.

We all relax, and Mick and I get along just as we used to. When I ask him if I can join the second part of the tour, he agrees to it without a thought. I'm not a perfect person and neither is he, but we're together and I don't want to live alone. Absence makes the heart grow fonder . . . *of someone else* is what I think to myself, and Ronee Blakley leaps to mind.

While we're here, we watch David on *The Dinah Shore Show*. He looks better than I thought he would, and he seems more lucid than he was when he appeared on *The Dick Cavett Show*. David plays 'Stay' off his new album *Station to Station*. He's dressed in black baggy pants and a dark-purple shirt, and I like his new hairstyle and look. At the end of his performance, he's a gentleman, helping Dinah on to her stool before he sits beside her; he's relaxed and as charming as ever. At the end of the show, a karate instructor appears with a leap and chop. David shares a short demonstration with him that's somehow neither silly nor contrived. I think David might be on the road to recovery.

David and Defries are no more, their partnership is done. David now lives in LA; he's finished his movie and is considering moving to Switzerland. I suspect taxes are the true reason. I can't help but wish we had that problem.

◆

I'm in a contented frame of mind as Mick and I fly down to Florida for the rehearsals in Clearwater. This is a part of America that I've never seen before, and in the springtime it's hard to imagine anywhere more beautiful. We're taken to the Biltmore Hotel, a true southern belle, the grounds filled with enormous old trees dripping with Spanish moss. It was built in 1925, which in American culture is truly historical; I'm told it's the biggest wooden structure in all the States, and I can believe it.

I step off the bus into southern splendour, warm sun and fragrant flowers. Rehearsals are in an hour, so Mick and I settle in and go back downstairs. We're warned by a porter about alligators that wander the grounds after dark. He says with a smile, 'Ole Jake's getting hungry!' I'm not quite sure how real 'ole Jake' might be.

The rehearsals are in a separate part of the hotel, and we walk across green lawns on a narrow path towards the hall. Inside, there's a stage with curtains and low-hanging lights. Drums and bass are playing and Bobby Neuwirth is at the mic. He calls out to Mick, who goes and joins them. Dylan's here, I'm sure of it; there's a force field around that man. Joan Baez and Roger McGuinn are sitting close to the stage.

The Rolling Thunder group is so relaxed; the Bowie tours were much more structured than this. After rehearsal there's a communal meal, and it's here I meet Jacques Levy, the producer, and his wife, Claudia. The night ends early, and the next morning a newsletter appears under our door. It's filled with gossip – someone makes up a bed with short sheets, someone else takes someone's shoes from outside their room, stuff like that. It's light-hearted and fun, and it's joined by an itinerary for the day. Today we're going on glass-bottomed boats to see the wonder of this paradise. We push off and see alligators lazing in the mud on the banks. Fish stream under the boat and colourful birds squawk and flap in the trees. Mick has some trinkets from the first tour, Indian things he wears around his neck. I want some mementos too and get a Rolling Thunder T-shirt as soon as I can.

Soon enough we leave for Lakeland and St Petersburg for the first shows of the tour. Bob drives his own Winnebago with a few chosen friends and a hound dog that doesn't have a name. The rest of us travel on two luxurious buses. There's a walkie-talkie in each vehicle so we can chat during the journey. On our bus, Rob brings out his bass, David a fiddle and someone else a guitar. Howie keeps a beat on a piece of rubber. They play old songs, new songs, songs from the show – the music's joyful. The bus is well supplied with a stocked fridge and a coffee maker, and before long a joint gets fired up and passed around. I take a puff or two and sit by the window watching the morning traffic.

The next time I see Bob Dylan he wears a scarf on his head, held in place by a thin tie. Somehow, he makes it look as if it belongs there. He still wears his leather jacket and jeans, the same clothes he wore when he had his flower-decorated fedora on. There's something about Bob that defies explanation: he's handsome but not classically so, and even though he's got a skinny figure he has marvellous shoulders, and his jacket hangs off them perfectly. His hair curls out of whatever headgear he has on. I'm drawn to his magnetism, as is everyone else. As a performer, he's mercurial. Some nights he's – well, he's awful, and other nights he's so good you could hear a pin drop in a 50,000-seater hall.

After the gig, we go back to the hotel. The tour usually takes a floor of a hotel and the music keeps going, everyone playing everywhere. A lot of musicians on the tour are late-nighters, staying up to play music and gamble. Mick stays up too; his playing has changed since he joined this tour, gaining another flavour from the musicians that surround him. Sometimes he doesn't make it to bed, and if I wake up and he's not with me I'll usually find him asleep in a chair somewhere. But not tonight. Tonight I find him asleep in the hospitality suite, asleep with a blonde girl. My heart races as I pour a large jug of water over them both.

Mick splutters, sits up: 'What did you do that fer?'

'Turn over, Mick,' I say angrily, and as he does, the blonde's head comes up, water dripping from her hair.

'Oh no . . .' Mick says, looking at me. 'I didn't know.'

I half believe him, but it's a humiliating situation all the same. I go to the lobby and sink into a chair, not knowing what to do. He comes down, still with the girl, and tries to introduce her to me. What is he thinking?! The girl slides on to his lap as he sits down, and he doesn't stop her. I'm beside myself. There's no excuse; he's not even drunk! I walk out of the lobby in a tearful fury.

Bobby Neuwirth's on my heels and I hear Mick's voice call out. Bobby tells me to get on his bus and I do. I don't want a big row, and I know if I push things I might be asked to go home. I'm seething at who I've become: a pathetic girl with no connection to this tour except my man. What Mick doesn't remember is that I was the one who pushed him up onstage at The Bitter End; he would never have been on this tour without me. Mick has never been big with groupies before, so why is he starting now? However, I have to accept the humiliation and at the first stop I get off Bobby's bus. Mick gets off his and we hug as he tells me nothing happened, that he's sorry, that he didn't even know she was there. I want to believe him. I know Mick's drinking is out of hand and that he's not the only one. More people get clean and sober after this tour than you can imagine; but I'm getting ahead of myself.

In Mobile, Alabama, a waitress laughs at my accent, and I can hear her in the kitchen imitating me. It makes me smile. We go on to New Orleans and it brings flashbacks to a different time, a different era with the Ziggy tours. While we're there, I learn that David's movie has been released in the UK. The reviews are mixed, with the famous Roger Ebert saying that David's performance 'flirts with the catatonic'. David has a history of playing someone else – Ziggy Stardust, Aladdin Sane and now Thomas

Jerome Newton – but all I ever see is David when he's on screen.

The South moves on its own time, with never a thought about its frenetic northern neighbours. I like the pace of life here, the lazy walks in the evening heat, the mint juleps, the men in seersucker suits. In Texas, the deep southern velvet voices change to a slightly harder twang; they both appeal to me.

As we're leaving Texas, the driver of the other bus runs over to ours, puffing and panting. There's some excited whispering before our driver gets on to the bus, and as we pull into the traffic he says:

'Yo'all ke'p off that ther' radio,' nodding to the walkie-talkie.

'What . . . ?' comes a reply.

'Ke'p off that ther' radio,' he repeats. 'Radio silence 'til fuurther notice.' He sits back. There's a dramatic pause, but by now we're all interested.

'Come on, what's going on?'

'Tha's all I know!' The bus driver continues, 'I'm be'n tol' to folla that bus in front and to ke'p up, destination unknown.'

We pepper him with more questions but soon give up. He knows no more than he's saying.

Houston comes and goes, and when we stop for gas, Neuwirth gets on our bus. I waste no time in cornering him, and Mick laughs as I start asking questions.

'All in good time,' is all he'll say, but when we turn off the Interstate and on to a country road, he breaks his silence. 'We're goin' to see a good friend of mine, Bobby Charles, who lives down here in Louisiana.'

'Bayou country,' someone says.

'That's righ'. Bobby has a spread and he's invited us to go stay a while.'

I don't know who Bobby Charles is, but I think his 'spread' must be huge to accommodate all of us. Neuwirth sits down and explains: 'Bobby's a real good friend of mine, haven't seen him for a while. He writes great songs he's be'n playing since he was really young.' Mick and I listen as he goes on. 'He wrote "See You Later, Alligator" when he was fourteen.' I gasp at that, and Neuwirth laughs.

'I used to sing "See You Later, Alligator" at school,' I cry. 'I can't believe it came from here!'

'Everyone knows that song,' Mick agrees.

'See You Later, Alligator' was recorded by Bill Haley and His Comets and was a huge hit everywhere, from Bayou country, Louisiana, all the way to Worsley Bridge Junior School in Beckenham. It's staggering how far music can go. Bobby Charles pioneered 'swamp pop' and wrote and recorded the Fats Domino hit 'Walking to New Orleans'.

We drive along highways in the rain and stop to stretch our legs before we pull off on to a real country road, small and rough. We cross over field after field before we enter a glade of trees where the sun filters through the leaves, pulling up at a long, low house. A couple of pick-up trucks sit by an old barn and a few men stand beside them looking at us as we pull in. There's a few dogs in the yard and they all bark as we park the bus; one howls as if it's the end of the world.

Neuwirth jumps out and walks towards the men, calling out: 'Bobby Charles, where are you?'

A man separates himself from the others and laughs as he sees him. He looks like a cowboy, wearing old jeans and a dark-red shirt along with boots and a cowboy hat. He's a little overweight but still a handsome man. He and Bobby Neuwirth act as though they saw each other only yesterday; there's a real brotherly camaraderie between them as they embrace in a bear hug. As they sweep into the house, Bobby Charles calls to his girl, 'Judy, they're here!'

Beer starts to flow and soon a bottle of Jack Daniels joins the party. Guitars come into the house and we're back to as we were. Being on the road with Bob Dylan is a far more bohemian affair than I'm used to; there's a lot of family and friends and a big crew. Usually there's an assortment of managers, promoters and record company people that hang around us, but not today; the crew are somewhere else and there's only one road manager here, along with security and our drivers. The buses park and hook up to power, tents materialise and lights are hung in the trees. It's a bit like a country fair, right down to a girl who reads palms and a man who does tarot readings. There's a tent for the tour doctor and one for the astronomer, whose telescope points to the stars.

A girl steps out from Bob's Winnebago carrying a coil of wire. She's in long culottes in a paisley fabric and a bolero-type top over a skinny T-shirt. She's with one of Bob's minders, whom I recognise; he takes the coil from her and attaches it to a tree, pulls it across to another tree and winches it tight. I feel foolish as I ask the girl:

'Are you going to walk on that?'

'Not tonight, the tension's not right, it needs some time to stretch. I might tomorrow.' She introduces herself as Stephanie and with a smile she turns and goes back to the Winnebago.

Another girl who's recently arrived is Jasmine, an exotic dancer. Jasmine is bejewelled, tanned and fully made-up, and today she wears a lot of blue net and some shocking-pink tulle; even with the clothes, there's a lot of skin to see. Her appearance makes us all look dull. A Hell's Angel leans on his bike as he looks down at her face, his big, tattooed arms bare and his long red hair falling to his shoulders. I recognise him as another of Bob's minders.

Bobby Charles's house has been set up for catering, a loose term for feeding us all. The barbecue is in use and a huge piece of meat is turning on a spit over the flames. I'm expecting hot dogs and hamburgers, maybe chicken, but Neuwirth says, 'This is a southern specialty: alligator tail.'

I'm a little repulsed as I watch it turn and be liberally basted, but Mick's all for it. I smile at Neuwirth, who tells me to try it before casting judgement, so I sigh and resolve to have a taste when it's done. I wonder where the tail came from . . . do you pick up alligator tail like a steak at the local supermarket? The rest of the food is southern-style too, and it looks a lot more appetising than the alligator: beans, rice and grits, with dark collard greens.

A man walks into the house chewing on a piece of wood, his straw-blond hair sticking out of a beat-up cowboy hat. He's wearing a faded blue plaid shirt with the sleeves cut off; on one arm there's a tattoo of a red flag and a gun, on the other an alligator crawls up his shoulder and down his back. His skin is like tanned leather, and when he smiles there's only a few teeth. At first glance, I think of the movie *Deliverance*.

'I wrestle' me an 'gator, down the swamp t'is mornin',' he says to no one in particular. He nods to the barbecue and smiles. I feel sick. Did he really kill that poor thing? 'Hi,' he says as he takes off his hat, 'I'm Bird.'

We're in 'good ole boy' country, that's for sure.

43
THE TURNING POINT

I sleep peacefully on the bus after a night of partying and music and get up early to look for Mick. It's a lovely day outside and people drift in and out of Bobby's house. I drink coffee on the porch in the morning sun. Judy and I look at the remnants of last night as Jenny comes in. We giggle together as we gather the empty beer bottles and clean overflowing ashtrays.

Mick's asleep in one of the chairs inside. He looks so young, all curled up like that. He wakes up bright and chipper and I hand him some toast and coffee. I want to ask why he didn't come to bed on the bus with me, but I haven't the heart. I know who Mick is; we're all different. Mick never seems to suffer a hangover, but I wish he did – it might slow him down a bit.

'What a great place this is, I luv it 'ere!' He seems to mean it, and I can see the appeal.

It's late morning before the rest of the men appear. They eat and stretch, belch and do whatever men do – I don't include Mick in this, he's a refined man, fastidious in his appearance and polite in his manner.

The day goes on and while the women cook and the men play cards, I go out to see Stephanie on her tightrope. She doesn't do much but even being able to walk the length of the wire is an achievement to me. Much of the day's gone by the time musicians start to play on the porch. I sit and listen as the sun goes down. The drinking has long started, and soon enough food is being served. I brave a small piece of the alligator and Bobby's right, it does taste like salty chicken.

I'm helping in the kitchen as Bird walks in, and I watch him join the card game, telling everyone that'll listen about his alligator tales. The men laugh as they play, excited yells rising up when someone wins a pot.

Then, suddenly, no one's laughing.

'What the fock?' It's Mick talking to Bird.

'Whaddaya mean?' returns Bird, shifting the stick in his mouth and standing up. When Mick has a few drinks he can be fearless, and he's had more than a few drinks this afternoon. He glares at Bird and says something I can't hear, staring at him straight across the table. He's not giving an inch. Bird glares back at him and no one blinks.

Words are spoken, angry words, and Bird steps back away from the table into the shadows. I hear something whistle across the room, and before anyone can do anything there's a large knife trembling in the wall behind Mick, passing within inches of his face. Mick looks pale but still doesn't back down, and neither does Bird. He escalates things by slowly taking his shotgun from where it's resting and laying it across the table between them, leaning forward as he does it. Mick doesn't move and holds Bird's gaze. The whole room is silent. I'm struck dumb with terror; I can't move, my feet are stuck to the floor. The stare-down goes on for what feels like eternity.

Bobby Neuwirth comes into the room, hard and fast. He takes in the scene before grabbing both the gun and Mick and walking outside.

◆

The night winds down after that, and Mick joins me on the bus.

'Don't drink so much, Mick, you nearly got killed in there!'

''e were cheatin',' he says indignantly. He sighs and flashes a smile at me, giving me a hug and agreeing: 'I know, I know,' he says, 'don't worry. I'll be all right, Suzi.'

It's an empty promise and I know it.

◆

We're barrelling down the Interstate when I hear the driver from the other bus call our driver's walkie-talkie:

'You got Bob's dawg on board that bus there?'

There's no dog on our bus. The brake lights on Dylan's Winnebago flash red, and the front bus too. We pull over behind them and the drivers get out. It seems that Bob left his dog tied up about a hundred miles ago when we last filled up with gas. The Hell's Angel offers to go and get the dog on his motorbike. He shows no ill will and with gratitude from Bob he sets off. We continue to our hotel and check in, and three or four hours later the dog is back, tied on to the pillion of the motorbike in a makeshift box and looking no worse for wear (and maybe even a bit superior at her rescue).

◆

I'm told that as part of the tour we're playing at a state school for boys in Gatesville, Texas, though I understand pretty quickly that this isn't a 'school' by any means of the word. We drive through some gates surrounded by razor wire and watch towers. From the bus window I see the 'inmates' – for want of a better word – circling a yard.

A young red-haired boy stands out in the group of dark heads, his skin blotchy and red from both sun and fighting. He wears ragged jeans and not much else, and one of his eyes is swollen shut while the other is screwed up. He looks so out of place; my heart goes out to him. They're said to be young, but not all of them look it. I quickly search for the colourful brochure that we were given about this place the day before, advertising it as a safe space for troubled teens with substance issues. The brochure looks nothing like I'm seeing here. In England, we call this a prison.

The bus feels like a haven in a sea of despair. The doors open and a few of us step out into the hot sun. The kids at the wire fence call out, and when they smile and laugh they look much younger. Joan Baez, love her soul, thinks she should go and mingle with the young men that are being held here. A few of us go with her, Jenny and me included. It's hot; the crowd is a seething mass and as we move through it the boys call out to Joan, who talks to them in both English and Spanish.

The band start to play and Joan leaves to perform. It's only now I realise that the kids aren't interested in listening to the music – they're interested in us. They want to hold my hand, Jenny's too. I can hear a suggestive remark and when other performers get up to leave, the kids get closer and closer. Suddenly, I don't feel so safe. I glance at Jenny, who has been fending off her own admirers, and we nod at each other. The boys call out as we leave, grabbing at our legs and asking for a kiss, and both of us swat away their hands as we make our way back to safety.

I admire Bob for doing this show, but he isn't Johnny Cash, and the inmates don't care. I, for one, am grateful when we drive out of the gates to go on to Fort Worth.

◆

Cocaine is a drug I haven't tried before and now it seems to be everywhere. It scares me a bit, and though I can't remember why I tried it, I did, and I took to it like a duck to water. Mick isn't that interested, which funnily enough makes it all the more appealing to me. Now when Mick hangs with his drinking buddies, I hang out with a different crowd. Cocaine gives me confidence, makes me feel interesting, it gives me everything – except sleep. I stay up with like-minded people and become part of what I think is an interesting group. As the days go by, I worry less about Mick and more about where the coke is.

A slim girl with tight curly black hair joins us midway through the tour. It's Felicity: she's been here before and is wildly popular. Her voice is quiet and high in pitch, her face pale and chiselled with a suggestion of a moustache over her top lip. She's pretty in an Edwardian kind of way, wearing sheer fabrics in romantic layers over jeans. She's not an artist, or a singer, and she doesn't seem to be with a man. Everyone I ask seems not to know who she is, but I soon find out after watching the trail of people going in and out of her room: she brings cocaine to the tour.

We become friends, and when we get to Kansas she asks me if I'd like to go to meet David Cassidy. I'm curious, of course, he's a massive star. The band are rehearsing for their last show, so I ask Mick and he tells me to go ahead. I pull on my cowboy boots, throw on a dress, fluff my hair and get in the car. We leave the tour behind us and drive into the majestic state of Colorado. The roads are narrow, and at one point we're so high up the clouds below give me the illusion that we're on a plane.

We follow a sign for Caribou Ranch and pull up at a barn beside a spread of buildings. The barn at Caribou Ranch is the studio; it's a large room with huge leather couches covered with cushions and blankets. The sound desk is in the middle of the room, the centre of attention. The unmistakable voice of David Cassidy rings out as we slide into seats and wait for the track to finish, and when it's over he comes to give Felicity a hug and kiss, before turning to me with that famous smile. I feel as if I'm in a scene from *The Partridge Family*.

I don't mention it now, but I remember when David came to London in 1974 as clear as day. The press compared the reception he received to that of The Beatles. Girls stood for hours outside his hotel and his performances created riots, with fans doing anything they could to get close to him. His concert in London was the scene of hysteria and disaster. The place was filled with 30,000 raving fans, and soon enough it got out of hand: in the frenzy of pushing and shoving, a fourteen-year-old girl died. This shook David to his core, and he immediately gave up live performances and cancelled the rest of his dates.

Now, though, David's at ease and there's a complete lack of ego on his part. He's wearing patched pale-blue jeans on slim hips, with a studded leather and turquoise belt, and on his feet are snakeskin boots. His necklace and bracelet are made of tooled silver. He looks like what he is: a pop star. Felicity chats away with him and the other engineers, and as they go back to the desk, she invites me to have a walk outside. It's early evening and the weather is spectacular. Mountains surround the studio, and there's a lake fed by a crystal-clear stream nearby. In the distance, a field with horses stretches to the woodlands and foothills.

David and the others call to us as they leave the barn. As we walk away, Felicity tells David that I'm with Mick Ronson, which elicits a look of surprise.

'I've heard of him, didn't he play with David Bowie?'

'That's right, and now he's on the road with Bob Dylan.'

'Wow,' he mouths.

We go into the main house to have drinks and dinner, and after a while David asks Felicity and me to go up to his room. Felicity wastes no time in bringing out her delivery; we all have some, and soon stories start. David tells me a bit about *The Partridge Family*, but it's a practised story from the past. He's twenty-six now and all he wants to do is get away from being Keith Partridge. He plays us a few songs that he's been working on, and in turn I entertain him with stories about Bowie. We talk managers and musicians, business and music, and the conversation comes easy. David listens to me – something Mick hasn't done for a long time. I can feel the magnetism, and he acknowledges it with a sly grin. Felicity's here and I'm glad of it. David's a temptation; I bite my lip and cross my legs.

The next morning after coffee he takes my hand, slips his telephone number into it, and says, 'Call me. Come and see me, I'll get you a ticket.'

His eyes hold mine for a long minute. He knows what he's doing and laughs at my face as he pulls me in for a long hug goodbye. Before he lets me go, he whispers in my ear.

'This isn't over. Come to California,' he says with that film-star smile. 'Promise? Bring her, Felicity!' he calls across to her, stepping back as he waves us off. I feel like a teenager and all the way back to the tour I'm on cloud nine.

We go back to Rolling Thunder, where the energy feels amplified as we hurtle towards the end of the tour. I'm sad about that, it's been a great time, though I'd be lying if I said I didn't think about

David Cassidy and his invitation. Eventually, I talk to Mick about him, tell him what a huge fan he is, of both him and Bowie.

'He's coming to New York, maybe you'll want to meet him, maybe work with him. He's got a record deal.'

'David Cassidy?' Mick laughs. 'You must be focking joking.'

44
BACK DOWN TO EARTH

Mick and I are on a high after recording the wonderful *Cardiff Rose* with Roger McGuinn and some of the Rolling Thunder boys. When we get back to New York, we decide it's finally time to stop living with Danny and find our own place. We move to a lovely two-bedroom duplex on Park Avenue and 19th Street and everything seems to be going swimmingly.

As if right on cue, though, Tony Defries calls us to the office. He looks grim as we walk in, holding some papers in his right hand. Without putting too fine a point on it, he's received a bill from the Rolling Thunder Revue instead of wages. Mick's expenditure has somehow outweighed his earnings and there's a sizeable sum to be settled. I look at Mick in amazement while Tony stares at us in stony silence. We wait for Mick to say something, to explain.

'I dunno, I don't really remember . . .'

Tony's speechless and I don't know what to say. Mick seems genuinely surprised. 'I'm sorr', Tony, I don't know 'ow that 'appened.'

I think I know how it happened: Mick gambles – and unfortunately, he's a rotten card player, especially when he's drunk.

We've been in debt to Tony from the start so anything Mick makes goes straight to him, and I'm sure he was expecting a nice bump from Bob Dylan. We have never had a full accounting statement from Tony, so we don't know how much we owe him – but however much it is, I doubt we'll ever be able to pay it back. Mick's sick of it and so am I. Both of us want to start again with a clean slate. We don't stay in the office long – the atmosphere is poisonous – but I do talk to Zee before we leave. He tells me that David's still making music with Iggy. I wonder who manages his crazy life now. It has to be Corinne. My God, that girl likes punishment.

◆

Tony Defries is going through some changes. He's found a new artist who he's convinced will be the next big thing and talks him into changing his name from John Mellencamp to Johnny Cougar. It's all anyone talks about at the office. Tony's so enamoured with his new find, and he invites me to meet him. When I call him Johnny, he politely asks me to call him John – it doesn't seem like he's a big fan of the name change. I'm excited all the same though. Maybe there's a chance for me to do something different, to work with this new artist instead of sitting around relying on Mick for everything, and sure enough I'm asked to work on a photo shoot with him.

John isn't tall but he has a sizeable attitude. He's brutally honest with everyone, including himself, and he's even more gorgeous than the photos I've seen. He's wearing a white T-shirt and a rough denim jacket pulled up around his face; he has that James Dean kind of quality. Jamie Andrews – who is part of the Warhol crew – is called in to be the photographer.

John's resistant to Tony's ideas, despising anything and everything Tony suggests. He doesn't want to wear make-up or take his shirt off, and even though we persuade him in the end, he complains about it the entire time. It reminds me a little of Mick and the *Play Don't Worry* album cover. Mick didn't want to become Tony's ideal teenage idol either, and he was bitter about it. John's more difficult and vocal about what he likes and what he doesn't.

Tony, determined to have his way, keeps pushing – he needs a star. He's lost Bowie and Mick isn't what he expects, so he needs to prove to himself and everyone else he can weave that magic again. But John isn't Bowie: his songs aren't as good and he's nowhere near as malleable. Ploughing on regardless, Tony books a studio and asks for Mick's help with recording. Mick goes down to see what's happening and comes home laughing.

'Guess who's producing it?' he asks me.

'Who?'

'Tony!'

'Defries . . . ? He's not a producer, what is he thinking?'

'Not much!' says Mick, and we both explode into laughter again. Tony thinks he can do everything, but producing is an art and Tony isn't musical. He should check his ego at the door and get a professional producer.

MainMan tell me that they are organising a 'Johnny Cougar' day in John's hometown of Seymour, Indiana. When I see John again, he's in despair.

'I used to live in that town; I know everybody there. I went to school with a lot of the kids, and now I'm meant to ride on a fire truck in a parade and wave?' His voice cracks with the indignity of it all. He's humiliated and hurt, and he swears that there'll never be another Johnny Cougar Day in Seymour, or anywhere else for that matter.

Tony is so preoccupied with John that his interest in us is almost non-existent.

Barry Imhoff is in New York and gets in touch with Mick. Barry is someone Mick met on the Dylan tour and he has expressed an interest in managing Mick. This could be the chance we've been waiting for. I haven't been asked to continue to work with John and it's just as well – I don't like what Tony's doing to him either. Eventually, John leaves Tony, changes his name back to John Mellencamp and has a huge hit: 'Little Pink Houses'. I salute him.

45

A FRESH START

Barry wants to give Mick a fresh start. He says he can get us green cards, which is music to our ears: we both like the States, and Mick wants to be able to work on both sides of the Atlantic. Barry's already concocting a plan and he tells Mick to put a band together before moving us to Woodstock. Suddenly, the world looks a little brighter.

Woodstock is in rural countryside, green and lush. It's a town full of live music, hippies and organic food; and apart from the obvious connection to the festival of the same name, it was also Bob Dylan's home for a couple of years. The Rolling Thunder Revue has inspired Mick, and his new group – Bobby Chen, Mick Barakan aka Shane Fonteyne, and a bass player from the South called Jay Davis – are young, eager and talented.

Mick and I go back to London for a quick Christmas break and it's there I find out I'm pregnant. I've always imagined I'd have a baby one day, but I didn't plan this. My parents are over the moon upon hearing the news and even though I'm a little nervous, I love Mick and I want his baby.

Returning to New York, I suddenly find that the excesses of touring are behind me, and I don't miss any of it as I take walks around Chinatown. Mick, for the most part, stays home too. He turns down a Peter Gabriel tour so I won't be alone during my delivery. The only cloud on the horizon is his drinking. I urge him to slow down and he promises he will, but as we live life as a normal couple his drinking becomes more apparent. Thankfully, he isn't a mean drunk.

When Defries hears about my pregnancy, he surprises us both by offering to pay my medical expenses. We're grateful, of course, but in the back of my mind I can't help but think that if Mick had been paid properly, we wouldn't need his help . . .

Regardless, Barry has the green cards in motion and advises us to get married as soon as possible so my card will be assured. We marry on the first day of spring in Bearsville, a stone's throw from Woodstock. The legendary music manager Albert Grossman made his base here and developed the hamlet, building a studio high in the hills as well as raising a theatre, his offices and three restaurants. We marry on the top floor of one of these restaurants.

I wear a purple smocked dress with black cowboy boots; my 'something new' is silver tips on my boots. Mick wears the blue leather jacket we got in the South of France, along with jeans and sunglasses. Only a few people are invited, new friends from Woodstock and the occupants of the bar downstairs. As I stand in front of the preacher, I find myself feeling nervous, not about marrying Mick – I love Mick, I want our baby to have his name and I'm not unhappy to get rid of the Fussey moniker – but rather about the way we are doing it. I never imagined getting married without my mum helping me dress and my dad giving me away. They're both hurt, as are Mick's parents, and that's to say nothing of our close friends Ian and Trudi. My only defence is that time was short: we only had a week to put everything together.

My mind rushes back to when I was plucked from a suburban hairdressing salon, whipped up in the frenzy of Ziggy Stardust and landing here, marrying the man of my dreams, Mick Ronson. It's almost impossible to process.

We stay in Woodstock over the summer, and it's another scorcher. There are riots and power outages in New York, and here I am, eight months pregnant, living in a barn that doesn't have any electricity. It doesn't faze me.

Lisa Anabelle Ronson is born in New York City on 10 August 1977. Mick and I only have eyes for each other and our daughter. We give up our apartment and Danny takes it (he never did get the power on in the house downtown). We drive with Lisa back to Woodstock, before leaving for London with the promise of green cards ringing in our ears. My parents are hanging over the rails at Heathrow airport when we arrive, and we go home together in familial bliss. I look at Mum: she's a bit older now, and I can't help but feel guilty at what an awful daughter I've been. I didn't invite her to my wedding, nor the birth of her grandchild. I swear I'll make it up to her, but she doesn't seem to care. She's just happy we're here, happy she's here to welcome us, glad she didn't move; 96 Cumberland Road is big enough for us all.

My parents are a lifesaver for us and the first couple of months are all the easier for it. Mum still works at the chemist and has become more involved with dispensing than serving in the shop. She tells me about the cost of some prescription pills. 'Shocking price they are,' she says over tea in the kitchen, 'but they're made so beautifully.'

'What are they for?'

'Well, Mr Jutton says they make you feel cheerful,' Mum smiles, 'and they do.'

She stands up, takes some bottles down from the kitchen cupboard and spills them out on the table to show me. The smooth black cylindrical tablets are as beautiful as she says, and she shows me another tube filled with Dexedrine, round pale-yellow capsules with a carved line across the middle. I don't think much of it. I've never done pills, but Mum's always had a little stash of something in the cupboard from the chemist. My mind goes back to when I was a teenager, sneaking home at 2 a.m. to find Mum meticulously laying tiles for a new kitchen floor. I should have twigged it then: Mother's little helpers.

Dad works in a grocery supply place. He 'accidentally' knocks over a pile of Pampers – the most dishonest thing he's ever done – and brings home the damaged boxes for Lisa. Mum and Dad's world now revolves around Lisa. It's fine, but soon enough that familiar feeling settles in: I'm bored. I don't want to live with my parents; I love them, I'm grateful to them, but I don't want to live with them. I want my own place, and I miss my American friends, not to mention my husband. Mick's always out, taking the car up to London, and sometimes he doesn't come home for days. He says he's looking for work, and while I'm sure he is, I'm also sure he drinks too much to even attempt to drive. I know he's depressed, and I can't help but feel the same way.

Glen Matlock comes back into our lives and Mick does some tracks with him and his new band, Rich Kids. It's a jolt of electricity, and another shock comes when Mick gets a call out of the blue from someone asking him if he wants to do some tracks with Roger Daltrey from The Who. Now this is more like it. I send him off with good luck kisses and hope to hear from him later, and even when I don't get a call from him, I'm not upset: I'm sure everything's going well, and I go to bed with a smile on my face.

A loud knock at the door wakes me up. I glance at the clock: 6 a.m. Getting up, I look out of the window to see a police car parked in front of the house. My heart racing, I run downstairs to find Mum, in her dressing gown, staring blankly at a policeman.

'Mrs Ronson? Married to Mick Ronson?' he asks me.

'Yes?' My mother grabs my arm.

'Your husband is being detained at Bromley police station.'

I sink on to the stairs. *At least he isn't dead*, I catch myself thinking.

We politely ask him to come in and walk him into the kitchen, where Mum puts the kettle on. He tells us that a minicab brought Mick to Bromley police station at 2 a.m. with no explanation from the driver other than the fact that he couldn't wake him up. He needed an address and didn't know what to do. Mick had been to the hospital, and after one whiff of him they sent him to the police station.

The police struggled to wake him up too, and when they finally did, he was fighting. '. . . he knocked my hat off,' the cop says, touching it with affection. 'We arrested him on the spot.'

He accepts a mug from Mum and takes a sip of tea before continuing. He tells us that Mick was asked to turn out his pockets, and when he did a pill fell on to the counter along with his tobacco, ciggy papers and some change. He tried to snatch it back, but they saw it and asked where he got it from.

'Me mother-in-law,' was his blurted answer.

My mother's mouth is moving but nothing's coming out. I glance at the kitchen cupboard: the prescription drugs are inches from the copper's helmet. I laugh, and flashing an encouraging look at Mum, I fib:

'Mick was coming back from a Who session. Someone must have given it to him.'

'Oh,' says the cop, looking interested. 'The Who, you say?'

'Yes, he was doing a session for one of them up in London. He prefers a drink, as you can see.' I act nonchalant. The Who and Roger Daltrey can look after themselves. The cop nods, as if this situation is entirely commonplace.

'You can come and bail him out as soon as you like,' he says, getting up to leave.

'Yes, we'll be right down,' I say, leading him to the front door. Walking down the garden path, he calls out over his shoulder, reminding us that we'll need some money to put up for Mick's bail. We close the door behind him and look at each other in silence before collapsing on the stairs.

'Mum, we have to hide those tablets, just in case they come back.'

'Come back? . . . What are we going to do with them?'

'I don't know, let's just get them out the house, hide them somewhere.' We're both quiet as we think.

'The compost heap,' whispers my mother. We run to the kitchen, wrap them tightly in plastic bags and bury them like bodies in the early-morning light. Afterwards, as we're having another cup of tea, Mum asks woefully: 'What if they do come back and find them?'

'They'll never find them,' I say, but she goes on as if she hasn't heard me.

'What if it's in the papers, and Mr Jutton finds out? He'll know I've taken them!' Her voice cracks. 'I'll be fired, everyone in Beckenham will know, and what about your dad?' She's getting shriller as tears creep in, and I calm her down before calling Barry. He's annoyed that I've woken him up, and even more so when I give him the news.

'Rocks stars . . .' is all he mutters at first, but I know that he's great in an emergency. 'I'll talk to someone and get back to you, don't say anything to anyone.'

'I said I'd go and bail him out,' I say miserably.

'Yeah, well, let him wait for a bit, there's nothing more I can do now.'

The lawyer calls later that afternoon and Mum and I meet them at Bromley police station. Barry tells me they represented the Stones in the past so I'm not feeling too worried. Mum, God bless her, comes through, and puts her house up for security to bail Mick out. There's press outside but Mick slips out of the side door and into the car. He looks bad and smells worse. There's a frosty silence for a few minutes, before he breaks it:

'They really 'urt me, twisted me arms right up me back.'

Obviously, I feel a little sorry for him, but I just have to ask: 'Why did you tell the police my mum gave you that pill?'

'Did I?' He looks at me quizzically, as if he can't remember. 'Well, she gi' me one before.'

Mum stares straight ahead.

'Mum . . . ?'

'Just trying to help . . .' she says quietly. I can't believe what I'm hearing – no wonder she was so worried.

When we get home, I ask what went on at the session. He said it hadn't gone too well.

'I dunno, they kept tellin' me what to play. I know what t'play, it might take me sum time, but I know what t'play!'

'But the rest of it, Mick, what about the rest of it?'

'Well, everyone were drinking, so I 'ad a couple.'

'A couple? The police said they couldn't wake you up!'

He doesn't say more, so I leave it at that and pray that Barry can save our green cards. Days go by and he doesn't call – maybe no news is good news, and gradually the drama fades into the background.

I see in the music papers that David's on tour with Iggy, and *Heroes* is in the charts. The photos of him look healthy. Maybe he's given up cocaine. I hope that he has. Defries and he have parted company, and thinking back I'm sure this didn't help Mick's career at all. Tony was too busy with David and the financial entanglement to focus on Mick or his career. If we'd known that then, our choices might have been different. Angie's running between London and Switzerland, and rumours are swirling that she and David are on the brink of a divorce. I don't see either of them, I haven't since Hammersmith, and I'm filled with a sense of loss. I had thought we were closer than that. I really had.

Life seems to have turned full circle. I'm back where I started, at 96 Cumberland Road. The life I created for myself has disappeared, and my career with it, and yet it isn't all doom and gloom by any means. My baby girl is lovely, and as I push her around the same streets my mother used to push me, I swear to her: this isn't going to be forever, and I pray I'm right . . .

Life did become better. We got our green cards, we returned to America. We moved just outside of Woodstock into Maria Muldaur's house, high in the hills overlooking the Ashokan Reservoir. Mick lands a production job and there's talk of a deal for his band. I'm happy, and Mick seems happy, but we both know life is precarious. Neither one of us knows what's on the horizon. Neither of us knows what's coming up next.

EPILOGUE

Three a.m. The phone rings. It's a UK number. I catch my breath – Lisa, my daughter, is in London.

'Hello?'

'Hello, Suzi. I'm so sorry, Suzi, so sorry for your loss. You must have heard?'

The voice is one I recognise: Tom Wilcox, my daughter's manager. He's offering me condolences, saying what a shame it was and how sorry he is . . .

'What happened?' I ask at last.

'David Bowie died.'

'David Bowie died!'

'Yes . . . he died of cancer this morning.' Tom pauses.

'David Bowie died . . .' I repeat the words to myself. A shiver runs down my spine.

My husband, the late Mick Ronson, David's musical partner in the 1970s, had died of the same cancer twenty-three years ago. I wondered briefly if David thought about Mick at all during his struggle. I knew he wasn't well – the photographer Mick Rock was still close to him, he had told me.

I turn on the TV, keeping the volume low. 'Starman' punctuates the news, the crawl on CNN full of it. David Bowie died of cancer in New York, aged sixty-nine. He had died an hour ago, and not a mile away from where I'm standing. Had it been just two days ago that Tony Visconti had urged us all to sing Happy Birthday to David down the phone at a Holy Holy gig?

My life flashes by in photographs: the day I met his mother; the day I met Angie; the day I met him; the day I did that iconic Ziggy haircut; the first time I saw them play. My life was all black and white until I met David, and afterwards it was glorious technicolour, as bright as the hair on his head.

Mick Rock says, 'Thank you, David, for giving us such a great time.' And he's right. I echo that. We had a great time.

I always hoped to see him one more time.

Acknowledgements

I want to take this chance to thank the people who helped me shape this book.

Richard Gardner and Frank Famiglietti, who introduced me to Meg Bowles, senior director at The Moth and host of the Peabody Award-winning Moth Radio Hour. Meg brilliantly edited my burgeoning story into 'The Girl From Beckenham', which I told on Moth stages both in the US and Europe. This started me on my journey.

My love and appreciation goes out to Mick and Jo Fussey, my brother and his wife, who were always there to say 'You can do it'.

I want to say thank you to Ian and Trudi Hunter, who told me to write the truth, and to Isabel Rose and Jeff Fagen, who gave me endless encouragement and support. Thank you to Maxine Marshall and Madeline Bocchiaro for sharing with me their encyclopedic knowledge of the time as well as Pati Rock for her generosity with photographs.

Thank you Lisa, my wonderful daughter, for your kindness and patience with me. Your wise words lifted me up whenever I became sad or stuck.

I'm inspired by Hanif Kureishi, who became my friend and led me to Faber. I would not be here if it were not for him and my manager, the invincible catalyst that is Tom Wilcox.

I had a lot of encouragement from Faber and from Mo Hafeez,

my editor, whose patience, understanding and superb skills make this book what it is today.

My greatest thanks, however, go to people I will never forget: David and Angie Bowie, Tony Defries and . . . of course . . . Mrs Jones!